D1292432

Springer Series on Behavior Therapy and Behavioral Medicine

Series Editors: Cyril M. Franks, Ph.D., and Frederick J. Evans, Ph.D.

Advisory Board: John Paul Brady, M.D., Robert P. Liberman, M.D., Neal E. Miller, Ph.D., and Stanley Rachman, Ph.D.

Johnny L. Matson, Ph.D., is an Associate Professor in the Department of Learning and Development at Northern Illinois University. Dr. Matson previously held positions as Assistant Professor of Psychiatry, Western Psychiatric Institute and Clinic, University of Pittsburgh School of Medicine and later, as Program and Research Director for their inpatient and outpatient services for mentally retarded and emotionally disturbed children. Additionally, he was Assistant Professor in Clinical Psychology at the University of Pittsburgh. Prior to these appointments, he served as Program Director of the Jemison Center, Partlow State School and Hospital, a large inpatient treatment center for mentally retarded adults. He received his doctoral degree from Indiana State University. Dr. Matson has published numerous book chapters, books, and journal articles. He is the founder and editor of the journal *Applied Research in Mental Retardation,* and he is on the editorial board or serves as reviewer for journals in clinical psychology and psychiatry.

Thomas M. DiLorenzo, M.A., is a resident in clinical psychology in the Department of Psychiatry and Human Behavior at the University of Mississippi Medical Center. For the past few years, he participated in the graduate clinical psychology program at West Virginia University. He also served as a research associate in the Department of Psychiatry, Western Psychiatric Institute and Clinic, University of Pittsburgh School of Medicine. He has published in a variety of behavioral and clinical psychology journals. His professional interests are in the areas of applied behavior analysis, behavioral assessment, social competence, and research design and methodology.

Punishment and Its Alternatives

A New Perspective for Behavior Modification

Johnny L. Matson, Ph.D.
Thomas M. DiLorenzo, M.A.

Foreword by Cyril M. Franks, Ph.D.

Springer Publishing Company
New York

Springer Publishing Company, Inc.
200 Park Avenue South
New York, New York 10003

84 85 86 87 88 / 10 9 8 7 6 5 4 3 2 1

Library of Congress Cataloging in Publication Data

Matson, Johnny L.
  Punishment and its alternatives.
  (Springer series on behavior therapy and behavioral medicine; v. 13)
  Includes bibliographies and index.
  1. Aversion therapy. 2. Punishment—Psychological aspects. I. DiLorenzo, Thomas M. II. Title. III. Series. [DNLM: 1. Punishment. 2. Behavior therapy. 3. Rehabilitation. W1 SP685NB v.13 / HV 8675 P984]
RC489.B4M37   1983   616.89′142   83-19625
ISBN 0-8261-4560-4

Printed in the United States of America

To our parents and families:
Walter, Mary, Deann, and Meggan Matson;
Emil and Viola DiLorenzo,
and Dawn and Nathan Cross-DiLorenzo

Contents

Foreword

It has been said on more than one occasion that the United Kingdom and the United States are divided by a common tongue. I can recall many instances where the British and the Americans met together, thought they were speaking the same language and that the same words had identical or similar meanings on either side of the ocean, only to find that this was not so. Regrettably, there was many an occasion when this assumption nearly had disastrous consequences. For example, I still recall an important war-time meeting between a small group of us working on a problem that was vital to the war effort, and the misunderstandings that arose because we assumed that we shared a common tongue. After many hours of heated discussion, the British contingent sought to draw closure by insisting that we table the motion there and then, whereupon the American group closed their books and walked out on the assumption that this meant that the day's meeting was at an end and that further talk would be postponed. It was not until many years later that I realized that the seemingly innocuous phrase "tabling the motion" had diametrically different meanings, depending on which side of the ocean it was uttered. No wonder that Alice complained in her Wonderland that words should mean what we want them to mean and that we should not let them control us.

In psychology, a similar state of affairs exists. Professionals use the same technical word to convey quite different notions, and misunderstandings thereby arise even among the so-called experts. For example, the word "inhibition" has a fairly precise physiological definition, a rather different meaning for the psychodynamic therapist, and a different meaning yet again for those who are concerned with behavioral inhibition. If such problems arise for those in the field, what chance has the lay person to achieve understanding or communication. The word "punishment" is very much a case in point. The image conjured up by the lay person is all too often related to sacrifice, "teaching them a lesson," revenge, or to procedures sadistically employed for the benefit of the administrator. All too often, the punishment meted out to criminals fails to decrease the frequency of their criminal acts. This may satisfy the everyday usage of the term punishment, but it is completely at variance with its precise psychological definition.

As all behavior therapists know well, there are three primary kinds of learning—classical conditioning, operant conditioning, and observational learning. To utilize the principles of operant conditioning, which is our primary concern here, it is necessary to describe precisely the relationships obtaining between behavior and the environmental events that influence behavior. In most applications of the principles of operant conditioning, the major emphasis is upon the consequences that follow behavior. Behavioral changes occur when certain consequences are *contingent* upon performance. For the consequence to be contingent, it has to be delivered only *after* the target behavior is performed and it must be otherwise not available. When delivered independently of what the individual is doing, the consequence is not contingent upon behavior and is therefore not going to result in systematic change. In much of our life, consequences are directly contingent upon our behavior: grades are contingent upon attention to the material to be learned and wages are contingent upon regular performance of our assigned tasks. By a *contingency* then, we mean the relationship between the behavior and the events that follow the behavior. This notion is focal to the principles of behavior modification and the numerous procedures that have been generated to alter behavior by modifying the contingencies that control the behavior in question.

Disregarding *extinction* for the moment, the three major contingent relationships between behavior and the events that follow this behavior are *positive reinforcement, negative reinforcement,* and *punishment.* Each has a precisely defined meaning that is often at variance with that attributed to these terms by the general public. Thus, the principle of reinforcement pertains to an increase in the frequency of a desired response when it is immediately followed by certain consequences, or—if we wish to be very precise indeed—an increase in the probability of this response occurring. Positive reinforcement refers to an increase in the frequency of a desired response that is followed by a favorable (reinforcing) event. This event is known as a positive reinforcer—in everyday parlance this is commonly referred to as a reward. But, it is important to distinguish between a "positive reinforcer" and a "reward." The positive reinforcer is defined exclusively in terms of its effects upon the behavior. If the event follows the behavior and the frequency of the behavior increases, the event is said to be a positive reinforcer. By contrast, rewards are usually defined as something given or received in return for service, merit, or achievement. Rewards may be highly valued in our society but they need not necessarily lead to an increase in the probability of the behavior they follow.

Somewhat related, negative reinforcement refers to the increase in the frequency of a desired response by the removal of an aversive event immediately following the performance of this response. Thus, the removal of the aversive event has to be contingent upon the response. The event becomes a *negative reinforcer* if and only if its removal after a response thereby increases the performance of that response. Events that seem to be annoying, unpleasant, or otherwise undesirable need not necessarily be negatively reinforcing. As with a positive reinforcer, a negative reinforcer is defined exclusively in terms of the effects it has on the behavior.

At this stage, it is important to note that both positive and negative reinforcement invariably refer to an increase to desired behavior. By sharp contrast, *punishment* is the presentation of an aversive event or the removal of a positive event following a response which decreases the frequency of an undesired response. This definition is quite different to the everyday usage of this term. Punishment, as defined in common usage, refers to a penalty imposed for performing a particular act. In everyday usage, it is by no means essential— even if it is advantageous—that the frequency of the response be decreased.

In everyday usage there are many negative connotations associated with the word punishment. For the lay person, all too often punishment implies pain, coercion, retribution, or "just payment" for a misdemeanor. Punishment, as used by behavior therapists, is defined exclusively in terms of its effects on behavior. Only if the frequency of an undesired response is reduced, can this activity be termed punishment. Punishment is thus quite different from negative reinforcement since it refers to procedures that decrease undesired responses, whereas reinforcement, be it positive or negative, refers to procedures for the increase of a desired response. Thus, just as the more general usage of the English language depends upon which side of the ocean we are, the word punishment is but

one example of the semantic gulf that separates the behavior therapist from the lay community.

Much of human learning is a result of contingent aversive conditioning occurring in the natural course of events—fires burn, beams
fall, provoked dogs bite, and hopefully, in most of these situations,
our behavior is altered accordingly. All that the skilled behavior
therapist does is to utilize these principles as one small part of a
carefully planned and comprehensive program of therapeutic intervention. If this be so, how then is it that there is such an outcry
against punishment? No one now seriously questions the fact that
conditioning occurs and that it can be systematically applied in therapy. When behavior modification was in doubt, it was not feared.
Now that its efficacy has been firmly established, behavior modification assumes the potential for becoming something to be feared,
distorted, and misinterpreted. The popular film *A Clockwork Orange*
shows the ultraviolent hero conditioned into a state of abject passiv-
ity by the use of behavioral conditioning. As "cinema," this film is
excellent and therefore, because of its widespread appeal, all the
more likely to further common misconceptions regarding the power
of behavior therapy and the "sinister" intent of behavior therapists.
The professional usage of punishment, as detailed above, is very
much at variance with the stereotypes and images evoked in the
minds of the general public, but unfortunately this precise distinction becomes blurred by the lay community.

In part, the responsibility for this unfortunate state of affairs
rests with behavior therapists. We who claim to be adept at modifying
the behavior of others can surely learn to modify our own behavior.
Certainly, we have not always been at pains to explain that the objectivity and precision with which we define and deploy our strategies in
no way negates our concerns for the welfare of the individual.

The typical lay person has no knowledge of learning theory, his
or her exposure to behavior therapy is often limited to a magazine
or popular movie in which aversive control is presented with either
no explanation at all, an explanation that is at best only partially
correct or, more usually, an explanation that is highly derogatory to
behavior therapy. It is too bad that behavior therapists do not take
pains to present definition of such terms as punishment and the
contexts within which aversive procedures are used more carefully.
Contrary to the popular belief of the Humanists, all therapists, regardless of orientation, are humanistically inclined and concerned
first and foremost with the welfare of their patients and the public
good. The discerning behavior therapist uses aversive conditioning

procedures rarely, only when there is little or no alternative (as in the case of extreme self-destructive behavior) and then only within a context of a careful consideration of pragmatic, ethical, and legal issues and the various guidelines that have been promulgated for their usage.

Contemporary behavior therapists recognize well the complexity and the uniqueness of all human beings. These days, except for the treatment of some relatively circumscribed learned habit such as smoking in an otherwise functionally intact individual, aversive conditioning is never applied in isolation. Following a careful behavioral analysis of the total life situation of the individual concerned, an evaluation that includes genetic, biological, social, ecological, and learned components, a provisional intervention program is established. This program will involve constant monitoring, the active, informed, and considered consent of the individuals or groups concerned and an emphasis upon behavioral and cognitive self-control rather than control by others. Throughout this multidimensional approach, a large range of procedures will be used of which punishment, as defined above, may or may not be one. If used at all, it will certainly be used with due regard to all the social, physiological, psychological, and other potential hazards. Such considerations will include the physical safety and validity of a particular procedure and the incremental success, if any, added by this procedure. Is it worth it? Do nonaversive alternatives exist? Is the use of aversion therapy implicitly or explicitly meeting some personal needs of the therapist rather than those of the patient? Do the ends really justify the means? Have the issues been presented fairly and squarely to all concerned, including the patient and the public? By what rights and criteria can any one group of individuals decide what is "good" for another individual or for society at large? What are the circumstances under which this becomes appropriate and what are the limitations? Thoughtful behavior therapists will constantly be addressing themselves to such issues.

Under these stringent circumstances, it is very likely that punishment will be used less and less in the future. But when it is used, it is likely to be deployed more and more effectively. It is within this context that Johnny Matson and Thomas DiLorenzo have prepared this important text on the use of punishment in behavior modification and it is of significance that the subtitle includes the phrase "A New Perspective." In thoughtful fashion, Matson and DiLorenzo take us step by step through virtually every aspect of punishment as deployed by the forward-looking behavior therapist.

In so doing, the potential for abuse is squarely faced and no apology is made for those who abuse the skills that their stringent training has provided. What is certain is that positive and negative reinforcers, punishments, and rewards are here to stay. They are inexplicably bound up with virtually every aspect of our everyday life and it is therefore extremely important that the record be set straight. To expect any one treatise to resolve these complex and pervasive issues once and for all would be unreasonable. To hope that this particular volume will provide a major step toward this general direction is very reasonable.

Matson and DiLorenzo are to be commended for their courage, their mastery of the behavioral principles involved, the clarity of their exposition, and their humane understanding of the needs of the individual. By their thoughtful contribution to this sensitive area, Matson and DiLorenzo shed a penetrating light through a region that is still shrouded in mystery and misperception.

Cyril M. Franks, Ph.D.
July 1983
Princeton, New Jersey

Preface

The concept of punishment is familiar to most persons. It encompasses many important aspects of everyday experience, including child-rearing, education, and law enforcement. However, the *therapeutic applications* of punishment, as well as the scientific definitions and analysis of the controlling variables derived from laboratory research, are less familiar. In this book, we describe the application of therapeutic punishment in the context of treatment, rehabilitation, and education. The research conducted in this area is evaluated, and the limitations and advantages, based on empirical findings presented in the treatment literature, are delineated. We also describe the conditions under which the application of punishment procedures are most suitable.

In developing a book on this topic, a few considerations are especially crucial. Perhaps the most significant consideration is that a book covering primarily punishment inadvertently might give the false impression that these techniques are advocated or endorsed for use in all instances. This belief would be unfortunate indeed, since recent evidence suggests that an overreliance upon punishment currently may be a problem. The purpose of this book is to exemplify (1) the conditions under which punishment may prove to be the best alternative treatment, (2) the criteria that need to be met to maximize the effectiveness of various punishment procedures, (3) the complexities and limitations of relying on punishment exclusively, and (4) the role of positive control in punishment programs.

Throughout the text are examples chosen from diverse treatment populations, including psychiatric clients, emotionally disturbed and mentally retarded children and adults, and normal children and adults with specific problem behaviors. Illustrations from a variety of settings are used, including examples from the classroom, home, and institutions. Finally, problems in administering punishment, as well as the ethical and legal considerations, are addressed.

We do not expect this book to be either exhaustive or "the last word" on the topic. Many times, the topics discussed or articles reviewed were selected based on our best guess as to trends in the field. From that perspective, the book is a reflection of our own interests and values; however, it is hoped that this book provides some direction in assimilating the massive literature on behavior decelerators. Additionally, some useful insights on that literature, relative to its practical implications, are presented.

Johnny L. Matson
Thomas M. DiLorenzo

Punishment and
Its Alternatives

1

Introduction

As its title implies, this book will address the application of punishment procedures to the modification of human behaviors. The systematic analysis of this phenomenon over the past two decades has elucidated the need for detailing this complex and often greatly misunderstood therapeutic tool. We will attempt to cover not only theoretical positions and definitions of various aspects of this procedure, but also practical, ethical, and legal issues and the role of punishment in the future of behavior modification.

At first, because of the lack of emphasis on this technique in the education of graduate and undergraduate students, the reaction of the reader may be, "How can a book be filled just with issues related to punishment?" We hope to show, through the many advances in research on this topic, that no longer will a mere chapter on punishment in a behavior modification book suffice and that the need for a comprehensive overview of punishment now is warranted.

Punishment and aversive techniques are not new. Kazdin (1975) pointed out that aversive techniques are deeply enmeshed in many social institutions including government and law (e.g., fines and imprisonment), education (e.g., failing grades on exams, explusion, and probation), religion (e.g., damnation), international relations (e.g., military coercion), and normal social intercourse (e.g., discrimination, disapproval, humiliation, and social stigma). Routine interactions of most individuals with both physical and social environments result in aversive events ranging from a burn on a hot stove to verbal abuse from an acquaintance [p. 146].

1

Because punishment is so much a part of our everyday lives, it is irrelevant to question whether or not punishing stimuli should be used. Rather, "behavioral science should undertake to understand and to control the results of their use" (Johnston, 1972, p. 1051). Additionally, the decision on which punishment procedures and stimuli are used should be made on the basis of scientific and empirical evidence rather than on gut-level feelings and/or a person's moral philosophy (Baer, 1970; Johnston, 1972; Solomon, 1964).

It could be asked, then, what the difference is between the aversive events just noted (Kazdin, 1975) and therapeutic punishment. When punishment is used therapeutically, behavior therapists systematically apply punishing stimuli to decelerate certain aberrant behaviors. Even though this definition appears straightforward and functional in nature, punishment remains the most misunderstood of behavior therapy techniques among professional and lay persons alike. While definitional problems will be addressed at a later point, the purpose of the ensuing section is to shed more light on the current beliefs and attitudes regarding this set of techniques.

Historical Perspectives

Although this book is clinically oriented, the great amount of animal literature on this subject cannot be ignored. Rather than attempt to review this massive literature, which certainly would double the books length, we will summarize briefly some of the more important points that derive from this research. Certainly a definitive work of its time and a basis for much of the later applied research was a chapter by Azrin and Holz (1966) entitled simply "Punishment." A complete synthesis was made in this paper of animal research findings up until 1966. Testimony to its comprehensiveness is that the review still is cited in many current research papers, emphasizing its relevance to clinical work today.

Almost all of the research conducted up to the time that Azrin and Holz (1966) completed their chapter was done with animals for the explicit purpose of defining characteristics, determinants, and outcomes of punishment procedures. As with prior animal research in designing the principles of learning and schedules of reinforcement, so too the results and conclusions of this classic chapter are easily transferable to human research and practice.

We will begin with Azrin and Holz's (1966) definition: "Punishment is a reduction of the future probability of a specific response as a result of the immediate delivery of a stimulus for that response" (p. 381). This definition adds parsimony to the field in that it is identical to the definition of reinforcement, except the direction of change is just the opposite, because positive reinforcement increases the probability that the response will occur again.

Although many aspects of punishment with animals were eloquently defined and explained by Azrin and Holz (1966), probably the most noted section of the thesis was the summarization of the circumstances that would make punishment maximally effective. The following 14 conclusions are taken from Azrin and Holz (1966) and will be addressed at different times in this book as they relate to the application of punishment with humans.

1. Escape from the punishing stimulus should be impossible.
2. The punishing stimulus should be intense.
3. The punishing stimulus should be delivered after every occurrence of the targeted behavior.
4. The punishing stimulus should be administered immediately after the response (no delay).
5. The punishing stimulus should be introduced at maximum intensity.
6. The punishing stimulus should be given in brief periods of time.
7. The punishing stimulus should not be differentially associated with the delivery of reinforcement.
8. The punishing stimulus should be a discriminative stimulus for extinction (no reinforcement will be provided for the response).
9. The degree of motivation to emit the punished response should be reduced.
10. An alternative response to the punished response should be available and reinforced.
11. If an alternative response is not available, a different situation should be available to receive reinforcement.
12. If the punishing stimulus cannot be delivered, then a conditioned aversive stimulus should be given.
13. If a punishing stimulus cannot be administered, then a reduction in positive reinforcement may be used as punishment (e.g., time-out and response cost).
14. The punished response should not be positively reinforced.

This last point may seem contradictory, but Dinsmoor (1952) cogently pointed out that reinforcement must control the emission of the maladaptive behavior. He stated, "In order that a person may learn to make a certain response in the first place, some type of reinforcement is presumably necessary. If the reinforcement follows as a simple physical consequence of the act, there seems to be no reason to assume that reinforcement should cease when punishment begins. Indeed, if the reinforcement is withheld for an extended time period, extinction sets in, and there may no longer be a response to be punished" (p. 27).

If Dinsmoor (1952) is correct, why not use extinction rather than punishment exclusively? Holz and Azrin (1963) addressed this question and compared five methods to reduce response rates: stimulus change, extinction, satiation, physical restraint, and punishment. Each method was evaluated along four criteria:

1. Does the method reduce the response rate immediately?
2. Does the method reduce the response rate as long as the contingencies are in effect?
3. Is the response rate reduced to zero while contingencies are in effect?
4. Does the reduced response rate maintain after the contingencies are removed?

Only punishment has an immediate effect and is maintained at a zero rate while the procedure is in effect and when it has been removed. Stated another way, punishment, when applied consistently, meets the four criteria as the most efficacious technique for eliminating behavior; that is, the answer to all four questions is "yes." We concur with Azrin and Holz (1966) that these effects are noted when each procedure is implemented as close to maximum effectiveness as possible.

An argument could be made that, if extinction were applied in the strictest sense, with absolutely no reinforcement for punished behavior, then punishment would not be necessary since extinction would be effective. Azrin and Holz (1966) aptly argue that: "this complete absence of reinforcement is impossible. The physical world often provides reinforcement contingencies that cannot be eliminated easily. The faster we move through space, the quicker we get to where we are going, whether the movement be walking or driving an auto. Hence, running and speeding will inevitably be reinforced" (p. 433). Extinction of running and speeding could be accomplished only if all reinforcing events that result from movement through space could be eliminated. This situation is of course impossible, and therefore some other reductive method, such as punishment, must be used.

Therapeutic Applications of Punishment

One of the major therapeutic tools in the modification of human behavior traditionally has been therapeutic punishment, which has been responsible for some of the most monumental successes in mental health. The use of procedures such as electric shock to eliminate autistic-like behavior of children is one of the most striking examples in the clinical literature. These methods have been a mixed blessing, however, because of the misuse of punishment procedures in some instances. In hindsight, these inappropriate applications seem to stem from a number of avenues, including the failure to try less aversive procedures when there was evidence that they might prove effective, the failure to get patient approval for the procedures used, failure to insure that the persons who would carry out the procedures were trained adequately, and, in general, frequent misuse of therapeutic punishment methods. The purpose of this book is to address many of these issues related to defining punishment and insuring that it is used appropriately with human populations. Our position is that reinforcement procedures should be used exclusively where possible, but that under many conditions punishment procedures are necessary and should not be avoided. Stringent application of safeguards should be used to decrease the possibilities of inappropriate use.

One reason for current negative beliefs is that many persons have confused therapeutic punishment with the lay definition. This situation has occurred even among members of the professional community. We hope to define the difference between these two forms of punishment in the ensuing pages, as well as review the therapeutic methods currently available for treating clients and attempt to delineate for the reader the differences between therapeutic and psychologically and/or physically harmful procedures. In addition, some of the controversies surrounding the use of such procedures and the disadvantages of these methods when used in a therapeutic manner will be described.

Controversy over the Definition and Use of Punishment

As previously noted, there are both lay and professional definitions of punishment, with the latter being espoused by behavior modifiers. The lay definition refers to any stimulus considered unpleasant to most people in our society. Thus, shouting, spanking, and cursing someone would serve as universal *a priori* punishers. This definition differs markedly from that used by those who adhere to a behavior modification perspective. As mentioned earlier, Azrin and Holz (1966) defined punishment as a reduction of the future probability of a specific response due to the immediate delivery of a stimulus for that response. Although this definition appears succinct, the definition of terminology is critically important as well. Morse and Kelleher (1977) cogently describe reinforcement and punishment on two levels, as reproducible behavioral processes and as operations. Thus, in common usage the terms "reinforcer" and "punisher" are emphasized as basic terms, while "reinforcement" and "punishment" are defined as the presentation of a reinforcer or punisher in specified temporal relation to an operant.

Typically, people have focused just on the event in defining a punisher. As Morse and Kelleher (1977) argue, we tend to ignore the antecedent and consequent behavior and the contingencies in effect. They posit that the modification of behavior by a punisher depends on a number of variables:

1. The actual application of an event (i.e., the presumed punisher).
2. The qualitative and quantitative properties of the behavior chosen to be modified.
3. The schedule under which the event is present.
4. Knowledge that events that were previously effective in reducing maladaptive behavior may not modify other responses in the same way.

We should never assume that particular events are punishers (e.g., spanking or electric shock) until a decrease in rate of responding is observed.

Furthermore, Morse and Kelleher (1977) point out, and we concur, clinically therapeutic applications of punishment should not be used in lieu of reinforcement procedures but rather as a supplement that can remediate difficult problem behaviors when used judiciously. Even with these stipulations, however, there is still considerable controversy as to whether such applications are ethical or appropriate in a civilized society. At least one psychiatrist (Bromberg, 1970) has opposed the use of punishment. In his view, punishment procedures are relatively ineffective in today's society in comparison to its general effects in and on society several generations ago. Despite the possible accuracy of this comment (at least in part), it should be noted that Bromberg's thesis is based on a lay definition of punishment, such as spanking children or placing persons in prison for breaking laws. As stated earlier, punishment cannot be defined topographically but must be defined functionally. The confusion with the therapeutic applications of this procedure noted by the behavior modifiers is striking when it is considered that this article appeared in the *American Journal of Psychiatry,* a prestigious, widely read journal considered most important in the field of mental health. Thus, therapeutic applications of punishment as we define them here are to some extent misunderstood and mystifying, even among some experts in mental health.

A closer analysis points to the fact that the controversy over punishment exists on at least three dimensions: definition, effectiveness, and types of punishers. We hope that the distinction between the application of therapeutic punishment and the lay definition has become clear with the preceding discussion. Bromberg's discussion that punishment procedures are ineffective does not correspond to the literature on therapeutic applications of punishment. Data in both the extensive animal literature and what research has been done with humans are optimistic (Honig & Staddon, 1977). Therapeutic punishment has in fact proven to be highly effective (Forehand & Baumeister, 1976).

The issue that has received the most emphasis has been the type of punishment procedures used. This situation is ironic in that many acts defined as highly aversive by the lay public may not prove to be punishing for a particular client from a therapeutic standpoint, since the behavior may not decrease in frequency contingent upon the application of the selected stimuli.

Likewise, some of the misunderstanding comes from the frequent confusion of procedures (such as electroconvulsive shock therapy and mood altering drugs) with therapeutic applications of punishment as the authors of this text and other behavior modifiers define them. Electroconvulsive shock therapy and mood altering drugs are not types of therapeutic punishment. Public reactions to such misinformation have been strong, so much so that behavior modifiers frequently have resorted to referring to therapeutic punishment in terms such as behavior decelerators to avoid the controversial and often emotional reactions engendered by the term punishment.

On the other hand, because specific types of therapeutic punishment are so widely misunderstood and/or the layman's concept of the punishment procedure is based on emotional reaction as opposed to research findings, some effective punishment procedures are no longer used. One of the most hotly debated of these procedures is contingent electric shock (Lichstein & Schreibman, 1976). This controversy has resulted despite the proven utility of the procedure in the suppression of behaviors that pose an immediate threat to a client's welfare. As noted, there are in fact two issues—the first concerns the use of punishment versus other behavior decelerators per se, and the second concerns the type of aversive stimuli used. These variables must be balanced in an equation based on the advantages and disadvantages of each procedure in particular situations.

The Need for Therapeutic Punishment Procedures

Because of the socially undesirable connotations associated with the use of punishment procedures, there has been some reluctance on the part of professionals to use them. Warren (1971) has noted that therapeutic punishment has received by far the most criticism of all the behavior modification procedures. Hewitt (1968) has gone farther by stating that punishment procedures have little value in the education of emotionally disturbed children. He also believes that appropriate behavior eventually will become reinforcing in and of itself. To believe that resilient maladaptive behaviors will decrease mysteriously and that appropriate behavior will somehow become intrinsically reinforcing is somewhat unrealistic.

Despite the sentiments that aversive contingencies should never be employed, punishment procedures remain in widespread use both in and out of the classroom. Sears, Maccoby, and Levin (1957) reported that 98 percent of the parents and teachers interviewed used physical punishment occasionally. Furthermore, Aronfreed (1968), among others, has written that this is one of the most striking examples of a conflict between social values (of at least some persons in our society) and naturalistic evidence. He states that "it seems doubtful that common observations of the interaction between par-

ents and children would lead anyone to the general conclusi
punishment was unnatural, ineffective or undesirable. Yet,
psychologists and educators for many years have argued pre
such a general case against punishment."

We hold to the contention that punishment is indeed a necessa
and important tool of the behavior modifier. Punishment has been
used effectively to facilitate children's learning (Meyer & Offenbach,
1962). Furthermore, these demonstrations have shown that such im-
provements frequently are greater than what can be attained with
reinforcement (Spence & Segner, 1967; Stevenson, Weir, & Zigler,
1959). Many observers have stressed that only reinforcement or extinction be used as methods of treatment (Warren, 1971); however,
such an approach frequently may be impractical. For example, simply ignoring the targeted behavior, as would be done in the use of
extinction, may not be possible in cases where physical aggression
occurs. Additionally, extinction typically requires a great deal of time
for effects to be noted. In the event the targeted behaviors are life
threatening (self-abuse), time is of the essence.

Church (1963) noted that extinction procedures require that
one identify the source of reinforcement so that it can be eliminated,
thus producing the appropriate conditions for extinction. This principle is often difficult to execute. For example, a child in a school
setting must not be allowed to gain reinforcement from other school
children. Teaching the classmates to avoid such behavior is often
hard to accomplish, if not impossible. Additionally, with reinforcement, the time needed to design and implement the procedures is
often unrealistic for staff and parents.

In the final cost-benefit analysis, the conclusion must be drawn
that therapeutic punishment is indeed necessary. At the same time,
we do not advocate the use of these procedures to the exclusion of
less aversive methods; however, we think that the type of behavior
modification procedure used should be evaluated on an individual
basis considering both the long-term benefits of these procedures
and the potential short-term effects.

Arguments for Using Punishment

As noted in the previous section, the advantages of using punishment
in a therapeutic manner often may outweigh the drawbacks. Paramount among the positive aspects of punishment to be considered is
that it is often rapidly effective in the treatment of harmful behaviors

(e.g., life-threatening rumination) that do not respond readily to other forms of treatment. Second, punishment procedures may result in the avoidance of more deleterious treatments. Third, while possible adverse side-effects may be observed, there are also a number of positive side-effects that have resulted from the administration of punishment. Fourth, these methods are time tested. The information generated by the prevailing literature is as great or greater than what is found with other treatment techniques.

There is a number of studies in which the effectiveness of therapeutic applications of punishment is described clearly. Among the most striking are the effects reported by Lovaas and his colleagues, who have had considerable success in eliminating a number of autistic behaviors (Lovaas, Schaeffer, & Simmons, 1965). Also, therapeutic punishment has been effective in eliminating life-threatening rumination (Sajwaj, Libet, & Agras, 1974). Results such as these make difficult the arguments against the total ban of such procedures. Repp and Deitz (1978) have taken this issue one step further by arguing that the withholding of such procedures, when research has demonstrated them to be effective with such problems, would be unethical.

In addition to the positive aspects of punishment, there are benefits to be achieved with respect to problem behaviors the client can avoid by employing punishment procedures. As we have mentioned, one of the major advantages of employing punishment is that it is more effective or works more rapidly than more positively oriented behavior modification procedures. Thus, for life-threatening behavior such as rumination or some extreme self-injurious behaviors, the use of punishment can serve as a means of avoiding undue pain.

Another instance in which punishment may be a humane method because of its effectiveness is when the alternative may be a medication administered or continuous physical restraint for an extended period of time. The most frequently cited example is the use of major tranquilizers such as Mellaril® or Thorazine® being given for aggressive–disruptive behavior. These behaviors require constant maintenance dosages over extended periods of time, usually the client's entire life, since the behaviors return after the drug is removed (Aman & Singh, 1979). This problem is widespread in institutions for chronic mental patients and the mentally retarded, where, on the average, 50 percent of the patients receive these medications for aggressive-disruptive behavior (Aman & Singh, 1979). Likewise, physical restraint, although effective in keeping an individual from self-injury, has definite debilitating effects (e.g., demineralization of bones, shortening of tendons, and loss of movement ability) (Rimm & Masters, 1974). Punishment procedures can be used with some persons to control these problems at least in part and do not have the disadvantages of inhibiting learning potential and producing irreversible neurological damage (e.g., tardive dyskinesia), as is the case with the major tranquilizers (Taylor, Zlutnick, & Hoehle, 1979).

A third major advantage of punishment procedures is that they can produce positive side-effects. Even what is considered by the layperson as the most severe of these therapeutic punishers, electric shock, has resulted in a plethora of positive responses including improved social skills (Birnbrauer, 1968); eye-to-face contact (Bucher & Lovaas, 1968); alertness, affection, and happiness (Lovaas, Schaeffer, & Simmons, 1965); smiling and hugging (Lovaas & Simmons, 1969); and calmness and playfulness (Tate & Baroff, 1966). At least some of these behaviors have been reported in the literature with other punishment techniques, such as overcorrection (Axelrod, Brantner, & Meddock, 1978).

Another important positive side-effect of punishment is response generalization, both across situations and across inappropriate behaviors. For example, Lovaas and Simmons (1969) reported that, for one of the childen they treated, a reduction occurred not only in self-destruction but in both whining and avoidance of an attending adult. Similarly, Azrin and Armstrong (1973) noted that another type of therapeutic punishment, overcorrection, contingent on spilling while eating, resulted in a corresponding decrease in other inappropriate mealtime behaviors.

These facts point to the importance of punishment as a viable therapeutic agent. It also will be apparent to the reader that decisions of when to use therapeutic punishment and the frequency and type of punishment tend to be complex and must be decided on an individual basis. Assuming that punishment is applicable for a given situation, the ensuing section describes types of therapeutic punishment that are at the clinician's disposal.

Types of Aversive Techniques

Two forms of treatment strategies have been described in the literature as related to aversion therapy: classical conditioning and operant conditioning (punishment). The basic elements of classical conditioning consist of pairing a neutral stimulus or event with a behavior that already elicits a particular reaction from a client. By repeatedly pairing stimuli and responses, separate events become associated in such a way that the client exhibits the same response when either stimulus is present. In aversive conditioning, the stimulus that occasions the maladaptive behavior would be paired with an aversive stimulus. Thus, after repeated pairings, the once-pleasurable stimulus will occasion fear. The experiment by Watson and Rayner (1920) is the traditional example of aversive therapy using a classical conditioning model. Albert, an 11-month-old boy, was the subject studied. He had played with a white rat for weeks and found it to be a pleasurable experience. The researchers began by pairing a loud noise, which produced a startle response and presumed fear by Albert, with the presentation of the rat. Albert soon developed the same reaction to the rat that he exhibited with the noise, whether or not the rat was paired with the noise. Furthermore, his "fear" soon generalized to other white objects.

Classical conditioning is considered to produce an involuntary response and generally is related to patterns of reflex behavior, while operant conditioning generally is considered to involve higher-order behaviors where the client can make a choice in responding. In addition, classical conditioning changes the stimulus value of the neutral stimulus, while operant conditioning focuses on changing the response pattern (Bootzin, 1975). Even though classical conditioning can be used in a number of different ways, the most prevalent aversion therapy methods are the operant procedures.

The use of aversive stimuli in operant procedures can be defined in four different ways (Church, 1963):

1. Escape training, a method in which the noxious stimulus is presented in a manner such that the client can terminate it by exhibiting a predefined adaptive behavior.
2. Avoidance training, a method in which the noxious stimulus is absent and the client is able to prolong the onset of the aversive stimulus.
3. Passive avoidance or punishment, where the noxious stimulus also is absent; however, in this case, when the client exhibits a predefined maladaptive behavior, the result is the onset of the punishment procedure.
4. Preservation, where the noxious stimulus is present, and when the client elicits a predefined behavior the presence of the noxious stimulus is prolonged.

It should be noted that in practice none of these procedures are implemented in a pure sense and any aversive program probably has some features of each.

To describe these principles more clearly, some examples of how aversive techniques might be employed will be presented. One of these precepts, referred to as escape training, is not used frequently with clients; however, one way in which it might be employed would be in a school setting. Assume that the therapist wishes to teach a child a designated set of arithmetic problems considered aversive for this particular student. The therapist tells the child that (s)he must get five math problems correct regardless of the number of trials required, thus the client must engage in the aversive task. However, if (s)he obtains correct performance on the first trial for each problem, the performance of additional trials can be avoided, so the child would have escaped practice of math problems.

The second operant aversive technique, avoidance, is different from escape in that the noxious stimulus is not presented initially. Let us suppose that a child is misbehaving in class. The teacher informs the child that s(he) will have to stay inside at recess and write sentences on the blackboard if the behavior persists. If the child then stops the designated problem behavior pointed out by the teacher, the punishing aversive consequence is avoided.

Passive avoidance (punishment) was mentioned as the third type of procedure. In this instance, as we have noted, a specific behavior of a client would result in the initiation of punishment. A teacher might apply this techniqe by using a noxious stimulus contingent upon fighting. Assume that the child does not like to write on the blackboard (noxious stimulus). When (s)he exhibits an inappropriate behavior (fighting), then the aversive or noxious consequence results.

The fourth type of technique defined as an operant method is preservation. An example of this method using the example of the child and the chalkboard might go as follows. First, the child has received a punishment and is writing at the chalkboard. Second, the child exhibits a specified inappropriate behavior such as talking out loud while writing. Third, because of the inappropriate behavior, the period of writing on the chalkboard is extended.

Of the aversive procedures described, the avoidance or passive avoidance (punishment) paradigms seem to be the most efficient. With escape, for example, the noxious stimulus must be presented first and then terminated when the client begins to desist from self-abuse. The problem is that the temporal arrangement of the stimulus event is such that the aversive stimulus is presented before the client has the opportunity to perform the desired response. In addition to the client being administered a greater number of aversive stimulus presentations, the time required to suppress the targeted behavior is greater. Furthermore, overpresentation of the aversive stimulus may result in habituation (Azrin & Holz, 1966).

Properties of Punishment

In the literature on therapeutic punishment, the technique's applicability for a wide range of human behaviors has been shown. There is no one theory, however, capable of adequately incorporating the range of phenomena observed in experimental studies on the effects and side-effects of punishment procedures with humans, since most of the well-controlled studies in the field have been conducted with infrahumans. A number of specific principles have been developed in the treatment of animals. Perhaps those most commonly agreed to with respect to the response of animals were proposed by Azrin and Holz (1966). While sufficient data do not exist as yet to demonstrate a direct one-to-one relationship in these effects, there are some data available to support the hypothesis that there are major similarities.

Azrin and Holz's (1966) 14 principles on how to achieve maximal effectiveness with punishment procedures were presented earlier. Our intuition tells us that these principles seem sound for use with humans as well; however, only with rigorous empirical research can we delineate definitive principles for the efficacious use of therapeutic punishment with humans.

Schedules of Punishment

In the previous section, reference was made to a number of properties of punishment. It was noted earlier that punishment should be administered every time the maladaptive target behavior occurs, a procedure known as continuous punishment. However, at times, this method of applying punishment can be difficult to maintain; thus, we would like to review briefly alternative schedules for applying punishment.

The term "schedule" refers to how often the punishment contingency is in effect. When the punishing stimulus is presented for every *n*th response, this is called *fixed-ratio punishment*. Alternatively, when the punishing stimulus is presented after a prescribed period of time, the schedule is known as *fixed-interval punishment.*

The early work with schedules of response consequation was done solely with reinforcement. This precedent was in large part due to the work of Ferster and Skinner (1957). Since that time, however, reports have been made regarding the use of punishment procedures. Typical studies include those of Brady (1969), Appel (1960), and Luiselli and Townsend (1980). As with the behavior modification literature in general, the early studies in this area dealt primarily with infrahuman subjects. An early study by Appel is a typical example. In this study, two Macaca Mulatta monkeys were the subjects. The experimental chamber was rigged using an old refrigerator compartment. The wall on which the discriminative stimuli (lights) were installed was electrified. After an initial training period to familiarize the animals with the setting and the discriminative cues, training began. The lights were green and white, and these colors were used as discriminative stimuli that forewarned the onset or the lack of a shock. The lights were used alternately as escape or as cues for the onset of the aversive stimulus. Schedules under which the aversive stimulus was delivered altered on a variable-interval schedule of six and then one. The general findings of this experiment were that mixing schedules of punishment and the opportunity to avoid it resulted in a very high number of attempts to avoid the punishing stimulus while both lights were being presented. This rate of responding decreased as the subjects were better able to assess the discriminative properties of the punishment schedules in force.

As the researchers began to evaluate the effects of different punishment schedules on humans, the situations under which these tests were made tended to be highly controlled and analog in nature. An example of the type of study conducted during this phase of development in schedules of punishment with both human and nonhuman subjects is a study by Crider, Schwartz, and Shapiro (1970). Two schedules of punishment were compared. These were punishment delivered after every response (spontaneous electrodermal responses were punished with an aversive tone) versus punishment delivered after every other response. The continuous punishment proved to be more effective. Similar types of effects have been found in more natural settings such as the treatment of aggressive behavior of children in a classroom (Deur & Parke, 1968).

The type of punishment schedule used has important practical implications. Luiselli and Townsend (1980) have described a number of benefits of schedules of punishment less frequent than a continuous schedule and the benefits that would accrue if these latter schedules proved effective. Among the points that they note are that less staff time would be required to administer the procedures. Also, the time that the child is removed from or actually receiving punishment should be decreased or at least spread over a greater period of time. Despite these generally agreed-upon benefits for less-than-continuous schedules and the mixed findings related to effectiveness of such schedules (Romanczyk, 1976), the continuous schedule still seems most practical. Frequently it is found that the more the punishment schedule approximates a continuous one the greater the response suppression with both humans and lower animals (Clark, Rowbury, Baer, & Baer, 1973; Estes, 1944). These are, however, tentative conclusions, since a great deal of research in this area is still needed and a number of variables such as type of behavior, subject treated, intensity of the behavior, and its frequency, as well as the therapeutic punishment procedure implemented, are important variables that could effect the general rule of schedule delivery and effectiveness.

Types of Punishment and Related Behavior Decelerators

There have been a number of punishment techniques employed in the behavior modification literature. The purpose of this section is to describe and define briefly some of the general categories of punishment. Definitions of specific punishment procedures will follow in chapters devoted to each of these major categories of punishment.

For purposes of this chaper we have decided to categorize punishment into three general types: presentation of aversive stimuli, removal of positive events, and punishment based on penalties and effort. In conceptualizing these three ways of giving punishing consequences, it is important to avoid confusing these pragmatic ways of reducing or eliminating inappropriate behavior with the methods in which aversive stimuli can be presented that are described under types of aversive techniques.

Presenting aversive stimuli can be defined broadly as using a noxious stimulus (as noted earlier, this must be determined on an individual basis) contingent on the occurrence of a selected behavior that the therapist wishes to decrease or eliminate. Pairing of a stimulus that is highly aversive for the client will result in the decrease or elimination of the target behavior. This approach is the most traditional view of punishment. The second form of aversive event is the removal of reinforcing stimuli from the client. Since, by definition, a person cannot be reinforced unless a deprivation state exists for that particular reinforcer, the removal of reinforcing stimuli produces a deprivation state and thus is an aversive consequence. Therefore, in the present instance, removal of reinforcing consequences is, by definition, a punishing event.

A third form of punishment is based on penalties and effort. These procedures differ from the first form of punishment primarily in the kind of aversive stimulus used. In the first form, reference is made to a noxious substance such as lemon juice, shock, or the like. With procedures for work and effort, however, reference is being made to a particular task that the subject must engage in as the form of punishment. A typical example of a work-and-effort procedure would be overcorrection, where the subject is required to put out a great deal of effort to perform the requested task. Thus, for example, the client might be required to sweep a floor or polish furniture.

Among the alternative adjuncts to punishment are reinforcement methods such as differential reinforcement of other behavior (DRO), the differential reinforcement of low rates of behavior (DRL), and differential reinforcement of incompatible behavior (DRI). The basis for all of these methods is to observe the client performing adaptive behavior and then reinforce him/her for it.

A second set of alternative adjunct techniques is the training of skills incompatible with the deleterious response. Typical examples are teaching the persons to give socially appropriate verbal responses rather than physically lashing out, or encouraging leisure and other adaptive behaviors in lieu of self-stimulation or other forms of aberrant behavior.

A final alternative adjunct to be reviewed is ecobehavioral management. This procedure refers to making manipulations in the environment as a means of enhancing positive rather than inappropriate behavior (e.g., arranging schedules to allow for more situations where cooperation and interaction might be planned).

Although all of these three procedures are termed "alternatives to punishment," it is our contention that when punishment is chosen as the treatment of choice, these alternative procedures should be included in the comprehensive program. As the reader may recall, Azrin and Holz (1966) delineated several principles to maximize the effectiveness of punishment procedures, principles that are in complete congruence with the procedures just discussed.

In this section, three general categories of punishment and some alternatives that have proven to be useful in past research have been presented. The following section will be devoted to a description of the populations and settings that have been used routinely in the treatment of problem behaviors with therapeutic punishment.

Settings and Populations

The range of settings and populations effectively treated with various behavior decelerators is perhaps as broad as the number of problem behaviors treated. The types of settings that are applicable for these techniques are limited only by the ingenuity of the persons employing them.

Briefly, we would like to point out some of the settings that have been used in the treatment of behavior problems with therapeutic punishment. Perhaps the most frequently cited setting for these treatments is large hopsitals for the mentally retarded and psychiatric populations. This situation is not unusual or even surprising when one considers that these populations are usually the hard-core groups with respect to frequency and intensity of problematic behaviors (e.g., self-injury and extreme physical aggression) (Forehand & Baumeister, 1976).

In one recently conducted case, Duker (1976) treated a profoundly mentally retarded female (age 16) for banging her head against the wall and hitting her cheeks, temple, and forehead with her fists. This setting was typical since it was conducted in a state hospital in which the child had been institutionalized for eight years. Other aspects of this problem were that the behavior had been occurring for several years, had steadily increased in intensity, and was resulting in marked physical injury to the child.

These procedures also have been used effectively in residential facilities for mentally retarded, autistic, and schizophrenic children. Lovaas and his colleagues have documented numerous cases of changing behavior with these procedures (Bucher & Lovaas, 1968; Lovaas, 1968; Lovaas, Freitag, Gold, & Kassorla, 1965; Lovaas, Freitag, Kinder, Rubenstein, Schaeffer, & Simmons, 1966; Lovaas, Schaeffer, & Simmons, 1965; Lovaas & Simmons, 1969; Simmons & Lovaas, 1969).

In addition, punishment and other behavior-decelerative procedures have been employed successfully in classrooms, short-term inpatient units, and in the home. Virtually any setting in which the behavior change agent can maximize control of the situation can be appropriate in the design of these types of programs.

Likewise, punishment techniques are effective with many different populations. The authors already have mentioned several: psychiatric patients, persons mentally retarded, autistic children, and self-abusive and physically aggressive individuals. These procedures have been used successfully on children with noncompliant behavior and learning deficits and with individuals of all ages.

Arguments against the Use of Punishment

There have been a number of arguments against the use of punishment. Nine of these are:

1. An undesirable emotional state is produced by some punishment methods.
2. Social disruption may occur after an individual receives punishment (Adler, 1930/1970; Skinner, 1953), which may lead to avoidance or escape of the situation.
3. The effects achieved with these procedures may be only temporary (Estes, 1944).
4. There is a potential that the procedure may have some socially reinforcing properties.
5. At times, social aggression appears to be a byproduct of physical punishment.
6. Punishment may teach the individual what behavior not to exhibit instead of teaching what behavior is appropriate.
7. Punishment is simply "unpleasant" for both the punisher and the recipient of the aversive stimuli.
8. There is great potential for abuse of the procedure.
9. Since the research that has been accumulated is minimal, the general concept of applying therapeutic punishment procedures to the treatment of humans does not have the benefit of decades of research.

All of these arguments against punishment must be taken into account. What follows is a more detailed description of each of these phenomena and the points to consider in their evaluation.

As with any treatment program implemented, punishment procedures need to be evaluated, not only with respect to their effects on the specific behaviors treated, but also to the effects and/or side-effects of these treatments on other behavior (Axelrod et al.,

1978). Discussion of such evaluations are popular and have a histori-
cal precedent of at least 30 years (e.g., Adler, 1930/1970; Skinner,
1953). However, in research that has been conducted to evaluate
side-effects of punishment, data tend to be anecdotal and these
issues rarely have been empirically addressed. Thus, at least to some
degree, there is disparity between the type of studies researchers
indicate are important and those conducted.

Despite this lack of research, punishment studies frequently have a
discussion of side-effects based on informal retrospective reports. It is
possible that, when using such a potentially unreliable system, many
positive and negative side-effects of punishment would go unreported.
Also, the frequency or intensity of these side-effects could be rated
inaccurately. Nonetheless, it is interesting to note that clear patterns
have emerged with respect to behaviors informally observed. Let us
now begin a discussion of the nine points just delineated.

Undesirable Emotional State. The first argument against the use
of punishment is the undesirable emotional state created. As Azrin
and Holz (1966) note, we need be concerned with this emotional
reaction only when a chronic behavioral disruption occurs. However,
as Hunt and Brady (1955) and Hearst (1965) found in their animal
experimentation, most disruptions were temporary in nature. Likewise, with humans, there appears to be no chronic emotional malad-
justment (Azrin & Holz, 1966). For instance, one experiment employing shock seems to indicate an emotional reaction related to the
device used as opposed to the procedure employed. Baroff and Tate
(1968) reported that the only deleterious effect observed in their
successful use of this procedure was a phobic response to buzzing
sounds. In another study, Simmons and Lovaas (1969) noted that
the child subject showed an aversion to the sight of the hand-held
shock stick, which had to be replaced with a remote-control device.
These findings are likely to be related to a pairing of a device (discriminative stimulus) and the ensuing shock (classical conditioning).

Emotional reactions also have been reported with other punishment procedures, including overcorrection. Typically, responses observed are crying (Matson, 1975) and increases in socially inappropriate collateral behaviors as the treated behavior decreases in
response rate (Epstein, Doke, Sajwaj, Sorrell, & Rimmer, 1974). Additionally, self-injury (Azrin, Gottlieb, Hughart, Wesolowski, &
Rahn, 1975) and increases in stereotypic behaviors (Rollings, Baumeister, & Baumeister, 1977) have emerged after the onset of treatment. However, in most cases, as noted earlier, these effects are
temporary and/or not as severe as the treated behavior.

Social Disruption. A second argument used to deter the use of punishment procedures is the creation of social disruption in the individual's life. This disruption could be severe, leading to avoidance or escape of the situation, resulting in a decrease in social relationships. Obviously, this decrease in socialization could have effects as profound as the original behaviors treated with punishment. However, several steps could be taken in the process and are suggested as part of the implementation of any punishment procedure, to minimize the chance of decreasing social contacts. Specifically, three aspects of the punishment process mentioned earlier would need to be monitored before starting a punishment program. First, the individual being treated should be on a rich reinforcement schedule. Second, avoidance or escape of the situation should be made impossible. Third, the behavior punished should be operationally defined and very specific. Therefore, the individual would learn that the behavior being punished was salient, while other behaviors in the same and other situations were richly reinforced.

Temporary Nature. The third argument, that punishment effects are temporary, is based on a study of Estes (1944) in which previously punished responses increased during a period of extinction. This study was used as a basis for extensive commentary that punishment only suppresses responses and does not weaken them; however, more recent punishment studies do not support this contention. If caution is taken so that (1) the punishing stimulus does not acquire discriminative reinforcing properties and (2) the punishing contingency is maintained during the extinction or follow-up, punished responses will not recover. Therefore, as long as the contingencies remain in effect after the initial treatment is completed, which should be the case with any behavioral intervention, the effects of punishment will be permanent and not temporary. If the punished behavior increases, Azrin and Holz (1966) have noted, "this recovery during extinction is probably not a function of the punishment process, but rather a function of the discriminative properties acquired by the 'punishing' stimulus" (p. 438).

Socially Reinforcing Properties. Another potential problem with punishment is that social contact provides reinforcement for the client in many cases. The degree to which this variable impacts on therapeutic punishment's effectiveness and general social desirability may vary considerably from person to person. For example, the amount of resistance a client demonstrates during administration of overcorrection can and does dictate the amount of physical guidance and, thus, the amount of contact that the trainer must have with the

client. In many cases, this additional contact can serve, at least in part, as a positive consequence. To date, however, few studies have been designed to evaluate this issue directly. In direct clinical work, the best way to alleviate this problem is to make a complete functional analysis of the situation and the punishing stimulus. Instead of assuming a stimulus is punishing, the clinician is advised to observe the effect of the assumed punishing stimulus on the subsequent frequency of the targeted behavior. If the response rate decreases, the stimulus may be considered a punisher.

Aggression. Another frequently cited side-effect of punishment is aggression. This behavior occurs in several forms. One type is operant aggression. It has been found that, when one individual delivers punishment to another, the punished individual often exhibits aggressive behavior against the punishing agent (Delgado, 1963). The functional purpose of this aggression would be to decrease or eliminate the punishment. Maintenance of this type of aggression would be controlled by the potentially positive effects of the aggression.

A second type of adverse emotional side-effect of an aggressive nature is termed elicited aggression. This type of aggression is exhibited against anyone in the client's view rather than being specific to the person administering the punishment (Ulrich & Azrin, 1962). However, despite the considerable evidence available to support the prevalence of this phenomenon among animals (Azrin & Holz, 1966), there is still some controversy as to whether it is present in humans (Lovaas & Simmons, 1969).

Appropriate Behavior Not Learned. A sixth argument against the use of punishment is that the punishment procedure teaches an individual which behavior to suppress but does not teach appropriate behavior. This statement is absolutely true if the punishment procedure is used exclusively. We, as well as other proponents of therapeutic punishment, have always maintained that punishment procedures should be used only in the context of a rich reinforcement schedule where the individual is taught that reinforcement will be provided when the person exhibits appropriate behavior and that only when the specific targeted inappropriate behavior is exhibited will punishment occur.

Unpleasantness. Another general comment about the use of punishment is that the entire procedure is unpleasant for both the punisher and the client. Any person who has been involved in an overcorrection procedure can attest to this fact; however, two comments seem appropriate. First, as will be noted in subsequent chapters, punishment procedures should be used only after previous attempts with less restrictive alternatives have been made (e.g., reinforcement procedures). Therefore, precautions are taken that punishment procedures are used only in situations where the behavior is particularly resilient or life-threatening to the client. In these situations, the benefits achieved through therapeutic punishment seem to outweigh the unpleasant aspects of the procedure. Second, punishment, when applied correctly, is effective in a relatively short period of time. Again, the benefits outweigh the short-term aversive costs.

Abuse. Probably the most persuasive argument against the use of punishment procedures is the possibility that the procedure will be abused. Such concerns are based on the frequent misuse of aversive contingencies in everyday life. However, the potential exists for any procedure to be abused (e.g., positive reinforcement is used incorrectly when given noncontingently or for inappropriate behavior). Likewise, Liberman and Davis (1975) have argued cogently that drugs have been inappropriately used as punishing agents in some psychiatric settings. We will present guidelines for the use of punishment procedures in a later chapter aimed at minimizing the abuse of therapeutic punishment.

Few Well-Controlled Studies   Lastly, it is recognized that the effects and side-effects of therapeutic punishment are not completely known. The application of therapeutic punishment with humans is in its infancy. Well-controlled studies are necessary to help evaluate potential effects and side-effects of the procedures (Lichstein & Schreibman, 1976).

As can be seen from a review of this section, there are a number of potential problems with punishment procedures. These difficulties are primarily of an emotional nature, although other problems such as the potential abuse of the procedure exist. Despite these disadvantages there are also a number of positive effects, which, when considered, make the use of punishment feasible at least in some instances. A description of some of these advantages is what will constitute the following three chapters.

Conclusion

The purpose of this chapter has been to present a professional definition of therapeutic punishment and how it differs from a lay definition. Also, some properties of therapeutic punishment and arguments for and against its use have been presented. Finally, different types of punishment procedures have been delineated briefly.

It was noted that initial studies on reinforcement and punishment schedules were conducted with animals. In the last 15 years in particular, however, there have been a number of applied studies with humans over a wide range of settings with diverse numbers and types of problem behaviors.

Likewise, the types of aversive stimuli and punishment procedures that have been developed are as diverse as the settings described and behaviors treated. In the 1960s and early 1970s the aversive stimuli used were more socially undesirable, at least to the lay public, than today. The most visible example is contingent electric shock. Because of the social restrictions applied to this procedure, it is rarely used at the present time.

In summary, therapeutic punishment has been shown to be an effective and warranted procedure in certain cases. We feel that this viable behavior change method should be explained in detail to dispel any misconceptions about its application and effectiveness. As with any program initiated on any level, from individuals to systems, the key word is consistency. We hope to point out repeatedly that therapeutic punishment must be applied from beginning to follow-up in a consistent manner to obtain optimal results.

We would make one final note before concluding this section. In each subsequent chapter, the term "punishment" will be used according to Azrin and Holz's (1966) definition. We do not intend to belabor this point any further; however, a clear understanding of the functional nature of this procedure is essential and the gross misconceptions and incorrect definitions in the past have warranted our concern.

In the following chapters, a more detailed review of potential alternative punishment procedures will be discussed, as well as how they are used with the specific behaviors and populations in which each has proven to be the most successful. Also, an attempt will be made to document some of the empirical data that are available to support each of these treatment methods.

2

Punishing Stimuli

Introduction: Terminology

As noted in the previous chapter, terminology in this area of behavioral psychology is greatly confused; therefore, we would like to begin this chapter with some definitions.

Many terms have been used in describing the process of decelerating aberrant behaviors. Some of these terms are *aversive therapy* (Abel, Levis, & Clancy, 1970; Cunningham & Linscheid, 1976; MacCulloch, Williams, & Birtles, 1971; Rachman & Teasdale, 1969), *aversive conditioning* (Caddy & Lovibond, 1976; Tanner, 1974), and *punishment* (Harris & Ersner-Hershfield, 1978; Kazdin, 1975, Romanczyk, Colletti, & Plotkin, 1980). These procedures have utilized *aversive consequences* (Conway & Bucher, 1974), *aversive techniques* (Bellack & Hersen, 1977; Berecz, 1976; Wilson & Davison, 1969), *aversive apparatus* (Weitzel, Horan, & Addis, 1977), *aversive stimuli* (Brownell & Barlow, 1980; Cautela & Wall, 1980), *aversion strategies* (Lichtenstein & Brown, 1980), *aversive events* (Kazdin, 1975), and *punishing stimuli* (Johnston, 1972).

In general, do all these terms explain the same phenomenon? More specifically, does the categorical term define the same procedure, method, or stimuli? We believe the answer to both questions is no.

Historically, aversion therapy and aversive conditioning were procedures to decelerate problematic behavior through a Pavlovian classical conditioning paradigm (Johnston, 1972; Rachman & Teasdale, 1969). The aversive therapy techniques were founded on this premise (Franks, 1964). There is still a general consensus that aversive conditioning through classical conditioning attempts to reduce behavior differently than punishment. Unfortunately, the many terms used to denote "aversive control" have been used interchangeably. We have tried to choose our terms carefully to avoid confusion and will include only research that addresses the decelerating of behavior utilizing punishment. Because of this problem, the title of this chapter, "Punishing Stimuli," was chosen instead of the more traditional term, "aversive stimuli."

Definition of
Punishing Stimuli

Another point of confusion has been the definition of punishing stimuli. Some researchers (Church, 1963; Kazdin, 1975; Rachman & Teasdale, 1969) have posited erroneously that certain stimuli can be considered primary and are inherently aversive. Kazdin (1975) further states, "Stimuli such as electric shock, intense physical assault, bright lights, and loud noises are primary aversive stimuli. Their aversive properties are unlearned and are universal" (p. 147). The problem with this line of reasoning is the further assumption that one of these stimuli (e.g., shock) will decrease universally the probability of the future occurrence of a response when administered contingently. This notion is simply untrue. As Morse and Kelleher (1977) cogently state,

> A remarkable diversity exists in the physical characteristics of events that can reinforce behavior. Included among these events are food, water, sex, electric shock, and intracranial stimulation; changes in lights, sounds, temperature, and gravity; opportunity to . . . fight; and the injection of various drugs. It has been assumed wrongly that the reinforcing or punishing effect of an event is a consistent property of the event itself; . . . the presentation of electric shock after a response has been considered an inherently negative event that will suppress subsequent responding. [p. 178]

Data are available, however, to show that shock can enhance and maintain responding (Byrd, 1969, 1972; Kelleher & Morse, 1968; Kelleher, Riddle, & Cook, 1963; McKearney, 1968, 1969; Waller & Waller, 1963). In observing the disparate effects the same event has on behavior, Morse and Kelleher (1977) report, "The evidence is overwhelming that behavior is more controlled by the nature of the prevailing schedule than by the nature of the scheduled events" (p. 193). From this point on, we can no longer refer to events as punishing unless we observe a reduction in response rate contingent on the administration of the stimulus (Johnston, 1972).

The Need for a
Funtional Analysis

The line of reasoning just noted was delinated further in a brief note by Berecz (1973) and subsequent critique by Danaher and Lichtenstein (1974). Berecz (1973) posits that "it is a general finding that experiments seem content to define aversiveness by fiat" (p. 112). A solution to this dilemma is to demonstrate aversiveness experimentally (Berecz, 1973) by independently assessing that "an aversive stimulus is really aversive" (Danaher & Lichtenstein, 1974; p. 112).

Romanczyk, Colletti, et al. (1980) carry the system of establishing punishing stimuli by empirical means a step further when they call for a complete behavioral analysis on every child they treat for self-injurious behavior. This functional assessment would insure the gathering of data noting the contingencies and schedules in effect at the time a stimulus is chosen for its potential to decrease the problematic behavior.

Punishing Stimuli
Need Not Be Painful

One final point of confusion is the belief that punishing stimuli must be physically painful. This simply is not the case. Kazdin (1975) asserts that a variey of procedures that do not entail physical discomfort have been used to decelerate behaviors. Johnston (1972) further notes that only a minority of punishing stimuli are physically noxious or painful. As a matter of fact, there have been reports where a punishing event, used to suppress behavior, was evaluated favorably by clients (Adams & Popelka, 1971).

For the remainder of this chapter, the discussion will center on specific punishing stimuli that have been used in the research literature. All punishment procedures described in this chapter have resulted in documented reductions in problematic behavior as a result of the consistent application of a specific stimulus. With this point made, all the stimuli now may be referred to as punishing stimuli in the specific studies noted.

Contingent Electric Shock

Misconceptions

A method of treatment traditionally used by behavior modifiers that has received considerable negative press has been contingent electric shock. The reluctance to use this procedure has risen to such heights that many states, at this writing, have put a virtual ban on the use of it, even in extreme circumstances (*Wyatt v. Stickney*, 1972). Despite the general reluctance to use this particular set of techniques, we take the position that they should not be completely rejected. Rather, it has been emphasized that under some situations it may be unethical not to use highly intrusive but empirically validated punishment procedures (Repp & Deitz, 1978).

Given this situation, it seems reasonable to discuss some of the reasons that have led to the current attitude toward this procedure before reviewing contingent electric shock as a treatment technique. This state of affairs has arisen due to at least two factors: misunderstanding of the procedure and misapplications of methods. The first problem surfaced in part due to the general misconceptions that the press has had concerning these techniques and in part due to the failure of behavior modifiers to educate the lay public adequately as to the value and appropriate use of such techniques. The major problem regarding misconceptions about therapeutic punishment has been the confusion over what constitutes therapeutic punishment. There have been a number of reports in the newspapers in which drugs and cruel and unusual forms of retribution, particularly in prisons, have been characterized as punishment procedures in the behavior modification tradition. A brief review of some of these problems seems relevant.

Mackey v. Procunier (1973) is one such case. A Folsom State Prison inmate was given a paralysis-inducing drug (succinylcholine) without his consent. In a similar program at Vacaville, a psychiatric facility for criminal offenders located in California, a similar case was reported. In still another case using this drug, there were confirmed reports that succinylcholine was used to intimidate inmates. In these instances, the drug was given on a haphazard basis for the "treatment" of harmless behavior within the general realm of social acceptability (pacing and grinning inappropriately). Because those in control (e.g., guards, administration, press, etc.) incorrectly label such misapplications of a drug as "punishment procedures" or "behavior modification," lay persons continue to receive the wrong impression of what therapeutic punishment is.

As noted earlier, a second problem has been the misapplication of behavior modification techniques, particularly those involving punishment. Misapplication has often resulted in the ineffectiveness of the procedures and harm and/or undue physical discomfort for the client. Consider, if you will, the 14 considerations posited by Azrin and Holz (1966) (see Chapter 1) necessary for maximal effectiveness of punishment. As each is discarded, or not addressed due to ignorance, the probability that the punishment procedure will be effective decreases.

In addition, persons who are well versed in the application of behavior modification methods are often too quick to employ punishment procedures without funtionally analyzing the situation and attempting to implement reinforcement procedures first. Premature implementation of punishment procedures may be due to the rapid effectiveness of these procedures in the deceleration of inappropriate behavior (Matson & Stephens, 1977; Risley, 1968). Also, they often tend to be easier to deploy than, for example, DRO (differential reinforcement of other behavior) programs, which require a great deal of staff time. Similarly, designing these reinforcement procedures is often difficult and requires suitable adjustments to make them effective. However, as Rimm and Masters (1974) and others have noted, "Aversive techniques, especially punishment, are rarely utilized alone: their effectiveness will be maximized and potential problems minimized when they are used in conjuction with other techniques designed to promote more effective behavior patterns" (p. 367).

Definition of Contingent Electric Shock

Contingent electric shock is the presentation, to the subject, of an electrical charge through two electrodes placed either on the fingers, forearms, legs, or feet (Rimm & Masters, 1974), immediately following an operationally defined event that the therapist is attempting to suppress. The electrodes are fastened with elastic or cloth strips, and electrode paste is often used to increase conductance (Bellack &

Hersen, 1977). The special equipment that is necessary includes an inductorium device to supply the electric current through the electrodes (Galbraith, Byrick, & Rutledge, 1970; Pfeiffer & Johnson, 1968; Royer, Rynearson, Rice, & Upper, 1971). Several types are available. Older models were designed to operate directly from house current, but the new and safer models are battery operated shock prods delivering a peak shock of 1400 volts at 0.4 milliamperes (Birnbrauer, 1968; Brandsma & Stein, 1973; Bucher & King, 1971; Corte, Wolf, & Locke, 1971; Hamilton & Standahl, 1969; Harris & Ersner-Hershfield, 1978; Kohlenberg, 1970; Kohlenberg, Levin, & Belcher, 1973; Lovaas & Simmons, 1969; Ludwig, Marx, Hill, & Browning, 1969; Merbaum, 1973; Rimm & Masters, 1974; Traugott & Campbell, 1981). Lovaas and Simmons (1969) described their apparatus as follows: "The inductorium was a 1-ft. long rod with two electrodes, 0.75 in. apart, protruding from its end. The shock, delivered from five 1.5-volt flashlight batteries, had spikes as high as 1400 volts at 50,000 ohms resistance" (p. 149).

Since the time between the behavior and the administration of shock should be kept between half a second (Hull, 1952) and one second (Bellack & Hersen, 1977), researchers have had to devise more efficient ways of administering shock. With some ingenuity, devices have been designed with long wires to allow the client some freedom of movement (Romanczyk & Goren, 1975). Harris and Ersner-Hershfield (1978) note an even more desirable solution to providing more subject mobility: the use of remote-control shock. The authors suggest that the discriminative cue of the prod is removed by the use of this device (Duker, 1976; Hamilton & Standahl, 1969; Luckey, Watson, & Musick, 1968; Prochaska, Smith, Marzilli, Colby, & Donovan, 1974; Simmons & Lovaas, 1969; Wilbur, Chandler, & Carpenter, 1974; Young & Wincze, 1974). Even more advanced equipment has been designed that delivers shock automatically when a client engages in self-injurious behavior (Whaley & Tough, 1970; Wilbur et al., 1974; Yeakel, Salisbury, Greer, & Marcus, 1970).

Contingent electric shock must be distinguished from electroconvulsive shock therapy (ECT). First of all, the purpose of ECT is to change the mood of an individual client with a particular type of diagnosed psychopathology such as depression. Thus, the aim is to curb a global response set that may entail many behaviors. Contingent electric shock, on the other hand, is aimed primarily at the deceleration of one particular undesirable response, such as head banging; thus, the focus of treatment with this latter procedure tends to be more localized.

A second difference between the two methods is the focus of the electrical charge. In the case of ECT, the current is always run through the brain (see the comprehensive review of this procedure by Scovern & Kilmann, 1980). This procedure results in brain damage, including retrograde amnesia, with the concomitant loss of important skills, for a short or indefinite period of time. As mentioned earlier, contingent electric shock typically is administered to one of the limbs, never to the brain or trunk, and involves no convulsions, no loss of consciousness, and no tissue damage (Craven, 1970).

Finally, the voltage used tends to be much higher for ECT than for contingent electric shock. The size of the charge and particularly the focus of the charge on the person's body are of considerable importance both in the purpose of treatment and the type of effects achieved.

In summary, ECT is aimed primarily at ameliorating a symptom complex and is not a behavior modification procedure. Due to this state of affairs, treatment is primarily focused on such broad-based disorders as depression or schizophrenia. While the treatment has been recommended for a broad range of problem behaviors, the empirical evidence available tends to support its use only for a few types of psychopathology, with severe depressive episodes being the most prevalent of these (Scovern & Kilmann, 1980).

Contingent electric shock, on the other hand, is a behavior modification method. It is applied for discrete behaviors such as head-banging or eye-gouging. Furthermore, as the term implies, it is given immediately and is contingent upon the occurrence of the behavior to be suppressed. The other rules of behavior modification usage also are followed. Interestingly, contingent electric shock has come under greater criticism than ECT, despite the research evidence that the former procedure has been found to be effective with a broader range of behaviors and is less physically dangerous if applied correctly.

Some Advantages and Drawbacks of Contingent Electric Shock

As noted already, one of the advantages of contingent electric shock is that when appropriately administered no physical harm results from its use. This factor is significant when it is considered that such a statement cannot be made about spanking and many other methods of punishment routinely used and considered to be less severe by the general public and many professionals.

A second advantage of contingent electric shock is that the administration of the procedure can be quite precise, perhaps more so than any other punishing stimulus (Rimm & Masters, 1974). It can be specified in terms of milliamperes and volts in minute amounts that are consistent across the time that the electrical discharge occurs and across administrations of the procedure. Also, the intensity of shock can vary with the sensitivity of the client.

Another technical advantage of contingent electric shock is that it can be applied specifically to the body part where the inappropriate behavior is most relevant. Thus, for a person hitting him/herself in the head, the shock can be applied directly to the hand administering the blows. This method may have the added advantage of making treatment more effective. While this hypothesis has not been verified with contingent electric shock, such findings have accrued with other forms of punishment (Ollendick, Matson, & Martin, 1978).

Besides the potential advantages of contingent electric shock over other forms of aversive procedures, there are also some disadvantages to these methods. Paramount among these are the general resistance to the use of such methods by the public and the misunderstanding of the method itself. Likewise, problems may arise in the area of generalization, maintenance, potential side-effects, methods of delivery, and schedules of punishment (Bachman, 1972; Birnbrauer, 1968; Corte et al., 1971; Griffin & Locke, 1974; Harris & Ersner-Hershfield, 1978; Lovaas & Simmons, 1969; Romanczyk & Goren, 1975).

Another problem with this technique is the potential for possible abuse. Butterfield (1975) outlines several safety factors that must be considered. He notes that current, not voltage, is the important variable in terms of lethalness of the shock. He also states that the path of the shock through the body should be considered and must never pass through the trunk. His third consideration deals with the possible risk to the client if the casing of the prod is touched while being shocked. His conclusion is that a number of important issues should be noted in each published article, including type of device, output characteristics, electrode material, design, area, placement, and amount of electrode paste.

Problems for Which Contingent Electric Shock Is Applicable

Contingent electric shock can be used for a variety of problem behaviors in a number of ways. One of the most common problems treated is self-injurious behavior (SIB). SIB is defined as the repetitive or stereotyped acts that produce self-inflicted injuries (Baumeister & Rollings, 1976). Numerous studies have noted the efficacy of contingent electric shock for SIB (Baroff & Tate, 1968; Browning, 1971; Bucher & Lovaas, 1968; Corte et al., 1971; Duker, 1976; Griffin, Locke, & Landers, 1975; Kohlenberg, et al., 1973; Lovaas & Simmons, 1969; McFarlain, Andy, Scott, & Wheatley, 1975; Merbaum, 1973; Prochaska et al., 1974; Romanczyk & Goren, 1975; Tate & Baroff, 1966; Traugott & Campbell, 1981; Whaley & Tough, 1970; Young & Wincze, 1974).

In their excellent review of the subject and the behavior modification procedures used to treat SIB, Baumeister and Rollings (1976) describe different types of SIB and deceleration methods. The procedure reported to be among the most frequently used was contingent electric shock. Although this method probably has wide applicability in regard to self-injurious behavior, most of the published literature concerning its effects has been plagued with inadequate experimental designs (Harris & Ersner-Hershfield, 1978). The primary function of most of these studies has been to suppress undesirable behavior rather than to evaluate treatment effects in a systematic fashion. Because of this emphasis, firm conclusions about treatment effectiveness are made more difficult. As Baumeister and Rollings (1976) note, the point that should be taken into consideration with all treatment techniques is that the published literature is skewed in a positive direction due to the tendency to publish only positive treatment results in professional journals.

Despite these methodological drawbacks, contingent electric shock does boast a most impressive record. In one often-cited demonstration of the technique's utility, Lovaas and Simmons (1969) were able rapidly to reduce self-injurious behavior in children. In their study, three children between eight and 11 years of age with severe-to-profound mental retardation were studied. Children were observed while "avoiding others." This behavior was defined as moving away from adults and whining without evincing tears, apprehension, or anger. At the same time, the children were hitting themselves. Shock was applied contingently and only for the latter behavior. Treatment was applied first while the child was on the experimenter's lap and then later while walking or standing in the room. Changes in the treated and nontreated behaviors were rapid when contingent electric shock was administered. A common finding here, which has been replicated in other research, is that the children readily distinguished between the persons who administered punishment and those who did not. Thus, rates of inappropriate behavior remained high when persons other than the therapist were with the child.

In another study, Tate and Baroff (1966) eliminated head-banging and face-slapping by an autistic child using contingent electric shock. During the initial baseline, the behaviors were occurring at five responses a minute. The rate of self-injurious behaviors dropped off to near zero after only one treatment session, and within four months the behaviors were totally absent.

These impressive findings have not been limited to the treatment of self-injurious behavior. Other problematic behaviors also treated with contingent electric shock have included tantrum behavior (Lovaas, Freitag, Kinder, Rubenstein, Schaeffer, & Simmons, 1966; Lovaas, Schaeffer, & Simmons, 1965), stereotyped screaming (Hamilton & Standahl, 1969), chronic ruminative vomiting (Cunningham & Linscheid, 1976; Kohlenberg, 1970; Lang & Melamed, 1969; Luckey et al., 1968; Toister, Colin, Worley, & Arthur, 1975; Watkins, 1972; White & Taylor, 1967), whining and inattention (Simmons & Lovaas, 1969), aggressive behavior (Birnbrauer, 1968; Brandsma & Stein, 1973; Browning, 1971; Ludwig et al., 1969; Risley, 1968), soiling pants and destroying property (Birnbrauer, 1968), excessive climbing behavior (Risley, 1968), self-stimulation (Baroff & Tate, 1968; Lovaas, Schaeffer & Simmons 1965; Lovaas, Freitag, et al., 1966; Tate & Baroff, 1966), self-induced seizures (Wright, 1973), saliva holding (Baroff & Tate, 1968; Tate & Baroff, 1966), and playing with electrical equipment (Bucher & King, 1971). The following behaviors also have been treated successfully with contingent electric shock: window breaking (Hamilton & Standahl, 1969), clinging (Tate & Baroff, 1966), incorrect picture identification (Kircher, Pear, & Martin, 1971), attempts to leave the setting (Bucher & Lovaas, 1968; Lovaas, Schaeffer et al., 1965), eating paper (Hamilton & Standahl, 1969), transvestism (Blakemore, Thorpe, Barker, Conway, & Lavin, 1963), sneezing (Kushner, 1968), spasms (Sachs & Mayhall, 1971), alcoholism (Ciminero, Doleys, & Davidson, 1975; Lovibond & Caddy, 1970; Vogler, Lunde, Johnson, & Martin, 1970; Vogler, Lunde, & Martin, 1971), and smoking (Berecz, 1976). Several of these studies will be reviewed.

Persistent vomiting can be a critical problem in need of amelioration. It has been found that this behavior and the ensuing weight loss that results can be damaging to one's health and in some cases even life threatening. In one such case, Kohlenberg (1970) treated this problem in a 21-year-old woman institutionalized since age two. Her diagnoses included mongolism and mild quadriplegia. It had been observed that the patient had vomited after every meal for three months, resulting in a loss of 13 pounds during this time period. At the beginning of the study the subject was 58.5 inches tall and weighted 74 pounds.

Treatment was instituted after mealtime in the ward dining room. The patient was brought into an adjacent private room and seated in a chair. She was given a glass of milk or juice which the author indicated facilitated the onset of a vomiting episode. The aversive contingency consisted of placing an electric prod on the patient's thigh for one second contingent on the occurrence of an abdominal contraction, which was observed to precede the onset of a vomiting episode. This treatment resulted in the rapid and long-term suppression of the problem behavior. It should be noted, however, that the delivery of shock in the manner described by the author is not advocated. Rather, the use of an electrode taped to the patient's body would result in a more precise, effective, as well as humane, treatment.

A related problem namely, chronic infant rumination, has also been treated effectively with contingent electric shock by Cunningham & Linscheid (1976). In this case, the subject was a nine-and-a-half-month-old boy who was hospitalized at a university medical center. At the point that the current intervention was contemplated, the child's presenting problems included malnutrition, dehydration, an electrolyte imbalance, and a considerable weight loss, all of which were caused by the rumination. Various methods of a less aversive nature had been tried and had proven ineffective. In this program, the shock was administered through electrodes attached to the calf (generally using adhesive tape). Shocks could be initiated using a remote-control hand switch and were administered for a half second contingent of each episode of rumination. In this case, antecedent behaviors were not treated, since the authors considered them to be unreliable. After the infant established control (suppression) over the target behavior while he was in bed, the authors generalized treatment effects while the subject was playing on the floor.

This latter study is important and is brought to the reader's attention since it incorporates many of the components of a successful contingent electric shock program. Furthermore, while the treatment in the Kohlenberg (1970) study was successful in suppressing the targeted behavior, the methods used were not as sound as the Cunningham and Linscheid (1976) procedures. In fairness to the author, this could have been due to the fact that the latter study is of more recent origin and thus incorporated the more current thinking on such treatment. Paramount among the admirable additions in the Cunningham and Linscheid (1976) study is that they tried a number of other treatments that proved ineffective before resorting to the contingent electric shock program. Additionally, they fastened electrodes to the patient to make for a more precise and consistent administration of the shock and used a remote-control box so that the punishing stimulus would not be associated only with the presence of the therapist, thus limiting the conditions under which the target behavior would be suppressed. Since the authors recognized that punishment procedures tend to be effective only under the stimulus conditions in which treatment is administered, they enhanced the likelihood that treatment effects would transfer to other stimulus conditions by providing treatment not only while the child was in bed but while the child was sitting, playing, and so on. These important considerations should be taken into account while employing contingent electric shock or other treatment procedures.

Another area that has received attention in the general area of health is alcoholism. An example of this approach is described by Ciminero et al. (1975). In their study, a 48-year-old married veteran, with a chronic drinking problem of 20 years, was treated. (The possibility of successful treatment was made more bleak by the fact that the patient had had five previous hospitalizations.) Each time the client was offered his favorite alcoholic beverage he was shocked on the arm (and later, as the movements decreased in strength, on the fingers) of the hand reaching for the drink. As with the other studies described, the treatment effects were rapid and were maintained for six months in laboratory conditions. In addition, while data taken in the everyday life situation were less stringent, the authors suggest that there was carryover of treatment effects to this latter situation.

Smoking is another common potentially harmful behavior that has been treated with contingent electric shock. An example of how this treatment can be employed with smoking is described by Berecz (1976), who treated 10 male smokers by shocking them when they were thinking of smoking. Contingent electric shock proved to be effective in a similar pattern to that described in the previously reported studies in alcoholism and weight loss due to vomiting or rumination.

A final example area in which contingent electric shock has proven effective is with various forms of undesirable sexual behavior. Although Brownell and Barlow (1980) posit that "electrical aversion has typically involved the pairing of a painful electric shock with a stimulus designed to elicit deviant sexual arousal" using "avoidance, escape, classical fear conditioning, and backward conditioning paradigms" (p. 608), punishment procedures have been used to treat exhibitionism, transvestism, use of fetish material such as trousers for sexual stimulation, and homosexual behavior (Abel et al., 1970; MacCulloch et al., 1971; Tanner, 1974). A good treatment plan for this type of behavior is described by Abel and his associates. In this case, the authors had five male clients describe situations within the general context of their problem behavior from least to most sexually arousing. These behaviors were of both a deviant and appropriate nature. A penile transducer was used to measure level of arousal and two silver electrodes were positioned on the left arm as a method of providing aversive stimulation. Tapes were made of deviant behaviors as described by the clients. The tapes were played and initially the clients were shocked after the final segment of each tape. The subjects were shocked earlier upon subsequent presentations of the tape. Finally, the clients were able to avoid the shock by verbalizing an appropriate socially acceptable sexual behavior that could be used in place of the deviant responses for sexual arousal. As in the other treatments described, this procedure was highly successful.

General Treatment Considerations for Contingent Electric Shock

When contingent electric shock is selected as the treatment of choice for a particular problem area, there are some practical treatment considerations that should be taken into account. First of all, the clinician should purchase high-quality brand-name equipment. When selecting such equipment, the unit must be of a fashion that allows variation of intensity from low to high values and may be monitored accurately and consistently. Additional factors associated with the use of such equipment can be obtained from the dealer. Second, the clinician should become well versed in the use of this equipment and the potential hazards that may accrue, prior to implementing a contingent electric shock program. Third, given that humans differ in their sensitivity to shock, it is inappropriate for the clinician to use a shock level that he feels is sufficiently aversive to produce physical injury or undue psychological pain. With respect to client safety, the paramount concern should be the client's response to various shock levels, using the minimal level that will produce the desired effects. Fourth, clients should not be allowed to choose levels of shock. This aspect of the program is important, since therapist choice of shock level significantly increases the therapeutic benefits for the patient.

Fifth, as we have noted earlier, electrodes should not be placed on the head. Additionally, placements on the torso or on opposite limbs should be discouraged. Placement of electrodes approximately two inches apart on the same limb insures that the current will travel only a short distance and that it will not travel through tissue where such a current could cause physical damage. Additional safety precautions include, but are not limited to, avoiding hazards such as water on the floor and objects such as chairs, pipes, and radiators that may contain metal. Finally, the electric shock unit should be powered by batteries, rather than by an electrical outlet. This should decrease the potential hazard of an undue amount of shock. Also, the battery units tend to be much smaller and are therefore more portable.

The production and testing of this type of equipment demands considerable expertise and training; therefore, the construction of a shock unit should be completed by a qualified engineer. Units sold across state lines in this country are subject to regulations posted by the FDA and ICC. Should the unit malfunction, the manufacturer is liable, in court; and if the clinician has built his own, then he's responsible for the integrity of the unit and any problems that arise from its use. If, however, the clinician uses equipment that has (1) passed federal standards, (2) is manufactured by a reputable firm, and (3) adheres to the safety precautions that accompany the unit, then malfunctions should be rare.

Consequently, it is noted that several investigations have used equipment intended for other purposes (e.g., cattle prods). These units should be avoided at all costs, since they are dangerous. Application of the shock with this instrument to the wrong part of the body might cause cardiac arrest or third-degree burns. It is to the credit of the organizations that manufacture such units that they (usually) emphasize that their equipment is not intended for use with humans. The clinician who disregards this sort of warning runs a very great risk of injuring his client and can be liable on both legal and ethical grounds. This latter point cannot be overemphasized.

Noxious Substances

Definition

The number of documented reports using noxious substances is fewer than what has appeared with contingent electric shock; however, there are still several research studies that lend credence to the use of these procedures in clinical practice. Also, it is worth nothing that the frequency of studies with noxious substances has increased markedly over the past few years, while the number of published studies using contingent electric shock have almost vanished (causes for the decreased use of contingent electric shock have been noted in previous sections of this chapter). It is our belief that these situations mirror the general clinical trend away from the use of contingent electric shock and toward the use of other punishment procedures that are viewed by both clinicians and the public as less intrusive.

For clinical purposes, a noxious substance is defined as any substance that is not physically harmful but is unpleasant for the client to either hear, ingest, or smell. Thus, for example, we would not typically consider a candy bar a noxious substance, since most people like to eat them. Likewise, we would not consider gasoline to be a noxious substance, since both smelling or drinking it could do physical harm to a person. Additionally, for a substance to be considered noxious it must fulfill all the other properties of punishing stimuli that we have discussed previously, such as consistent and immediate application. Typical noxious substances used in the past include, but are not limited to, 100 percent lemon juice, Lysterine®, ammonia capsules, and noise. We do not imply that these substances are universally noxious; as always, they must be proven on an individual basis.

Advantages and Disadvantages of Use of Noxious Substances

There are a number of advantages to the use of these procedures. First, as with contingent electric shock, they can be administered in a precise, topographically specific manner. This factor is of considerable importance, since with some severely mentally retarded and some psychologically disturbed persons making the connection between the punishment and the targeted behavior is difficult. However, there exists variability in how specifically these procedures are linked to the behavior, since noxious substances include a broad range of stimuli and a number of focal points to which the potentially punishing stimuli can be administered. For example, placing a distasteful solution in the mouth of a child after he has bitten his lip, a behavior that has been causing him considerable tissue damage, might be useful. A stimulus that might eventuate in a less topographical administration might be noise. This stimulus should be applied only to a specific problem behavior in a case where a child was hitting herself in the ear, and even then the topographical specificity might not be as precise as with some other methods. (It should be noted that topographical specificity is not an essential characteristic in all cases. We are referring here to those situations where it may be an asset. It remains an empirical question as to the most efficacious stimulus for each problem behavior, each individual, each setting, and so on.

A second important advantage of noxious stimuli, one that can be said of many of the other punishment procedures, is their rapid effectiveness. This factor has been well documented in the treatment literature. These findings are further enhanced by the fact that such changes occur with some severe and highly resistant behaviors.

A third advantage of this method over contingent electric shock is a point alluded to earlier: Noxious stimuli are generally considered less objectionable than contingent electric shock (Luiselli, 1981). Since noxious stimuli have been found to be effective with a number of behaviors that also have been treated successfully with contingent electric shock, this factor becomes more important.

The two major disadvantages of this method of therapeutic punishment are the potentials for physical harm and for abuse, each of which could lead to mistreatment of the client. These two problems go hand in hand, since physical harm usually results when the methods are not used properly. A typical example concerning the inappropriate use of such procedures would be the excessive use of a substance such as 100 percent lemon juice. Excessive amounts of such a substance conceivably could cause the client to become nauseous. Certainly, the thoughtful clinician will wish to consider these variables before instituting such treatments.

Types of Noxious Substances and Applicable Problems

A number of substances have been used systematically to decrease problematic behavior and therefore warrant the title "noxious." These include lemon juice (Apolito & Sulzer-Azaroff, 1981; Becker, Turner, & Sajwaj, 1978; Cook, Altman, Shaw, & Blaylock, 1978; Marholin, Luiselli, Robinson, & Lott, 1980; O'Neil, White, King, & Carek, 1979; Sajwaj, Libet, & Agras, 1974; Turner, Sajwaj, & Becker, 1977), shaving cream (Conway & Bucher, 1974), Tabasco sauce (Bright & Whaley, 1968), aromatic ammonia (Altman, Haavik, & Cook, 1978; LeBoeuf & Boeverts, 1981; Tanner & Zeiler, 1975), ice (Drabman, Ross, Lynd, & Cordua, 1978), noise (Barrett, 1962; Flanagan, Goldiamond, & Azrin, 1958; Goldiamond, 1967), water squirts (Robinson, Hughes, Wilson, Lahey, & Haynes, 1974), and mouthwash (Matson & Ollendick, 1976; Pollow, McPhee, Luiselli, & Marholin, 1980). These substances have been used to control tantrums, chronic vomiting, public masturbation, postural abnormalties, SIB, self-stimulation, and aggressive behavior.

To allow the reader to get a more thorough understanding of this particular set of treatment procedures we would like to present examples from the preceding references. One behavior frequently targeted has been chronic rumination. Sajwaj et al. (1974) treated a six-month-old infant at a large medical school for chronic rumination using the lemon juice method. The rumination had resulted in considerable weight loss and had led many professionals to conclude that the present condition was life threatening. Treatment consisted of squirting 5 to 10 cc. of lemon juice into the child's mouth with a 30-cc syringe when vigorous tongue movements (the antecedent of rumination) were detected. The procedure was used at each of the child's meals. During baseline (which had to be kept short due to the severity of the problem), the number of time intervals in which ruminations were monitored was very high. However, when treatment was introduced, changes in a positive direction rapidly occurred. The authors suggest this approach as an alternative to massive noncontingent attention or contingent electric shock. These findings have been replicated by Marholin, Luiselli, Robinson, & Lott, 1980.

Another study that involved the use of a noxious substance placed in a person's mouth was described by Conway and Bucher (1974). In their study, a profoundly mentally retarded child was treated for tantrum behavior. The child had been treated with a number of other procedures such as positive reinforcement, extinction, and time-out, all without success; hence the authors resorted to the use of a squirt of shaving cream in the child's mouth contingent on screaming, which preceded the tantrum episodes. While this method was effective, we would recommend that less aversive solutions be tried first, such as reinforcement for incompatible behavior. Should this prove ineffective a safer form of punishing stimulus could be tried. In a similar study where the child was biting others, Lysterine® sprayed in the mouth proved effective (Matson & Ollendick, 1976). Alternative stimuli such as Lysterine®, lemon juice, or cold water are recommended.

Another type of punishment briefly referred to earlier in this chapter is the use of sound as a conditioned punishing stimulus.

Although an analogous demonstration, it has been shown that various levels of pure tones could markedly decrease error rate on a memory task when used in a contingent fashion (Erickson, 1970). Certainly, the applicability of this stimulus to other problem areas is worth considering; however, the potential for ear damage with such methods exists, so specialists in audiology and related disciplines familiar with sound levels and their potential effect on clients should be consulted in all cases. In addition, a physical examination of each person should be made, to establish the potential for damage.

A final example case of the varied applications of noxious substances involves aromatic ammonia used to treat the self-injurious behavior of two mentally retarded children (Altman et al., 1978). This procedure consisted of breaking an ammonia capsule and holding it under the child's nose contingent on hair-pulling and held in place for the duration of the episode. If necessary, the child's head was held in position by the trainer. Figures 2–1 and 2–2 show the results of such treatment with a four-year-old severely mentally retarded cerebral-palsied child with a seizure disorder. Changes were rapid but switched rapidly back to inappropriate levels when the treatment was withdrawn. (Additionally, the child received reinforcement if she could go a fixed interval without hitting. Time intervals were increased as behavior improved.)

Figure 2–3 contrasts hair-pulling in the clinic with hair-pulling in three other settings, home, grandparents' home, and school. As can be readily seen, effects generalized across settings, as evinced by the downward trends in the latter portions of baseline. Generally, behavior improved after treatment was introduced. Dates in Figure 2–3 are particularly interesting, since generalization is demonstrated, which contrasts with the effects obtained in the Lovaas and Simmons (1969) study. Thus, the generalization properties of such procedures would seem to vacillate based on the problem, its strength, the person treated, and other pertinent variables.

Drugs as Punishment

One of the important considerations in the use of therapeutic punishment is that the punishing stimuli should be applied immediately after the problematic behaviors. Since it is extremely difficult to control the effects of drugs with sufficient precision to meet this aim, there are few reports in the literature on the use of drugs as contin-

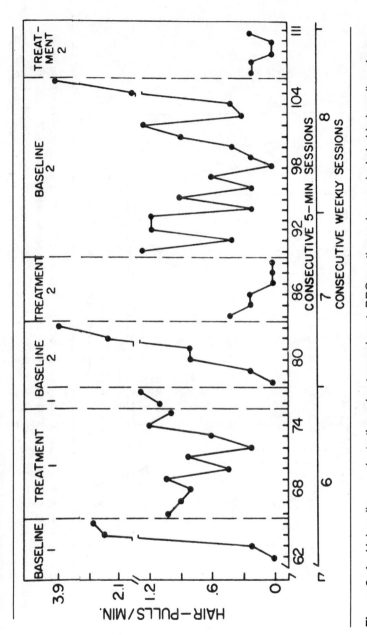

Figure 2–1. Hair-pulls per minute throughout experiment. DRO contingencies are included in baseline phases. Treatment consists of DRO contingency plus momentary ammonia contingency. The upper abscissa indicates consecutive five-minute sessions while the lower indicates consecutive weekly treatment sessions.

(*Source:* From Altman, K., Haavik, S., & Cook, J.W. Punishment of self-injurious behavior in natural settings using contingent aromatic ammonia. *Behaviour Research and Therapy,* 1978, *16,* 85–96. Reprinted with permission from authors and Pergamon Press, Ltd.)

43

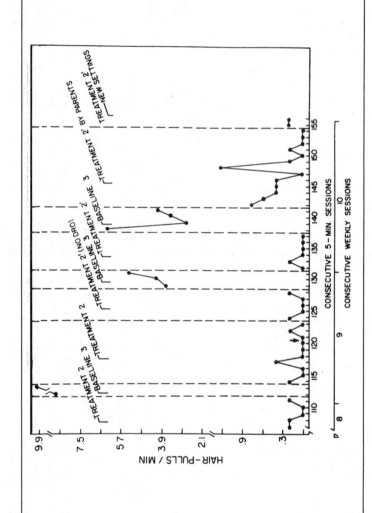

Figure 2–2. Hair-pulls per minute throughout experiment. Treatment 2' implemented by parents in a variety of settings. The arrow after session 120 indicates the point at which fading of DRO was initiated.

Source: From Altman, K., Haavik, S., & Cook, J.W. Punishment of self-injurious behavior in natural settings using contingent aromatic ammonia. *Behaviour Research and Therapy*, 1978, *16*, 85–96. Reprinted with permission from authors and Pergamon Press Ltd.

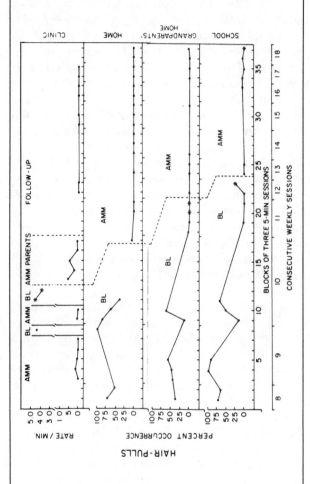

Figure 2–3. The upper graph represents frequency of hair-pulling per minute in the clinic during two alternations of ammonia treatment and baseline, followed by ammonia treatment administered by parents and follow-up. The remainder of the graph shows percentage occurrence of hair-pulls during baseline and ammonia treatment conditions in the home, grandparents' home, and school. Asterisks represent blocks of two 5-minute sessions.

Source: From Altman, K., Haavik, S., & Cook, J.W. Punishment of self-injurious behavior in natural settings using contingent aromatic ammonia. *Behaviour Research and Therapy,* 1978, *16,* 85–96. Reprinted with permission from authors and Pergamon Press Ltd.

gent punishment. However, studies that meet the necessary criteria for therapeutic punishment have been achieved in a few cases.

A very powerful drug that has been employed is Anectine. One use of this substance is described by Blanchard, Libet, & Young (1973). In their study, a 19-year-old man was treated for a long history of inhaling various substances to "get high." These episodes included inhaling spray-paint vapor, which can have deleterious physical effects. Four aversion sessions in which Anectine-induced apnea was paired with inhalation of paint fumes were given. This procedure was conducted by an anesthesiologist. The client was told that he would receive an injection that might affect his breathing and might cause him to dislike "paint sniffing." After he was seated on a table, an intravenous saline drip was started. He then proceeded to spray paint into a bag and bring it to his face to inhale. At that point the anesthesiologist, from behind the screen, added 20 mg of succinylcholine chloride (Anectine) to the injection, which caused paralysis and apnea approximately 20 seconds later. Apnea was allowed to continue for 30 seconds before the subject was artificially respirated. (It is generally reported by clients that this treatment produces extreme anxiety and fear.) The treatment was reported to be highly effective; however, as can be seen from this case, it should be used only in extreme cases and should involve close supervision and highly trained personnel.

Another area that has received attention with drugs is the treatment of alcoholism. An example of this treatment approach is presented by Boland, Mellor, and Revusky (1978). They used lithium carbonate capsules to induce "sickness" (i.e., nausea, gas, headaches, tremors, and vomiting) in alcoholic clients. Treatment consisted of having the person wash down capsules with alcohol and continue consuming a preferred alcoholic drink until the client became nauseous. Nine of 25 clients remained abstinent at six-months follow-up. The authors note that this abstinence rate was reliably higher than the control group where four of 25 clients remained abstinent at six-month follow-up. Although the success of this treatment approach is questionable, Lamon, Wilson, and Leaf (1977) report that drugs that are foul tasting are a more effective method of controlling alcoholism than contingent electric shock. Despite this conclusion, there is some justifiable controversy as to whether such aversive measures for the treatment of this problem are warranted (Pohl, Revusky, & Mellor, 1980). The principle argument centers around the fact that such a treatment is most unpleasant for the client and is attached to considerable social undesirability. (See Miller & Hester, 1980, for a more extensive review on the use of drugs to control alcoholism.)

Covert Sensitization

"Covert sensitization is analogous to the punishment procedure of the operant paradigm" (Cautela & Wall, 1980, p. 153). This procedure involves the presentation of punishing stimuli, through imagery, contingent on imagining a maladaptive behavior. This procedure has been applied successfully to a host of problematic behaviors including sexual disorders (Barlow, Leitenberg, & Agras, 1969; Curtis & Presley, 1972; Gershman, 1970; Kolvin, 1967; Segal & Sims, 1972), smoking (Cautela, 1970a; Irey, 1972; Lawson & May, 1970; Mullen, 1968; Tooley & Pratt, 1967; Wagner & Bragg, 1970), delinquent behavior (Cautela, 1967), obesity (Cautela, 1966, 1972; Janda & Rimm, 1972; Manno & Marston, 1972; Stuart, 1967), sadistic fantasies (Davison, 1968), alcoholism (Anant, 1968; Ashem & Donner, 1968; Cautela, 1970b; Cautela & Wisocki, 1969), and drug abuse (Cautela & Rosenstiel, 1975; Wisocki, 1973).

A number of steps are involved in the application. The clinician first must gather relevant data on the problem behavior, antecedents to that behavior, important stimuli that can be imagined readily by the client and are tied to the situation, and client's self-report of punishing consequential effects of the problem behavior. This information then is written into a script of vivid images and presented to the client.

Although covert sensitization, in a general sense, meets the definitional criteria for labeling it a punishment procedure, few considerations for maximizing the effectiveness of punishment can be assessed since little control may be obtained by the therapist. Effectiveness of the procedure seems to be contingent on the client's ability to imagine consequential punishing events. [See Cautela & Wall (1980) for a complete review of the treatment procedure.]

Other Forms of
Punishing Stimuli

There are a number of other stimuli that have decreased the frequency of targeted behavior when applied contingently. Some of these stimuli are hair-pulls (Banks & Locke, 1966), slaps (Birnbrauer, 1968; Koegel & Covert, 1972; Koegel, Firestone, Kramme, & Dunlap, 1974; Lovaas, Berberich, Perloff, & Schaeffer, 1966; Marshall, 1966; Morrison, 1972; Romanczyk, 1977), reprimands or verbal commands (Baumeister & Forehand, 1972; Hall, Axelrod, Foundopoulos, Shellman, Campbell, & Cranston, 1971; Kazdin, 1971; O'Leary, Kaufman, Kass,

& Drabman, 1970; Phillips, Phillips, Fixsen, & Wolf, 1971; Wells, Forehand, & Hickey, 1977), shaking (Risley, 1968; Stark, Meisel, & Wright, 1969), aversive tickling (Greene & Hoats, 1971), and facial screening (Lutzker, 1978; Spencer & Lutzker, 1974; Zegiob, Alford, & House, 1978; Zegiob, Becker, Jenkins, & Bristow, 1976). These punishing stimuli have successfully altered problematic behaviors in such areas as SIB, disruptive behavior, self-stimulation, and toileting. As can be seen from the references, many of these procedures have been developed within the past 10 years. As punishment procedures become more defined, these as well as other stimuli will be used more often.

Conclusions

Because of their wide applicability to a broad range of behaviors, noxious substances are beginning to be suggested as an alternative to the use of contingent electric shock. This development has occurred since contingent electric shock has come under close and sometimes critical evaluation. A trend of this type also highlights that professionals, advocating such treatments, have an alternative for difficult inappropriate behaviors such as extreme physical aggression.

   In this chapter we have reviewed some of the most controversial of the therapeutic procedures. Despite the fact that there has been considerable reluctance to use these methods, they are appropriate in a limited number of cases, if used judiciously. This includes insuring that (1) the methods are the only possible alternative among the behavior modification procedures available and (2) reinforcement programs are used concomitantly. Also, where possible, other more socially desirable methods should be employed. Following these steps should safeguard the clinician without having to compromise the client's right to a potentially effective treatment.

3

Work and Penalty Procedures

Introduction

In this chapter, a second general category of therapeutic punishment will be described. This group is categorized under two headings: (1) work and effort procedures and (2) penalty procedures. These terms have been used somewhat unsystematically in the past; however, for the present book, we feel the procedures, descriptive of some of the most commonly used punishment techniques in applied settings today, fall under the same general rubric. Unlike contingent electric shock and noxious substances, previously described for the treatment of inappropriate behaviors, these methods require the client to exert physical effort in the form of work, or receive fines, rather than await the delivery of a punishing stimulus. Thus, the client is involved in treatment in a much different way. These methods have become increasingly popular among professionals since they have received generally good public acceptance.

We will discuss each technique separately, beginning with work procedures. These include overcorrection and negative practice. Following this section will be a discussion of response cost, a penalty procedure used frequently to curb problem behavior.

Overcorrection

Definition

Researchers and clinicians have always believed that electric shock, as defined in Chapter 2, is a punishment procedure that should be utilized when other less intrusive measures have failed or when imminent danger is present due to the severity of self-mutilative behavior. Until the early 1970s, however, no other procedure was available that was as "effective" and "less intrusive." Clinicians, working with autistic and mentally retarded individuals, were wondering what could possibly be done to control self-stimulation, self-injurious behavior, and aggressive and disruptive acts.

Procedures were attempted but met with little success. Mulhern and Baumeister (1969) were able to reduce "rocking" by only one-third in two mentally retarded individuals by reinforcing sitting still. Hollis (1968) and Baumeister and Forehand (1971) were able to eliminate self-stimulation in mentally retarded individuals but only during brief operant reinforcement periods. Results from other experiments were equally discouraging.

Then, Azrin and Foxx introduced a procedure, overcorrection, that appeared to control resilient behavior and was indeed less intrusive than contingent electric shock (Azrin & Foxx, 1971; Foxx & Azrin, 1972, 1973b). As originally conceptualized, "The general rationale of the proposed restitution procedure is to educate the offender to assume individual responsibility for the disruption caused by his misbehavior by requiring him to restore the disturbed situation to a greatly improved state" (Foxx & Azrin, 1972, p. 16). Practically speaking, overcorrection is the punishing consequence of time-out from reinforcement; during time-out the client is required to perform some work compatible with his/her misbehavior (Matson & Cahill, 1976).

This technique was refined into a two-stage process. The first component, referred to as restitution overcorrection, required the offender to restore the disturbed area. For example, if a client made a mess in a hallway by kicking over a bucket of water, (s)he would be required to (1) clean up the mess and (2) straighten (e.g., dust, mop, scrub) other parts of the hallway. The work and effort required, therefore, would result in considerably more than merely reinstating the area disrupted. The purpose for the extended effort is to make the task particularly punishing by doing these additional repetitive tasks that result in expenditure of effort. One group with which this method has been most effective is chronically institutionalized persons who are sedentary and who are adverse to procedures that require physical exertion.

The second stage, defined as positive practice overcorrection, requires the offender to practice appropriate modes of responding in situations where (s)he normally misbehaves (Azrin & Powers, 1975; Foxx & Martin, 1975). Going back to the original example, after the individual completed restitution overcorrection, the bucket would be set up again in the hallway and the client might be required to walk past and around the bucket appropriately. This task would be repeated 10 to 20 times and differs from restitution in the purpose of the enforced practice.

At this point, after the preceding example, the reader may have observed that overcorrection is made up of any number of component procedures. Along with time-out, other strategies employed are reprimands, social isolation, feedback, negative reinforcement of incompatible behaviors, graduated guidance, verbal instruction, physical restraint, reinforcement, avoidance contingencies, and response prevention (Foxx & Azrin, 1972, 1973b; Hobbs, 1976; Ollendick & Matson, 1978). The number of such components in treatment may vary due to the pragmatic differences in overcorrection methods developed for the treatment of different problem behaviors. Because of this reason, one overcorrection procedure may look, topographically, very different from any other overcorrection procedure. Axelrod et al. (1978) went so far as to suggest that "it is not clear exactly what overcorrection is and is not" (p. 387). Therefore, overcorrection is still a greatly misunderstood method. We have attempted in Table 3–1 to delineate globally the procedural steps involved in overcorrection and the individual intervention techniques associated with each. Remember that any given step may be omitted, according to the presenting problem and contingencies in effect at the time the program is designed. Note that positive reinforcement is not a component part of the procedure (Axelrod et al., 1978; Foxx & Azrin, 1972).

Ever since the two forms of overcorrection were originated, there has been a discrepancy in the literature on how to classify each of the forms. Both have been considered punishment procedures by many researchers and clinicians; however, there have been attempts to classify one form of overcorrection, positive practice, as a type of positive reinforcing event, or education rather than punishment. These attempts have met with opposition from many professionals.

Table 3-1. Procedural Steps and Specific Techniques Involved in Restitution and Positive Practice Overcorrection.

Steps	*Intervention*
Restitution:	
1. Request to stop responding (e.g., No)	Reprimand
2. Notation of behavior to be corrected	Feedback
3. Interruption of ongoing activity	Time-out and response prevention
4. Removal from others	Social isolation
5. Requirement to do work	Verbal instructions
6. Manually assisting	Physical restraints
7. Proceed to only verbal prompting	Graduated guidance
8. Performance required repetitiously	Aversive contingencies
Positive Practice:	
9. Requirement to perform appropriate behavior	Presentation of alternative incompatible behaviors
10. Performance required repetitiously	Aversive contingencies
Conclusion:	
11. Return to activity interrupted	Negative reinforcement of appropriate behavior and decreased probability of reinforcement of avoidance behavior

A cogent and representative presentation of this argument is made by Axelrod et al. (1978), who base their argument on specific definitions within operant conditioning. They refer to Azrin and Holz's (1966) definition of a punishing stimulus: "A consequence of behavior that reduces the future probability of that behavior" (p. 381). Axelrod et al. (1978) note that since the purpose of overcorrection is to decrease the frequency, duration, and/or intensity of the inappropriate behavior that precedes the application of the overcorrection technique, it is, by definition, punishment.

With restitution, the procedures developed to treat individual behaviors seem to be generally in line with the rationale for punishment; however, positive practice was designed to teach the client new and more appropriate behaviors. Again, though, we must take the position that it is often difficult to envision how treatment will result in new alternative socially appropriate responses; that is, can we assume that what we attempt to teach is what is learned?

An example of this situation is functional movement training. With this procedure, the client is required to raise, lower, or hold her/his hands out straight for 15-second intervals at the command of the trainer. One of the earlier studies using this method was conducted by Foxx and Azrin (1973b) for hand-clapping. They noted, "Any time that Mike began clapping, he was immediately given Functional Movement Training for 5 min. . . . Mike was instructed to move his hands in one of five positions: above his head, straight out in front of him, into his pockets, held together and held behind his back by the teacher" (p. 7). The authors note that the functional movement training procedure taught and motivated the hand-clapper to hold his hands stationary and move them only for functional reasons, upon command from staff. Despite the fact that this method has been used in a number of published cases, there has never been an attempt to measure such positive educative effects of functional movement training.

Wells, Forehand, Hickey, and Green (1977) did attempt to measure the acquisition of a functional behavior, toy play, utilized as the repetition response in an overcorrection paradigm. The procedure was effective in decelerating a number of stereotyped responses; however, acquisition of the toy play behavior was observed in only one of two subjects.

One final note on this area is that some researchers (Foxx, 1976b; Foxx & Martin, 1975; Marholin & Townsend, 1978; Martin, Weller, & Matson, 1977) have not been able to fade guidance of the overcorrection response totally. Additionally, DeCatanzaro & Baldwin (1978) and Ward (1976) successfully suppressed self-injurious behavior and self-stimulatory behavior, respectively, without incorporating fading of guidance into their procedure. This strategy would suggest that independent instructional control is not necessary to suppress maladaptive behavior. Marholin, Luiselli, & Townsend (1980) further state that "the purported educative function of the procedure may be unwarranted" (p. 55). We concur and accept the logic of the preceding researchers, but the reader should be aware of the disagreement among experts over this issue.

Advantages and Disadvantages of Overcorrection

There are a number of reasons why overcorrection should be considered for use. First, it has been found to be rapidly effective. Controlling a maladaptive behavior in a few sessions is more the rule than the exception. Additionally, comparative studies have indicated that overcorrection is superior to other forms of treatment, including time-out (Azrin & Wesolowski, 1975a; Foxx & Azrin, 1972), verbal warnings and loss of recess (Azrin & Powers, 1975), physical restraint (Foxx & Azrin, 1972; Foxx & Martin, 1975), simple awakening to an alarm to control enuresis (Azrin, Sneed, & Foxx, 1973), simple correction (Azrin & Wesolowski, 1974, 1975b; Foxx & Martin, 1975), contingent social isolation and physical restraint (Foxx, 1976b), extinction/reinforcement (Matson, Stephens, & Horne, 1978), and reinforcement of other behaviors (Azrin, Kaplan, & Foxx, 1973; Duker & Seys, 1977; Foxx & Azrin, 1973b; Luiselli, Pemberton, & Helfen, 1978; Matson & Stephens, 1977; Sumner, Meuser, Hsu, & Morales, 1974). Even though some of the aforementioned studies contain methodological problems and inadequate comparisons (Forehand & Baumeister, 1976) and some projects (Doleys, Wells, Hobbs, Roberts, & Cartelli, 1976; Rollings, Baumeister, & Baumeister, 1977) indicate other treatments to be as effective or more effective than overcorrection, the data to date indicate that overcorrection "is an effective procedure for reducing and eliminating a wide range of maladaptive behaviors" (Marholin, Luiselli, & Townsend, 1980, p. 72).

Perhaps the greatest advantage next to effectiveness is acceptability of the procedure. Generally, institutional policies have banned contingent electric shock and, to a lesser degree, time-out. In these same settings, overcorrection typically has been accepted as a standard operating procedure.

A third advantage is its marked effectiveness with such a broad range of problematic behaviors. Overcorrection has been used effectively to treat behaviors ranging from aggression (Foxx & Azrin, 1972; Matson & Stephens, 1977; Ollendick & Matson, 1976) to nervous tics (Azrin & Nunn, 1973; Ollendick, 1981). (A more extensive list is presented later in this chapter in our discussion of the types of problems for which overcorrection procedures are applicable.) No other therapeutic punishment procedure can lay claim to such a diversified and empirically validated clinical base of effectiveness, with perhaps one exception, time-out from reinforcement.

A fourth advantage is its applicability to a wide range of populations and settings. Overcorrection procedures have been used with both children and adults. These individuals have come from normal, emotionally disturbed, mentally retarded, autistic, and psychiatric populations. Additionally, the techniques have been applied successfully in homes, schools, and institutional settings (Harris & Ersner-Hershfield, 1978; Marholin, Luiselli, & Townsend, 1980).

Finally, the consequences seem logical to laypersons and professionals not familiar with behavior modification. As a result it generally is not difficult to convince these persons that cleaning up an area where a disruption has occurred is a reasonable punishment.

We now will highlight some of the disadvantages of this particular treatment procedure that the practitioner should consider when picking a therapeutic strategy. One major consideration is the potential for physical injury. The potential exists when the trainer must physically guide the client through the requisite set of tasks. Such guidance could result in bruises, contusions, and, in some cases, broken bones. In cases where injury to the client has occurred, however, the therapists have proved to be poorly trained and improperly conducting overcorrection. If done correctly, the likelihood of serious injury is minimal. Certainly though, the possibility of such injuries should not be discounted and close monitoring of such treatment is a necessity.

Second, despite the fact that these procedures are effective for a wide range of problem behaviors, they are not applicable for everyone. This situation is particularly true with aggressive behavior of adults or where the possibility of physical injury is great (e.g., with clients who are extremely noncompliant and struggle during the procedure). In the situation just presented, as well as situations involving large clients, it is recommended that overcorrection not be the treatment of choice unless the person readily complies.

General Treatment Considerations

When Foxx and Azrin (1972) originally proposed overcorrection as a viable punishment procedure, they delineated four parameters that, at the time, were suspected to lead to maximal effectiveness. In their original treatise, Foxx and Azrin's (1972) rationale for each of the parameters was based on not only empirical data but also clinical intuition or face validity. Too often, in reviews of this article, a great deal is lost by simply summarizing the four characteristics in a few words. (In actuality, we have noted nine.) The four precepts were as follows:

1. *Topographical Similarity.* The restitution should be directly related to the misbehavior, lest it become arbitrary and punitive. This characteristic of relevance also should motivate the educator to apply the restitution procedure, since the educator would otherwise be forced to correct the general distur-

bance himself. Further, the offender experiences directly
the effort normally required by others to undo the disruption created by the misbehavior.
2. *Latency of Implementation.* The restitution should be required
immediately after the misbehavior, thereby accomplishing
two objectives. First, extinction of the offense will be provided, since the offender will have little or no time to enjoy
(be reinforced by) the product of the aggressive offense (Azrin & Hutchison, 1967). Second, greater inhibition of future
misbehaviors should result, since immediate negative consequences are known to be more effective than nonimmediate
consequences (Azrin, 1956; Azrin & Holz, 1966).
3. *Duration.* The restitution should be extended in duration.
While engaging in the restitution, the offender cannot engage in other activities that are reinforcing, so the restriction
period constitutes a time-out from reinforcement. This time-
out is known to be more effective at longer durations
(Ferster & Appel, 1961; Zimmerman & Bayden, 1963;
Zimmerman & Ferster, 1963).
4. *Intensity.* The offender should be performing the restitution
very actively and without pausing. Restitution constitutes
work and effort. An increased work or effort requirement is
known to be annoying and serves as an inhibitory event
(Applezweig, 1951). [Foxx & Azrin, 1972, p. 16]

Subsequent careful experimentation that has attempted to sift
out the critical variables in overcorrection has shown that not all of
Foxx and Azrin's (1972) original assumptions are still true. Each will
be addressed with emphasis on more recent data.

Topographical Similarity. We have noted three characteristics
under this one title. The most obvious and most heavily researched
point is the need of the overcorrection response to be similar to the
misbehavior. However, the research is equivocal. Many early studies
in the area of overcorrection utilized responses that were topographically similar to the maladaptive behavior. For example, Foxx
and Azrin's oral-hygiene procedure had been used for mouthing of
objects (Foxx & Azrin, 1973b), biting (Foxx & Azrin, 1972), and
coprophagy (Foxx & Martn, 1975). Foxx and Azrin (1972) required
an offender to apologize and restore the environment for aggressive
behavior. Also, Harris and Romanczyk (1976) required arm and
head exercises contingent on head-banging.

However, a series of studies demonstrated the same suppressive effects with topographically dissimilar behaviors. Epstein, Doke, Sajwaj, Sorrell, and Rimmer (1974) and Doke and Epstein (1975) successfully treated inappropriate vocalizations and inappropriate nonoral behaviors with topographically dissimilar overcorrection responses (i.e., functional hand and arm training and appropriate oral behaviors) after demonstrating suppressive effects with the use of topographically similar responses. Additionally, Ollendick, Matson, and Martin (1978) and Wells, Forehand, Hickey, and Green (1977) demonstrated that an overcorrection procedure that was not related to the misbehavior could reduce the incidence of the response before it was applied to topographically similar behaviors. However, these studies indicated that overcorrection may be more effective and durable when topographically similar responses are chosen and that the learning of appropriate incompatible behaviors occurred only when topographically similar responses were used (Ollendick & Matson, 1978).

Osborne (1976) takes this notion one step further. He states, "Although there is a logical basis for a belief in topographical incompatibility, the concept, as all concepts in the analysis of behavior, is derived *post hoc* and inductively" (p. 16). He posits that functionality of overcorrection responses and misbehavior may be the critical factor.

Foxx and Azrin's (1972) second point is that using a similar overcorrection response will motivate the educator to perform the procedure, since (s)he would have to clean up the mess anyway. This raises an important unresearched area. Would using topographically similar responses increase staff compliance in completing the procedure—since they potentially would be saving time and effort—and thereby increase the effectiveness of the program?

Foxx and Azrin's (1972) final point is that the offender should experience, firsthand, the amount of work and effort necessary to correct the consequence of his/her misbehavior. An opposing, and as intuitively feasible a viewpoint, would be to choose those topographically incompatible responses that would lead to the greatest socially facilitative responding (Osborne, 1976). Again, we have an unanswered empirical question.

Latency of Implementation. Foxx and Azrin (1972) define two procedures in operation when administering overcorrection immediately after the misbehavior: (1) extinction and (2) increased inhibition of future misbehaviors when they are consequated immediately. These are interesting concepts, but they are virtually unresearched. Azrin and Powers (1975) demonstrated equal effectiveness of both immediate and delayed application of the overcorrection contingency; however, a number of methodological shortcomings are evident. A second study (Bornstein, Hamilton, & Quevillon, 1977) did not compare immediate and delayed application, but did find that, even with delay, overcorrection was still effective.

Intuitively, we suspect that the combination of the procedures posited to be in operation would be more effective than delaying the contingency; however, no data exist to confirm this hypothesis.

Duration of the Procedure. Foxx and Azrin (1972) suggest that the procedure should be "extended in duration" (p. 16); however, the data do not confirm this hypothesis. As can be seen in Table 3–2, a wide variety of durations have been used successfully to control maladaptive behaviors. This is critical information in the implementation of a procedure, not only in terms of its effectiveness but also in terms of staff compliance.

Some degree of flexibility with the program is also useful. In several studies (Foxx, 1977; Foxx & Azrin, 1973b; Ollendick & Matson, 1976; Sumner et al., 1974) increasing the duration of the overcorrection procedure increased its effectiveness. Marholin and Townsend (1978) also demonstrated that different durations of overcorrection have varied effects on behavior.

Foxx and Azrin's (1972) second component in this parameter is a type of time-out. They suggest that the individual should not be able to participate in other reinforcing activities. This statement certainly has face validity, but no research has been done in the area. Such an issue may be important in practice when, for example, a decision is made whether to conduct overcorrection at a child's desk, in full view of peers, or in an adjoining empty room.

Intensity of Work or Effort Requirement. Foxx and Azrin (1972) have suggested that (1) overcorrection should be an "active" process and (2) it should consist of an increased work or effort requirement. These parameters are two different ways to conceptualize intensity, and Marholin, Luiselli, & Townsend (1980) suggest that the difficulty in adequately operationalizing intensity is the reason for there being no published research regarding this issue.

The first parameter has been assessed indirectly through the observation of vicarious effects of overcorrection. Sumner et al. (1974) and Doke and Epstein (1975) reported decreases in inappropriate behavior of subjects who viewed peers being treated through overcorrection. However, Matson and Stephens (1981) and Wells, Forehand, Hickey, and Green (1977) observed no such effects.

The second parameter could be operationalized as number of repetitions needed to suppress the behavior. This may be the most

Table 3-2. Duration of Successful Overcorrection Procedures and
Related Studies.

Time	Study
30 seconds	Smeets, Elson, & Clement (1975)
40 seconds	Doleys, Wells, Hobbs, Roberts, & Cartelli (1976)
1 minute	Freeman, Graham, & Ritvo (1975)
	Luiselli, Helfen, Pemberton, & Reisman (1977)
	Luiselli, Pemberton, & Helfen (1978)
2.5 minutes	Epstein, Doke, Sajwaj, Sorrell, & Rimmer (1974)
3 minutes	Nunn & Azrin (1976)
5 minutes	Azrin & Powers (1975)
	Foxx & Azrin (1973b)
	Martin, Weller, & Matson (1977)
	Matson & Stephens (1977)
	Ollendick & Matson (1976)
	Ollendick, Matson, & Martin (1978)
	Rollings, Baumeister, & Baumeister (1977)
	Townsend & Marholin (1978)
10 minutes	Harris & Romanczyk (1976)
	Kelly & Drabman (1977)
	Measel & Alfieri (1976)
12 minutes	Azrin & Wesolowski (1975a)
20 minutes	Azrin, Kaplan, & Foxx (1973)
	Foxx & Azrin (1972)
30 minutes	Azrin, Gottlieb, Hughart, Wesolowski, & Rahn (1975)
	Foxx & Azrin (1972)
	Foxx & Martin (1975)
	Sumner, Meuser, Hsu, & Morales (1974)
1 hour	Azrin & Wesolowski (1975b)
	Klinge, Thrasher, & Myers (1975)
2 hours	Foxx (1976a)
	Webster & Azrin (1973)

critical factor of all, and no research has been conducted to date
assessing this characteristic.

As can be seen from the preceding section, Foxx and Azrin's
(1972) original four parameters easily can be viewed as nine separate
research areas. Because of the relatively recent introduction of overcorrection, a paucity of data exists to answer the many treatment
considerations in terms of specific active components. However, this

particular method has been shown to be effective for the treatment of a wide range of problems. Furthermore, despite the potential for physical harm with this procedure, no such reports have been made in the literature. The method is popular and generally accepted by most professionals and laypersons as an acceptable alternative to contingent electric shock. Researchers and clinicians are limited only by their own ingenuity.

Types of Problems for Which Overcorrection Procedures Are Applicable

In the following sections, we will review a number of areas in which overcorrection treatment strategies have been employed. The methodology may vary, but the studies are representative of overcorrection procedures typically used.

Self-Stimulation. One area that has received much attention with overcorrection is self-stimulation or stereotypic behaviors. Foxx and Azrin (1973b) present a nice definition of self-stimulation:

> From a reinforcement orientation, profoundly mentally retarded persons can be considered to suffer from a deficit of functional (reinforced) behaviors directed toward their physical and social environment because of their intellectual, physical, and perceptual deficits, which probably cause such behaviors to be extinguished or punished. Autistic children, by definition of autism as self-directed, similarly receive little reinforcement from outward-directed activities, presumably because of emotional, physical, or other non-intellectual factors. For both the mentally retarded and autistic person, the process can be considered self-perpetuating. [p. 13]

Given this definition, Foxx and Azrin (1973b) delineated a treatment strategy for self-stimulation and overcorrection that proved to be the prototype for future research. In that study, they treated mentally retarded children for a number of behaviors, including mouthing objects, hand-clapping, hand-mouthing, and head-weaving. The general procedure used for all these children involved the repeated practice of behavior incompatible with the target response. The authors state that this method could be used to teach and motivate the head-weaver to hold her head in a sustained orientation and move only for functional reasons.

In the same article, the authors employed hand functional movement training (described earlier in this chapter) for stereotyped hand-clapping. Two additional children were treated for self-stimulatory mouthing. An oral hygiene procedure was used consisting of a firm "no" and subsequent brushing of the gums and teeth with a toothbrush which had been immersed in an oral antiseptic. Mouthwash was used instead of toothpaste since the children had been exposed to a large number of germs from object mouthing. These seven- and eight-year-old mentally retarded children were treated successfully in rapid fashion for all the behaviors just described.

These effects were replicated in later research. Additionally, it has been found that the hand functional movement training method was particularly effective when overcorrection was related directly to the undesirable behavior (Ollendick et al., 1978). Table 3–3 has an extensive list of studies using overcorrection to suppress self-stimulatory behavior.

Self-Injurious Behavior. As noted earlier, self-injury also has been treated effectively with overcorrection. A typical case is reported by Kelly and Drabman (1977). The problem behavior, eye-poking, had resulted in a substantial loss of eyesight in this three-year-old child. Medical reports indicated that continued poking would result in John losing his remaining vision.

John was seated in a chair with an attached table in an area isolated from other children. When he raised either hand and made contact with his eye, the teacher firmly took the child's arm and lowered it to his side. The arm was immediately raised 180 degrees, until his hand was above his head, motorically simulating an eye poke, but without actually touching the eye. John's arm was firmly raised and lowered 12 times by the teacher when poking occurred. Ten-second intervals without eye pokes were reinforced with verbal praise. Thus, treatment followed the general rationale for functional movement training described for stereotypic behavior (Foxx & Azrin, 1972) and was rapidly effective for this problem.

Matson, Stephens, and Smith (1978) treated pica and hair-pulling using a multiple-baseline design with overcorrection. The treatment for pica was similar to the oral hygiene procedure previously presented in the Foxx & Azrin (1973b) study. However, since the client in this study enjoyed drinking the mouthwash, it served as a reinforcer and therefore, a punishing stimulus was sought. A mild solution of water and hot sauce proved aversive. One important aspect of this study was that the client's gums and mouth were monitored closely by the staff physician. The treatment for hair-pulling consisted of contingent applications of overcorrection via a verbal reprimand followed by appropriate hair-brushing for 10 minutes. Reductions in both behaviors were noted immediately contingent on

Table 3–3. Studies Employing Overcorrection for Self-Stimulation.

Study	Number of Subjects	Population	Behaviors Treated
Azrin, Kaplan, & Foxx (1973)	9	Retarded adults	Rocking and hand movements
Azrin & Nunn (1973)	12	Adults and normal children	Tics and nervous habits
Cinciripini, Epstein, & Kotanchik (1980)	1	Seizure-disordered child	Hand movements
Doke & Epstein (1975)	2	Disadvantaged children	Thumbsucking
Epstein, Doke, Sajway, Sorrell, & Rimmer (1974)	2	Schizophrenic children	Hand and foot movements
Foxx & Azrin (1973b)	4	Retarded and autistic children	Mouthing and head-weaving
Freeman, Moss, Somerset, & Ritvo (1977)	1	Autistic child	Thumbsucking
Luiselli, Helfen, Pemberton, & Reisman (1977)	1	Retarded child	Repetitive masturbation
Luiselli, Pemberton, & Helfen (1978)	1	Autistic child	Hand movements
Martin, Weller, & Matson (1977)	1	Retarded adult	Object-transferring
Matson & Stephens (1981)	4	Retarded adults	Various stereotypes
Nunn & Azrin (1976)	13	Normal adults and children	Nailbiting
Ollendick (1981)	2	Normal children	Eye-twitching
Ollendick, Matson, & Martin (1978)	2	Retarded adults	Handshaking and nose-touching
Rollings, Baumeister, & Baumeister (1977)	1	Retarded adult	Rocking
Townsend & Marholin (1978)	1	Retarded child	Rocking
Wells, Forehand, Hickey, & Green (1977)	2	Autistic children	Mouthing objects and hand-flapping

the overcorrection phase. Studies using overcorrection to control self-injurious behavior are listed in Table 3–4.

   Aggressive, Disruptive, and Other Behaviors. The third area receiving the most attention with overcorrection has been aggressive behavior. A typical example of a treatment for this problem is described by Ollendick and Matson (1976). They treated a target behavior, hitting, in two young boys (ages two and two and a half years). The first step in treatment consisted of a verbal warning. If the children did not stop the problem behavior, it was followed by requiring the child to pat lightly for 30 seconds the area struck, while verbally apologizing. This procedure was repeated 10 times after each episode of hitting. The procedure proved effective, although the children often were noncompliant (e.g., crying) when required to perform the overcorrection response. However, these problems

Table 3–4. Studies Employing Overcorrection of Self-Injurious Behaviors.

Study	Number of Subjects	Population	Behavior Treated
Azrin, Gottlieb, Hughart, Wesolowski, & Rahn (1975)	11	Autistic and retarded children	Different forms of self-injury
Azrin & Wesolowski (1975a)	1	Retarded adult	Vomiting
Barrett & Shapiro (1980)	1	Retarded child	Hair-pulling
Duker & Seys (1977)	1	Retarded adult	Vomiting
Foxx & Martin (1975)	4	Retarded adults	Pica and coprophagy
Freeman, Graham, & Ritvo (1975)	1	Aphasic child	Excessive nail-picking
Harris & Romanczyk (1976)	1	Retarded child	Head-banging and chin-banging
Kelly & Drabman (1977)	1	Visually handicapped child	Eye-poking
Marholin, Luiselli, Robinson, & Lott (1980)	2	Retarded children	Vomiting
Matson, Stephens, & Smith (1978)	1	Retarded adult	Pica and hair-pulling
Measel & Alfieri (1976)	2	Retarded children	Head-banging
Zehr & Theobald (1977)	2	Retarded adults	Fist-to-head contacts

decreased in frequency as treatment progressed. This approach appears to be a reasonably good one since the positive findings were replicated and extended with children four to six years of age who were hitting and kicking other children at a nursery school (Matson, Stephens, & Horne, 1978).

Matson and Stephens (1977) report an example of overcorrection used with aggression in adults. In this study, a chronically institutionalized mentally retarded woman was treated for throwing objects in the face of other patients and staff. Treatment consisted of having the woman apologize for her actions. If she refused, the trainer verbalized the apology for her and prompted June to nod in agreement. The apology was followed by five minutes of training, which required June to pick up trash in the day room or hallways and place it in a garbage can. This simulated the disruption she caused by throwing objects.

June was manually guided through required activities when she refused to carry them out. Guidance was discontinued after a few sessions, since she voluntarily began performing the desired response. On one occasion during the first few days of overcorrection, June became so disruptive that it was impossible to guide her through the procedure without a physical struggle. On these occasions this treatment was interrupted and she was placed in the "quiet room" until agitation subsided to a manageable level. She was then taken back to the ward to complete training. Overcorrection was extremely effective. Additionally, effects were greater than those that could be obtained with reinforcement alone (differential reinforcement of other behavior was attempted) and they were maintained for an 11-week follow-up.

Bornstein et al. (1977) demonstrated another variation of overcorrection by treating a nine-year-old boy for out-of-seat behavior in the classroom. An interesting twist to treatment was the exclusive use of long-distance consultation necessitated by the isolated rural environment where treatment occurred. Overcorrection consisted of instructing Herbie that leaving his seat without permission was against the rules and that if he did this he would have three minutes deducted from his lunch or recess. During this penalty, he was required to remain in class and perform positive practice exercises, which consisted of reciting, upon request, the classroom rules: (1) "Do not get out of your seat without permission" and (2) "Raise your hand, upon being acknowledged by the teacher, ask permission to leave the seat." This sequence was repeated until the full penalty time of three minutes had elapsed.

Another overcorrection program that proved successful was described by Doleys et al. (1976). Four mentally retarded children between eight and 10 years of age were treated for noncompliance. The goal was to increase appropriate play. Thus, positive practice overcorrection required the experimenter to lead subjects to the designated task and manually guide them in appropriate play. Manual guidance consisted of assuming a position behind the subject, taking the subject's hand, and directing the task-related activity for 40 seconds. The amount of pressure or force necessary for compliance was applied.

Overcorrection also has been used to treat a number of novel behaviors. One such behavior is floor-sprawling (Azrin & Wesolowski, 1975b). Criteria for inclusion in the study included three or more incidences of lying on the floor during a 12-day baseline period. Participants included three males and eight females (mean age = 35 years) who were all classified profoundly mentally retarded. As can be seen in Figure 3–1, simple correction, which consisted of having the clients stand when they were found lying or sitting on the floor, had little effect. Positive practice, however, consisted of having clients practice sitting in appropriate places. Therefore, when found sprawling on the floor, the person was instructed not to do so and was asked to rise, walk to a nearby chair, sit down on it for approximately one minute, then proceed to another chair and repeat the exercise. This procedure was repeated with 10 chairs, requiring approximately 12 minutes to complete. The trainer encouraged clients to complete the procedure independently; therefore, he guided them only when they did not react to the verbal instructions. This treatment was effective, and treatment effects were maintained at a six-month follow-up.

There is not sufficient space here to describe all of the other types of problems with which overcorrection has proven to be effective; however, the procedures we have described are representative of techniques successfully employed. Some additional examples of behaviors similarly and effectively treated are presented in Table 3–5.

Negative Practice

Definition

Negative practice is similar to positive practice in that both procedures require the client to practice a behavior repeatedly. Hull (1943) proposed that the consequence of the repeated performance

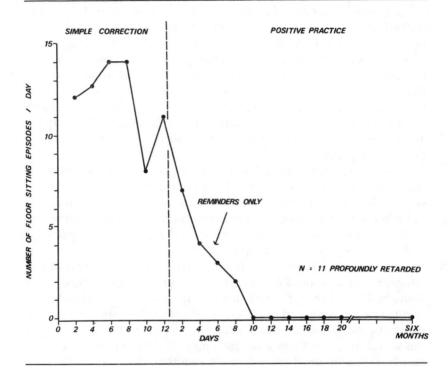

Figure 3–1. The effect of positive practice on floor-sprawling behavior is shown. Each data point designates the number of times per day, averaged over two-day periods, that the 11 retarded residents sat on the floor. During simple correction, the trainer required an individual found sprawling to stand up. During positive practice the trainer required the person to practice sitting on several chairs for a brief interval on each. The graph shows all two-day periods until the third week after positive practice was initiated, and for a sample day, six months later. The arrow designates the point after which only reminders were given and no further positive practice periods were needed since all residents arose when given the simple reminder.

Source: From Azrin, N. H., & Wesolowski, M. D. The use of positive practice to eliminate persistent floor sprawling by profoundly retarded persons. *Behavior Therapy,* 1975, *6,* 627–631. Reprinted with permission from authors and Association for Advancement of Behavior Therapy.

of a behavior is the buildup of fatigue, which is aversive. Thus, the client must perform the requisite behavior with little rest (Rimm & Masters, 1979). Theoretical and empirical support for the procedure comes primarily from laboratory work with nonhumans.

The difference between the two approaches is the requirement; that is, in negative practice the offender must perform the *incorrect* response repeatedly. The technique involves practicing the maladaptive behavior, not to perfect it but rather to eliminate it. Foxx & Azrin (1972) prefer overcorrection to negative practice because the former technique is seen as reeducative, since the purpose of treatment is either to teach new behaviors or consequences for a particular inappropriate response. A second difference is that the focus of treatment differs from a theoretical perspective. Overcorrection training is viewed as an attempt to teach or reeducate the client, while in the case of negative practice, the simple elimination of a behavior is the thrust. The viability of the former rationale has not been demonstrated empirically, although it has face validity. Axelrod et al. (1978) contend that it is doubtful that the effects of positive practice overcorrection would transfer from the control of the trainer to spontaneous emission by the client in the natural environment unless reinforcement for the desired responding occurred. Such issues, however, are empirical questions yet to be resolved.

Advantages and Disadvantages of Negative Practice

One of the primary advantages of negative practice is that it is relatively easy to conceptualize and implement. Treatment simply consists of determining what behavior is to be modified, followed by teaching the client to perform the behavior a requisite number of times. A second advantage of negative practice over a number of other procedures that fall into the area of therapeutic punishment is that it generally is considered to be an acceptable treatment alternative by professionals, particularly for tics and other nervous disorders (Rimm & Masters, 1979).

Among the disadvantages specific to this particular treatment is the fact that it has been a little-used procedure relative to the other techniques described in this chapter. This problem is exacerbated by the fact that little scientific information about the treatment's utility has occurred in the past few years. Another shortcoming of this particular procedure is the potential for harm due to noncompliance

Table 3-5. Studies Employing Overcorrection for Aggressive, Disruptive, and Other Behaviors.

Study	Number of Subjects	Population	Behaviors Treated
Azrin & Armstrong (1973)	22	Retarded adults	Eating behavior
Azrin & Foxx (1971)	9	Retarded adults	Toileting
Azrin & Powers (1975)	6	Emotionally disturbed children	Talking out and out of seat
Azrin, Sneed, & Foxx (1973)	12	Retarded adults	Enuresis
Azrin, Sneed, & Foxx (1974)	24	Normal children	Enuresis
Azrin & Wesolowski (1974)	34	Retarded adults	Stealing
Azrin & Wesolowski (1975b)	11	Retarded adults	Floor-sprawling
Barton & Osborne (1978)	Kindergarten Class	Hearing-impaired children	Lack of sharing
Bornstein, Hamilton, & Quevillon (1977)	1	Normal child	Out of seat
Butler (1976)	1	Spina bifida child	Toileting
Butler (1977)	3	Normal children	Encopresis
Doleys, Wells, Hobbs, Roberts, & Cartelli (1976)	4	Developmentally handicapped children	Noncompliance
Drabman, Cruz, Ross, & Lynd (1979)	5	Retarded children	Drooling
Foxx (1976a)	1	Retarded adult	Inattendance
Foxx (1976b)	1	Retarded adult	Public disrobing
Foxx (1977)	3	Retarded and autistic children	Lack of eye contact
Foxx & Azrin (1972)	3	Retarded adults	Various aggressions
Foxx & Azrin (1973a)	34	Normal children	Toileting
Klinge, Thrasher, & Myers (1975)	1	Schizophrenic adult	Verbal and physical aggression
Luce & Hall (1981)	3	Emotionally disturbed children	Inappropriate verbal behavior

(continued)

Table 3–5 (continued)

Study	Number of Subjects	Population	Behaviors Treated
Martin & Matson (1978)	1	Retarded adult	Disruptive vocalizations
Matson, Esvelt-Dawson, & O'Donnell (1979)	1	Emotionally disturbed children	Elective mutism
Matson, Horne, Ollendick, & Ollendick (1978)	20	"Adjustment" disordered children	Various disruptive behavior
Matson & Stephens (1977)	1	Schizophrenic adult	Throwing objects
Matson, Stephens, & Horne (1978)	10	Nursery-school children	Inappropriate disruptive behavior
O'Brien & Azrin (1972a)	6	Retarded adults	Eating behavior
Ollendick & Matson (1976)	2	Children	Aggressive outbursts
Smeets, Elson, & Clement (1975)	1	Multihandicapped child	Nasal discharge
Song, Song, & Grant (1976)	1	Retarded child	Toileting
Sumner, Meuser, Hsu, & Morales (1974)	4	Psychiatric patients	Aggressive outbursts
Taylor, Zlutnick, & Hoehle (1979)	2	Schizophrenic adult	Behaviors associated with tardive dyskinesia
Webster & Azrin (1973)	8	Retarded adults	Disruptive behaviors

on the part of the client, which may result in the necessity for physical prompts and guidance of the client by the staff. These problems are similar to those discussed with the overcorrection procedures in the preceding section.

Other areas in need of exploration, and thus a liability in using the technique, are duration of practice, intensity of implementation, and other related parameters that would lead to its most efficacious use. These problems make it difficult to recommend this particular therapeutic punishment technique over other judicious procedures.

Problems for Which
Negative Practice Is Applicable

As noted, there have not been a great number of situations in which
negative practice has been reported; however, of those described
dealing primarily with nervous habits, the findings have been encouraging. One such behavior that has been treated is nail-biting.
Vargas and Adesso (1976) solicited adult volunteers to receive treatment for this problem. Clients met in groups of eight and were
asked to begin biting their nails when the therapist gave a cue. They
were to continue to bite their nails for 10 consecutive minutes,
spending one minute per finger. Throughout this period, the therapist interjected comments aimed at enhancing the client's concen-
tration on this response. Typical comments were "Let's go, bite, bite,
bite, keep biting"; "harder, harder, keep pressing, don't let up" (p.
324). Also, the clients were instructed to bite their nails for a continuous three-minute period each evening. This treatment proved to
be effective in eliminating the problem behavior.

Lahey, McNees, and McNees (1973), using negative practice,
attempted to teach a 10-year-old boy to reduce obscene vocalizations.
Sessions were 15 minutes long and required the child to repeat
continuously the most frequently used obscenities as quickly as possible. Negative practice did not prove effective. The child ultimately
did reduce these vocalizations under a time-out contingency.

Walton (1961) treated a young boy with multiple tics by giving
him prolonged practice on the primary tic. This procedure required
him to engage in the tic-like behavior repetitively, and it proved to
be effective in suppressing the behavior. Walton (1964) treated
another child presenting three problem behaviors: shaking his head
for extended periods of time, hiccups, and explosive exhaling. All
these behaviors responded well to treatment by having the child
repeat the behavior in a repetitive fashion. In addition, effects of the
treatment were maintained at the five-month follow-up. In both of
these cases, however, the negative practice was combined with the
use of a sedative drug; thus, the degree to which treatment effects
could be attributed to the negative practice itself is unclear.

A final example of this procedure is that of Clark (1967), who
used this procedure with children to treat Gilles de la Tourette syndrome (involuntary utterances of obscene words). After a short period of practice, the two treated children remained free of obscene
utterances for over two years.

By these examples we can see the general effectiveness and potential utility of this form of therapeutic punishment; however, its application has been relatively infrequent, despite the fact that the technique was one of the first therapeutic punishment procedures described in the literature. No rationale for this state of affairs is available.

Response Cost

Definition

Response cost is a punishment procedure based primarily on the principle of fines for inappropriate behavior. Kazdin (1975) notes that fines, such as for parking or speeding, are familiar to all of us, so this technique employs a concept that already has its place in our daily lives.

Typically, response cost procedures are embedded in token economy systems. In token economies, individuals either may be given tokens or may have to earn them for appropriate behavior. Later, they are given the opportunity to trade the tokens for tangible reinforcers (e.g., candy, cigarettes). If the individual exhibits inappropriate behavior, tokens will be removed or fines assessed. This is the response cost component of the program.

A typical example of response cost is a study conducted by Winkler (1970). He employed a token reinforcement system, for chronic psychiatric patients, similar to that described in the classic work of Ayllon and Azrin (1968). These tokens were small plastic discs that could be earned for various appropriate behaviors the patients performed. In addition to this standard token system, however, was a fine or response cost system in which the patients lost tokens if they displayed operationally defined behaviors that had been deemed to be unacceptable. In the case of the present study, this consisted of violence and excessively loud noise.

Several techniques may be confused with response cost and should be discussed when defining the method. One of these is extinction, where a reinforcing consequence, which previously followed the behavior, is discontinued. In response cost, an aversive event, the removal of a reinforcer in the possession of the patient follows the occurrence of a particular target behavior. Although both the nonreward of extinction and the token loss of response cost may be aversive and result in response suppression, in extinction procedures, nothing is lost as a result of responding, as it is with response cost.

Response cost also should not be confused with time-out from reinforcement. With time-out, there is a fixed period of time following inappropriate respondings in which reinforcement is not available. In the case of response cost, however, there are no such temporal restrictions on reinforcement.

Response cost also should be distinguished from the exchange of tokens for backup reinforcers used in a token economy. When tokens are used to purchase events, privileges, food, or other primary reinforcers, there is a net gain in reinforcing events. On the other hand, response cost involves a loss of reinforcement and results in response suppression. Also, there usually is a difference in the temporal order of yielding tokens. In token economies, exchange of tokens precedes reinforcement and, hence, behavior is not suppressed. Response cost, however, follows a response and leads to suppression and, therefore, is a punishment procedure.

Response cost procedures have been utilized in a number of diverse settings, such as classrooms (Hall, Fox, Willard, Goldsmith, Emerson, Owen, Davis, & Porcia, 1971; Wolf, Hanley, King, Lachowicz, & Giles, 1970), homes for predelinquent boys (Phillips, 1968), and psychiatric facilities (Upper, 1973). Additionally, numerous forms of activities have been withdrawn and fines imposed in response cost programs, for example, loss of privileges, money, personal possessions, tokens, and minutes from recess (Kazdin, 1975).

Advantages and Disadvantages of Response Cost

One of the major selling points for response cost is its documented effectiveness for a wide range of behaviors and populations over an extended period of time. In line with its documented effectiveness, this method has received wide acceptance (especially when used in conjunction with token economies), unlike contingent electric shock and other related punishment procedures. Despite these positive aspects of the procedure, it has not been studied extensively (Kazdin, 1975).

As with all the treatment methods that we have discussed, there are a number of negative aspects of response cost. Perhaps the one mentioned most often is the generally negative orientation of the method compared with other punishment procedures. This stems from the fact that the basis of the technique is to take away items (reinforcers) that already have been given to the client. This can be particularly problematic with the mentally retarded and children, if they do not understand the rationale for this type of contingency. Although no empirical evidence is available, it would appear that undue emotional reactions could be produced around the removal of items. For those persons that become particularly upset, a struggle may ensue between the client and therapist over possession of reinforcers.

A second problem may involve the types of reinforcers administered. If primary reinforcers are earned instead of tokens, the individual has the opportunity to consume the item prior to the period when fines are levied, in which case no aversive contingency would exist.

A final problem comes from the individual who continually loses tokens and becomes so deeply in debt that no further points can be lost, thus making the program ineffective. A requirement for response cost is that tokens are present so they can be withdrawn (Kazdin, 1975). Additionally, the system should be reinforcing enough (e.g., no matter what infractions occur during the day, an individual still has a few tokens remaining) so that the individual remains motivated to stay in the system and exhibit positive behaviors.

All of the negative aspects of the procedure can be dealt with by judicious use of response cost, which has shown it can be very effective in suppressing behavior (Kazdin, 1975).

Types of Response Cost and Examples

Weiner, who was one of the early pioneers in the development of this technique, described two different forms of response cost. In the first, points can be given, noncontingently, and then the individual loses them for inappropriate behavior (Weiner, 1963). In the second, the individual earns points for appropriate responding and then loses them for inappropriate responding (Weiner, 1962).

An example of this first method of response cost is described by Sanok and Striefel (1979) in the treatment of an 11-year-old electively mute girl. First, they presented the girl with a "pool" of pennies. The child then was asked to give responses to target stimuli. Contingent on no response, an incorrect response, or a nonverbal response, a penny was taken away. This procedure, in addition to a reinforcement component, was effective in reinstating speech.

Alexander, Corbett, and Smigel (1976) also employed the response cost method where items are first given, then taken away for inappropriate behavior. In their study they were attempting to decrease curfew violations and increase school attendance of predelinquent adolescents. On Sunday evening, each student was told that lunch money would be available for that week; however, for anyone to receive the money, every student must attend 100 percent of his classes for any given day. Everyone would either receive $1.00 or no one would receive money. As in the previous study, this use of response cost proved highly effective.

A third example of this form of response cost is presented by Clark, Greene, MacRae, McNees, Davis, and Risley (1977). Their program involved a parent management model in which parents attempted to teach good shopping behavior to their children. The parents laid out guidelines for the children about what constituted appropriate and inappropriate behavior in the store. In addition, the children were told that 50¢ of their allowances were still available to spend at the end of the trip if they followed the guidelines. However, any time a child did not follow a guideline the parent would hold back 5¢ of the allowance. If the child failed to follow the guidelines again, another 5¢ would be deducted, and so on. After the parent finished shopping, each child was informed of how much money could be spent and the children were allowed 10 minutes to shop. This treatment was highly effective.

The second type of response cost involves first allowing an individual to earn points or tokens for appropriate behavior and then removing them for inappropriate responses. This is generally considered a "token system with response cost." Doty, McInnis, and Paul (1974) used such a program with 28 chronic mental patients. Response cost, in the form of token fines, was applied contingently upon specific inappropriate behavior (tokens could be earned for appropriate performance). If a "finable" behavior occurred, the client was informed of the consequence, including concrete specification of the offense. As can be seen in Figures 3–3 and 3–4, all the cases that described response cost proved to be highly effective.

Additionally, in some cases, response cost has advantages over other procedures. Kazdin (1973) compared response cost (withdrawal of tokens), aversive sound stimulation (loud noise), information feedback, and a no-treatment control to suppress speech dysfluencies (e.g., repetitions of a sound) in 40 mentally retarded adults. Posttest assessment and a subsequent one-month follow-up indicated that response cost was more effective than aversive stimulation, and both were superior to feedback and the no-treatment control. Response cost also led to greater response generalization (i.e., suppression of related but nonpunished speech dysfluencies).

Another application of response cost that demonstrates the di-

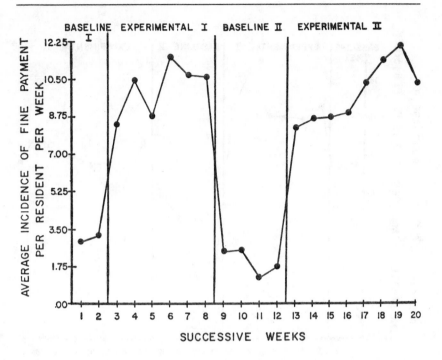

Figure 3–2. Average incidence of fine payments for residents with standing
fines under conditions in which less than total fine payments
served only to reduce fines (baseline) and conditions in which
eligibility to purchase other backup reinforcers could be obtained by an additional fine payment (experimental).

Source: From Doty, D. W., McInnis, T., & Paul, G. L. Remediation of negative side
effects of an ongoing response cost system with chronic mental patients. *Journal of
Applied Behavior Analysis*, 1974, 7, 191–198. Copyright 1974 by the Society for the
Experimental Analysis of Behavior, Inc. Reprinted with permission from authors and
publisher.

versity of the technique was described by Marholin and Gray (1976).
They employed a group response cost procedure to decrease cash
shortages in a small business. Treatment consisted of subtracting
cash shortages that exceeded 1 percent of total sales from the six
cashiers' salaries. The magnitude of daily shortages sharply decreased after the program was implemented despite the fact that
penalties were needed infrequently; $8.70 was the total penalized in
three episodes over a 41-day span.

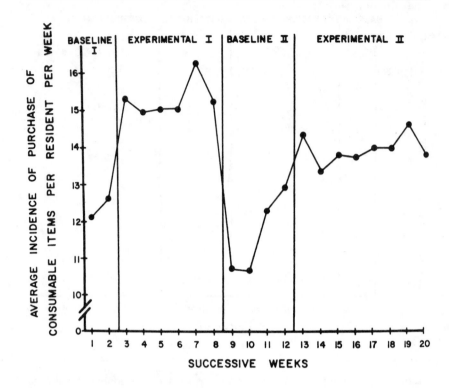

Figure 3–3. Average incidence of consumable purchases under conditions
in which standing fines allowed purchase of only regular meals
(baseline) and conditions in which eligibility to purchase all con-
sumables could be obtained contingently by an additional fine
payment (experimental).

Source: From Doty, D. W., McInnis, T., & Paul, G. L. Remediation of negative side
effects of an ongoing response cost system with chronic mental patients. *Journal of
Applied Behavior Analysis,* 1974, 7, 191–198. Copyright 1974 by the Society for the
Experimental Analysis of Behavior, Inc. Reprinted with permission from authors and
publisher.

A final example case (McLaughlin & Nay, 1975) involves the
treatment of compulsive hair-pulling (of six years' duration) in a
17-year-old woman. Treatment involved (1) relaxation training, as
she exhibited this behavior only when anxious and (2) a response
cost program wherein contingent on each episode of hair-pulling,
she was to write an account of the incident in a log. In addition, if

she did not pull her hair when the urge to do so arose, she earned the opportunity to reward herself by imagining one of a number of predetermined positive cognitions, such as imagining herself with a full head of hair or imagining a desirable man stroking her hair. The rate of hair-pulling decreased steadily through the first three months of therapy, although there was a marked peak during weeks 13 and 14, when she reported extreme tension over an advanced placement exam. Subsequently, daily hair-pulling decreased to zero and remained there for the remaining 12 weeks of the study.

Conclusions

The three procedures described in this chapter on work and penalty procedures are those that have been used most frequently in the past and have research to support their efficacy. All of these methods generally are well accepted as viable alternative treatment methods by both the professional and lay communities. For these reasons, such methods should be considered strongly as treatment alternatives to decelerate maladaptive behaviors.

The reader should be cautioned about the potential abuses that may arise from the use of these methods. This situation is particularly the case with the work and effort procedures, since physical force in the form of manual prompts and guidance frequently are necessary to insure the effective implementation of the technique. In these cases considerable training, supervision, and attention to detail are required to insure that abuses and potential harm to the clients do not occur.

One final note on an issue that is frequently raised regarding these procedures, especially overcorrection: Some individuals argue that generalization is poor or that the educative features of the procedures are obscure. These were, at one time, viable arguments, since researchers were claiming that overcorrection "could do it all."

It is our contention that overcorrection, as well as the other procedures presented, succinctly fit Azrin and Holz's (1966) definition of punishment; that is, overcorrection's expressed purpose is to suppress behavior, no more and no less. To this end, data suggest the procedures to be quite effective. However, if generalization of treatment gains is a goal, then it must be programmed (Osborne, 1976), as is the case with all treatment strategies (Stokes & Baer, 1977). Likewise, professionals should not expect spontaneous increases in other, more adaptive behaviors without programming (e.g., concurrent DRO schedules). To argue against overcorrection, or any punishment procedure, because of a lack of generalization or because increases in other positive behaviors do not occur as side-effects does not seem to be a cogent argument. These points will be addressed in detail in later chapters.

4

Removal from Reinforcing Events and Extinction Procedures

Introduction

The two preceding chapters reviewed punishment procedures that emphasized the presentation of a punishing stimulus contingent on the emission of some targeted behavior. Another form of punishment procedure is globally defined as the removal of the opportunity to obtain positive reinforcement. Three specific types of procedures fall under this general heading. They are time-out, physical restraint (a special case of time-out), and extinction. A fair amount of controversy surrounds the exact definitions of these procedures, as well as the essential elements of each. This chapter is designed to review each procedure, delineate the uses and restrictions of each, and compare the procedures to other forms of so-called therapeutic techniques (e.g., seclusion).

Time-Out

Definition

Time-out from positive reinforcement has been defined and categorized in a number of different ways in the extensive research
literature on the subject. Several authors define time-out as the
removal of all positive reinforcers for a certain period of time (Kazdin, 1980b; Wells & Forehand, 1981). Others define time-out as
removing an individual from positively reinforcing events (Bellack &
Hersen, 1977). Still others define time-out as a combination of the
two (Harris & Ersner-Hershfield, 1978; Plummer, Baer, & LeBlanc,
1977; Rimm & Masters; 1979).

Additionally, there appears to be a problem in deciding exactly
what time-out is. At times, the term has been used interchangeably
with extinction (Harris & Ersner-Hershfield, 1978). Other researchers have determined that sometimes time-out is a punishment
procedure and somtimes it is an extinction procedure (Rimm &
Masters, 1979).

A final confusion lies in noting the essential elements and parameters of time-out (Forehand & MacDonough, 1975; Hobbs &
Forehand, 1977; Johnston, 1972; Leitenberg, 1965; MacDonough &
Forehand, 1973; White, Nielsen, & Johnson, 1972). Even though
time-out has been the most widely used punishment procedure
(Drabman, 1976; Solnick, Rincover, & Peterson, 1977), few studies
have noted the exact parameters by which time-out is maximally
effective (Hobbs & Forehand, 1977).

Since one of the earliest documentations of time-out (Wolf, Risley, & Mees, 1964), the purpose of the procedure has clearly fit the
definition for punishment posited by Azrin and Holz (1966): An
attempt is made to reduce the future probability of a response by
contingently applying a specific stimulus. Therefore, time-out from
reinforcement is simply and clearly a "punishment procedure." For
the purpose of the present chapter, Harris and Ersner-Hershfield's
(1978) definition of "contingent removal of reinforcement" will be
used to define time-out. That is, time-out is

> . . . removing attention or another reinforcing event upon emission of
> the target behavior. This removal is marked clearly by such events as
> removing the subject from the room, physical withdrawal of the thera-
> pist, or other discrete acts that signal the withdrawal of reinforcement.
> Return of access to reinforcement may be contingent upon cessation of
> the target behavior. This procedure is often called time-out but is more
> actively punishing than most definitions of time-out permit. [p. 1356]

The specific characteristics of time-out are included in the next section.

Parameters of Time-Out

A number of empirically derived or intuitively defined parameters of time-out have been indentified (Hobbs & Forehand, 1977; Mac-Donough & Forehand, 1973; Solnick et al., 1977; White et al., 1972). These include:

1. Duration of time-out.
2. Presence or absence of a stimulus to indicate the onset and end of a time-out period.
3. Use of instructional versus physical administration of time-out.
4. Schedule of time-out administration (continuous versus intermittent).
5. Location of time-out.
6. Type of release from time-out (contingent versus noncontingent).
7. Use of a warning prior to time-out.
8. Use of an explanation in conjunction with time-out.
9. Reinforcing value of natural environment.
10. Presence versus absence of adult during time-out (more globally defined as subject removal versus reinforcer removal).

Each of these parameters now will be discussed.

Duration. Even though duration is probably the most researched parameter in time-out, the findings are equivocal. Effective time-out durations have ranged from 10 seconds (Solnick et al., 1977) to three hours (Burchard & Tyler, 1965). Additionally, methodological problems (e.g., sequence effects) have plagued this area of research (Burchard & Barrera, 1972; Kendall, Nay, & Jeffers, 1975; White et al., 1972). Some research suggests that longer periods of time-out are more effective in reducing targeted behavior (Burchard & Barrera, 1972), while others show that shorter periods of time-out are more effective (Kendall et al., 1975).

Although most studies have used time-out durations of from 5 to 20 minutes (MacDonough & Forehand, 1973; Patterson & White, 1970), great variability exists (Barton, Guess, Garcia, & Baer, 1970; Bostow & Bailey, 1969; Cayner & Kiland, 1974; Foxx & Azrin, 1972; Hobbs, Forehand, & Murray, 1978; Pendergrass, 1971; Ramp, Ulrich, & Dulaney, 1971; Resick, Forehand, & McWhorter, 1976; Tyler & Brown, 1967). Rimm & Masters (1979) suggest that "5 minutes is a reasonable rule-of-thumb for intitial implementation" (p. 187). Several points to consider when designing time-out durations are that periods that are too short may be ineffective (Rimm & Masters, 1979; Sailor, Guess, Rutherford, & Baer, 1968) and time-out durations that are too long may have several effects: (1) decreased opportunity to learn desirable behavior and an increase in the cost of program time (Sailor et al., 1968), (2) time-out durations longer than effectively needed subject a person to unnecessary aversive experience (White et al., 1972), and (3) time-out durations that are functionally too long or too short may increase the rate of deviant behavior (White et al., 1972).

Presence or Absence of Stimulus. The presence of a stimulus to indicate the onset of time-out refers to a nonverbal signal that time-out is beginning or has ended. Typically, a staff member/parent will place the client/child in a time-out room or remove the opportunity to gain reinforcement and then notify her/him when time-out is over (MacDonough & Forehand, 1973). Therefore, in this case, a signal is not used. However, a few studies (Adams & Popelka, 1971; Baron & Kaufman, 1966; Hamilton & Stephens, 1967; Holz, Azrin, & Ayllon, 1963; Martin, 1975; Pendergrass, 1971) have used nonverbal signals to initiate and terminate time-out. No definitive data are available concerning the efficacy of this procedure, however, MacDonough and Forehand (1973) suggest that if a client/child knew when her/his time-out was complete (using a nonhuman signal like a buzzer), this would allow a self-regulation response to occur, rather than requiring staff/parent monitoring.

Instructional versus Physical Administration. The third parameter asks whether to instruct a client/child to go to a time-out room or to physically place him/her in the room. This is an interesting variable, posited by MacDonough and Forehand (1973); however, no comparative data exist at this time. The researchers suggest three reasons for preferring the use of instructions over physical force on theoretical grounds. First, aggressive behavior would not be modeled. Second, less interaction between staff members/parents and clients/children would occur (which research has shown to be reinforcing at times). Third, responsibility for administering part of the time-out is put in the hands of the client/child.

Schedule. Relatively few studies have addressed schedules of time-out. Only one study (Pendergrass, 1971) compared continuous time-out (every incident of the targeted behavior was consequated with time-out) with a quasi-intermittent time-out (the targeted behavior was consequated with time-out every other day). The results indicated that only the continuous time-out condition was effective.

Studies comparing only intermittent schedules of time-out (Calhoun & Lima, 1977; Calhoun & Matherne, 1975) have indicated moderate effectiveness. However, Clark, Rowbury, Baer, and Baer (1973) studied the effects of four intermittent schedules of time-out, and their results suggested an inverse, nonlinear relationship between the percentage of responses punished and the frequency of the response. At this time, the data suggest that a continuous schedule should be used for initial suppression of the targeted behavior, while an intermittent schedule may be effective for maintenance.

Location. The fifth parameter, location of time-out, refers to the actual physical location where the client/child is placed.[1] The client/child may be placed either in a separate area (e.g., empty rooms or bathrooms) (Allison & Allison, 1971; Cayner & Kiland, 1974; Hawkins, Peterson, Schweid, & Bijou, 1966; Miller & Kratochwill, 1979; Sachs, 1973; Sloane, Johnston, & Bijou, 1967; Wahler & Fox, 1980; Wasik, Senn, Welch, & Cooper, 1969; Wolf et al., 1964) or isolated in the same area where the act took place. Examples of this type of time-out would be a requirement to stand in the corner (Barrett, 1969; Hobbs, Forehand, & Murray, 1978), use a time-out chair (Carlson, Arnold, Becker, & Madsen, 1968), or use of modified portable time-out rooms located in the treatment setting (Harris, Ersner-Hershfield, Kaffashan, & Romanczyk, 1974; Kendall et al., 1975). MacDonough and Forehand (1973) suggest that the major advantage to the separate-area technique is the probability that positive reinforcement will be effectively removed during time-out. Additionally, the separate-area time-out can be enforced with closed or locked doors, whereas the same-area time-out requires more responsibility on the administrator to enforce the time-out. If adequate facilities are not available, however, the same-area technique would be useful.

Parents often make the mistake of designating a child's own room as the time-out area. This technique will not be effective if the room contains toys, games, a television set, and/or other play items. The purpose of time-out is to remove sources of reinforcement. On the other hand, physically noxious settings (e.g., cages or pens) are

---

[1]Parameter 10, subject removal versus reinforcer removal, has been confused with location in the past literature. Parameter 5 refers to the removal of the subject from all reinforcement, while parameter 10 attempts to remove a specific stimulus (e.g., food).

also prohibited (Bellack & Hersen, 1977). The suggestion often made to parents is to make the bathroom a time-out area.

Type of Release. Patterson and White (1970) suggest a response-contingent release from time-out over a fixed-duration time-out. This suggestion is consistent with basic research evidence. Ferster and Skinner (1957) have shown that the removal of an aversive stimulus will increase the probability of the response occurrence that produces the removal. Therefore, to increase adaptive behavior, the client/child should be removed only after terminating the maladaptive behavior and exhibiting quiet, calm behavior. This may be one of the most critical features of time-out.

A number of studies have used this type of time-out (Bostow & Bailey, 1969; Brawley, Harris, Allen, Fleming, & Peterson, 1969; Burchard & Tyler, 1965; Clark et al., 1973; Hawkins et al., 1966; Lahey, McNees, & McNees, 1973; Martin, MacDonald, & Omichinski, 1971; McReynolds, 1969; O'Leary, O'Leary, & Becker, 1967; Ritschl, Mongrella, & Presbie, 1972; Sachs, 1973; Wahler, 1969; Wahler, Winkel, Peterson & Morrison, 1965; Wetzel, Baker, Roney, & Martin, 1966; Wiesen & Watson, 1967; Wolf, Risley, Johnston, Harris, & Allen, 1967; Zegiob, Becker, Jenkins, & Bristow, 1976; Zeilberger, Sampen, & Sloane, 1968). MacDonough & Forehand (1973) suggest three types of contingent release from time-out: (1) release based on a specified period of desirable (quiet) behavior, (2) release based on minimum duration of desirable behavior with subsequent extensions imposed until undesirable behavior is terminated, and (3) time-out extended for a fixed duration (e.g., one hour) following undesirable behavior in time-out.

Warning. Several studies have reported the use of the seventh parameter, a verbal warning before the administration of contingent time-out (Adams, Klinge, & Keiser, 1973; Hawkins et al., 1966; Kendall et al., 1975; Ritschl et al., 1972; Sibley, Abbott, & Cooper, 1969; Wasik et al., 1969; Wiesen & Watson, 1967; Zeilberger et al., 1968). This usually consisted of a brief statement that if the behavior persisted, time-out would be administered. No data are available contrasting the use or omission of warnings.

Explanation. Few studies have reported the use of an explanation of time-out before its administration (Alevizos & Alevizos, 1975; Gardner, Forehand, & Roberts, 1976; Pendergrass, 1971; Sachs, 1973). The comparative studies (Alevizos & Alevizos 1975; Gardner et al., 1976) indicated that the explanation did not facilitate the effectiveness of time-out.

Reinforcing Value of Natural Environment. Theoretically, time-out from reinforcement assumes the prior establishment of reinforcement in the natural environment. Spitalnik & Drabman (1976) continue this argument and suggest that the effects of time-out may be due to the aversive nature of the time-out room and not the removal of reinforcement. Drabman & Spitalnik (1973) suggest that sending a client/child to a restrictive room, in the absence of demonstrable reinforcement in the natural environment, should be labeled social isolation and not time-out. This argument, carried one step further, suggests that time-out may fit a negative reinforcement paradigm or serve as an escape (Plummer et al., 1977; Solnick et al., 1977) from the dreary institutional environment or demanding learning situations to which client/children are exposed (Carr, Newsom, & Binkoff, 1976).

One researcher (Baum, 1973) has suggested that the relationship between situations before and after a stimulus is introduced may define the reinforcing and punishing effects of the stimulus better than simply referring to the "post" situation. Solnick et al. (1977) examined this phenomenon by establishing a time-out contingency with a 16-year-old mentally retarded boy in both an enriched and an impoverished environment. Time-out was effective only in the enriched environment condition, suggesting the reinforcing value of the natural environment is an important parameter.

Removal of Reinforcing Stimulus. The final parameter has been defined by Hobbs and Forehand (1977) as "presence versus absence of an adult during time-out." We have chosen to define this category more globally as subject removal versus specific reinforcer removal.

Hobbs and Forehand (1977) referred to two studies (Forehand, Roberts, Doleys, Hobbs, & Resnick, 1976; Scarboro & Forehand, 1975) that were designed to compare the effects of time-out when mothers stayed in the same room as their child during time-out (i.e., removed attention and physical proximity) to when mothers left the room (i.e., removed attention and presence). Both were equally effective in reducing the targeted behavior, although the out-of-room condition worked faster. This appears to be one case of removing assumed specific reinforcing stimuli from the subject. Other forms of innovative "reinforcer removal" have been noted in the literature.

Several researchers (Brawley et al., 1969; Martin, 1975; McReynolds, 1969; Rimm & Masters, 1979; Sachs, 1973; Solnick et al., 1977) also have suggested that some form of removal of attention may serve as a time-out condition. Other specific sources of reinforcement that have been removed include television or music

(Greene & Hoats, 1969; Greene, Hoats, & Hornick, 1970; Hauck & Martin, 1970; Ritschl et al., 1972), food (Barton et al., 1970; Martin et al., 1971; O'Brien & Azrin, 1972a), and eyesight (by covering a child's face with a bib) (Zegiob et al., 1976).

Several researchers (Detrich, 1982; Foxx & Shapiro, 1978; Glaven, 1974; Husted, Hall, & Agin, 1971; LeBlanc, Busby, & Thomson, 1974; Porterfield, Herbert-Jackson, & Risley, 1976; Spitalnik & Drabman, 1976) have advanced or suggested extremely innovative forms of nonexclusionary time-out procedures. Three of the reports suggested "the opportunity to receive reinforcement" as the specific source of reinforcement to be removed.

Detrich (1982) designed a token economy, using "point cards," to be used with adolescents. If a situation arose such that the removal of points was necessitated, due to noncompliant or aggressive behavior, the adolescent was to turn over his point card to a staff member. If he refused, he was placed in "point time-out" and no additional points could be earned until the card was turned over.

Foxx & Shapiro (1978) designed a similar procedure. During a reinforcement period, mentally retarded children were given different colored "ribbons" to wear as reinforcers. If an instance of misbehavior occurred, the ribbon was removed and teacher attention ceased for three minutes or until the targeted behavior stopped.

A final example is presented by Spitalnik and Drabman (1976). A reinforcement program initially had been designed and implemented with two mentally retarded children. Additionally, a time-out contingency had been developed. Time-out was defined as "the interruption of an ongoing reinforcement system, for a fixed time period, contingent upon the emission of inappropriate behavior" (p. 17). At the time time-out was administered, an orange card was placed on the child's desk at which time reinforcement was not dispensed.

As with all punishment procedures, a great deal is yet to be learned about the effectiveness of time-out from reinforcement procedures. One important point must be delineated. Although a number of procedures have been suggested, "there can be no 'standard' time-out procedure that will reliably reduce problem behavior" (Solnick et al., 1977, p. 423). The clinician and researcher must not fall into the trap of designing "procedural time-out" (Plummer et al., 1977). Instead, the reinforcing and punishing qualities of the stimuli and situations and the relationships and interactions of the various combinations and schedules must be assessed to design "functional time-out" adequately.

Safeguards for Time-Out

Recently, the use of time-out has come under considerable criticism by teachers, principals, parents, school districts, and other institutions (Foxx & Shapiro, 1978; Jones & Kazdin, 1981; Sulzer-Azaroff & Mayer, 1977). Several reasons have been posited for this concern. First, the term "punishment," as defined by the lay community, carries extremely aversive overtones. Second, the relative ease and effective results of time-out often lead to its overuse and misuse, often in the absence of an adequate reinforcement system. Third, other punitive procedures (e.g., seclusion) have been mislabeled as time-out. Fourth, adequate facilities often are not available to use time-out effectively (Foxx & Shapiro, 1978; Jones & Kazdin, 1981). This may exacerbate the situation by allowing escape or reinforcing the maladaptive behaviors. To allay some of the fears of using time-out, as well as to create an atmosphere where learning alternative adaptive behaviors is encouraged, some safeguards are suggested.

The overall goal of all programs designed to assure the greatest quantity and quality of appropriate responding is to maximize the reinforcing and minimize the punishing aspects of the client's/child's environment (Jones & Kazdin, 1981). The first safeguard, therefore, would be to insure the maximal amount of reinforcement possible in the environment. This fact has been stated elsewhere but is emphasized here since it never can be overstressed. As a matter of fact, it was mentioned in the preceding section that the underlying theoretical assumption of time-out is that reinforcement exists before the program can be started. The following safeguards address a number of viable methods for enhancing the humane nature of treatment without detracting from its therapeutic value. Most of these recommendations involve the use of a time-out room; however, a number of points to consider relative to the method by which staff/parents administer time-out also are delineated.

When a room is designated as part of the treatment, it should be used only for administrations of time-out. Sulzer-Azaroff & Mayer (1977) suggest the use of the term "quiet place." This room should be kept completely empty: no furniture or items on the walls and, if possible, no closets, sharp corners, or objects that could be thrown or ingested. These factors are important since an agitated client/child easily could hurt himself/herself on these objects, whether it be by accident or intent. In addition, to enhance the punishing aspects of a time-out room, clients/childen should not be permitted to spend time in the room other than strict time-out periods, or they will become desensitized. Also, we have found that time-out rooms on an inpatient ward of emotionally disturbed children can be abused if unlocked when not in use. In these instances, the children often play in the room, time-out other children, hide contraband in the room, and use it as a place to hide from staff and other children. All of these are seen as antitherapeutic behaviors and certainly compound an already difficult situation.

The size of the room is another important physical characteristic. It should be large enough to allow for ample movement but small enough to insure that the client/child can be monitored easily through a one-way mirror placed in the door of the time-out room. Also, an unbreakable convex mirror placed out of the client's reach should be affixed to the room's back wall to insure monitoring of the client while at the side of the door. A diagram of a functional room is presented in Figure 4–1.

A final concern is to insure the room has adequate lighting and heating, which should be controlled from outside the room.

A modified version of a time-out area for children is a portable room. Harris et al. (1974) described such a room, which consisted simply of a three-panel room divider purchased at Sears. It could be used in the corner of a classroom or a room in the child's home. By closing the panels around the child, tantrum behavior can be timed-out effectively while minimizing the opportunity for self-stimulatory behavior. Figure 4–2 shows how this device was used.

There are also a number of procedural details that are important to follow in administering time-out. Some of these are specific to the time-out administration in a time-out room, while others can be considered of general applicability in all instances of time-out. To begin, we will describe routine procedures that staff should follow in every administraton of time-out.

First, if a verbal prompt is to be delivered to signal the onset of time-out, it should be done in a calm but firm voice. Shouting at the client or responding in tones that convey a marked amount of emotion can result only in reinforcing disruptive behavior, particularly when the purpose of the client's behavior is to gain staff attention. Second, the prompt's length should always be short. Frequently, the tendency of staff is to get into lengthy discussions with clients about why time-out is being used and what the behavior was that caused the staff person to initiate the time-out. Furthermore, with young children, the mentally retarded, and some psychotic individuals, there often can be increased confusion associated with the advent of lengthy verbal prompts. A third variable is the type of sentence that

Time-out room

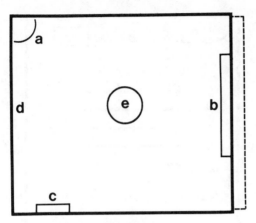

a. convex mirror
b. one-way mirror and
   observation room
c. locked door with window
d. no lead paint, no nails, etc.
e. no furniture

Figure 4–1. An overhead view of a time-out room that takes into account the features presented in this chapter.

staff use in announcing time-out. It should always be a statement such as, "You are getting a time-out now." Comments like, "Would it be all right with you to have time-out now?" or "I think you should have a time-out," can lead to additional debate or failure on the client's part to perceive the fact that the staff person is serious about the delivery of the consequences.

Fourth, the client should not be threatened with a consequence, such as time-out, unless the staff person fully intends to use the procedure. This point may seem self-evident, but we frequently have observed staff who will allow a client to exhibit behaviors repeatedly, followed by numerous staff warnings, without administration of the stated consequences. Also, in line with administering therapeutic punishment in a consistent manner, the client should never be in-

Classroom

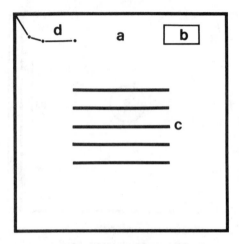

a. front of classroom
b. teacher's desk
c. student seating
d. time-out room

Figure 4–2. An overhead view of a portable time-out room (d) located in an elementary-school classroom.

formed that a behavior is to be consequated with therapeutic punishment unless the staff member is assured that there are ample staff to guide or carry the person physically to the time-out room. This procedure should be followed, for the safety of both the staff and client.

Another form of safeguard to insure the efficacious use of time-out is to devise a decision-making tree that outlines the procedural steps from the inappropriate behavior to release from time-out. Those issues, discussed in a previous section, should be discussed thoroughly prior to implementation of the program by all persons who will be involved. Additionally, antecedent behaviors in the chain that eventually lead to the targeted behavior should be identified for several reasons. First, in many instances, the identification of these behaviors may allow the staff/parent to avert the disruptive behavior by interrupting the sequence of behaviors and getting the client involved in another task. We are not suggesting that consequating the targeted behavior be ignored once it occurs. However, if a good funtional analysis has been performed, antecedent conditions may be observed and treated (e.g., problem solving) before the extreme disruptive behavior occurs. Even if this is not possible, a second reason to assess antecedent behaviors accurately would be to generate more time to alert other staff so that requisite persons can be at the scene at the time of the disruptive behavior. A final point to consider, with respect to anticipation, is what type of response to expect from the client when inappropriate behavior is exhibited and attempts are made to consequate it.

The physical condition of the client should be considered in all cases. Physical problems, due to age or other factors, that worsen when agitated may obviate the use of time-out. Problems that are frequently difficult and for which screening should be done are high or low blood pressure and diabetes. Persons with particularly severe problems in these areas may not be appropriate candidates for time-out procedures due to the possible physical harm that may result from the procedures (e.g., onset of insulin shock due to excessive agitation).

In addition to closely adhering to the points just noted, the personnel in charge of implementing closed-door time-out, which is often the case with extremely maladaptive behavior, should follow this additional guideline. The client's shoes, belt, money, sharp objects, and any other potentially harmful items should be taken until after time-out is completed. This precaution is necessary to safeguard the physical well-being of the client.

Sulzer-Azaroff & Mayer (1977) suggest two additional guidelines. First, informed consent should be obtained from the client and/or client's parent or guardian. Also, the procedure should conform to agency regulations and current policies and laws. Second, before visitors observe the procedure, the steps involved in time-out should be explained and data should be offered that show its effectiveness. [2]

Advantages and Disadvantages of Time-Out

A number of advantages have been proclaimed for this type of punishment procedure. First, in terms of effective durations, brevity is a major advantage. As a matter of fact, Cayner & Kiland (1974) sug-

[2]All these general rules may not be applicable for all types of persons who require time-out in a room or who require time-out in general. However, the authors are striving to present a solution here that best typifies a situation where the greatest number of desired precautions for the use of time-out are provided.

gest that with time-out, punitive prolonged confinement periods are eliminated, leaving more time for appropriate, alternative behavior to occur and be reinforced. Second, time-out does not involve pain (Johnston, 1972; Kazdin, 1980). Another advantage is that it can be rather portable (Harris et al., 1974; Kendall et al., 1975) or adaptable (Detrich, 1982; Foxx & Shapiro, 1978; Kazdin, 1980b; LeBlanc et al., 1974; Porterfield et al., 1976; Spitalnik & Drabman, 1976). A fourth plus for this procedure is that it replaces harsher forms of punishment, including reprimands and corporal punishment (Kazdin, 1980b). Additionally, time-out removes the individual from the situation that may be reinforcing the maladaptive behavior (Bellack & Hersen, 1977).

Also, there have been a few positive side-effects noted when time-out was required. Several researchers (Barrett, 1969; Bostow & Bailey, 1969; Brawley et al., 1969; Hamilton et al., 1967; Sachs, 1973) have viewed increases in participation in ward activities and interactions. Eating behavior also has been modified appropriately as a side-effect of the time-out procedure (Edwards & Lilly, 1966; Martin et al., 1971).

Another advantage of time-out may be the potential for decreasing the likelihood of physical harm to the individual, others around her/him, and/or the physical environment (Bellack & Hersen, 1977; Matson, Ollendick, & DiLorenzo, 1980). In these instances, only three options are possible: (1) the client is restrained physically, (2) the client is restrained by medication, or (3) the client is contained in a time-out room. If one of these procedures is not followed, the possibility for physical harm of not only self but others is greatly enhanced, since the client can move in an unfettered and agitated state around others. In many such instances containment in a time-out room while agitation persists may be the most reasonable option. Rimm & Masters (1979) suggest that this individual also is sequestered from others who may be eliciting or reinforcing the maladaptive behavior.

The procedure also appears to be rather robust in terms of the populations that have been treated successfully. A few examples include paranoid schizophrenics (Cayner & Kiland, 1974), delinquents (Kendall et al., 1975; Tyler & Brown, 1967), normal adults (Murray & Hobbs, 1977), mentally retarded children (Calhoun & Lima, 1977; Clark et al., 1973), mentally retarded adults (Matson, Ollendick, & Dilorenzo, 1980), autistic children (Solnick et al., 1977; Wolf et al., 1964), emotionally disturbed children (Drabman & Spitalnik, 1973; Sachs, 1973), school children (Ramp et al.,

1971), and normal children (Miller & Kratochwill, 1979; O'Leary et al., 1967).

Much research confirms that the techniques are readily taught (Barrett, 1969; Davison, 1964, 1965; Laws, Brown, Epstein, & Hocking, 1971; Nordquist & Wahler, 1973; Wahler, 1969). A method such as time-out, when effective, also decreases the need of psychotropic medications used as chemical restraints. This contention is supported by the rate at which psychotropic medication is given to institutionalized mentally retarded persons—generally reported to be approximately 50 percent in the United States (Lipman, 1970; Sprague & Baxley, 1978). This rate is far above the number of persons with identified psychiatric disorders.

In addition, release from time-out can be made contingent upon both the lapse of some designated time interval and the cessation of undesirable behavior (Matson, Ollendick, & Dilorenzo, 1980), insuring the exhibition of appropriate behaviors. Consequently, the release from time-out may serve as a negative reinforcer for the development of behavior incompatible with the undesired behavior (Matson, Ollendick, & Dilorenzo, 1980).

A final advantage of time-out is that it interrupts an interaction that has explosive potential for escalation. Both staff and the time-out recipient can use this interval to consider their own behavior, to calm down, and to renew alternative appropriate behavior (Kanfer & Phillips, 1970).

The potential disadvantages of time-out are analogous to those observed with most punishment procedures. These include overuse, negative emotional side-effects, the potential for physical harm, and the failure to apply the procedures accurately. One factor that is somewhat unique to time-out, overcorrection, and physical restraint is that the amount of physical contact between client and staff member may be greater than what might be observed with other punishment procedures. This factor not only enhances the likelihood of physical harm but increases the possibility that the attention received through these acts might be reinforcing. The degree to which any or all of these facts will influence the client depends on the degree of noncompliance, type of time-out used, client and staff characteristics, and so on. These of course must be evaluated on an individual basis.

Another disadvantage is that time-out decreases the opportunity to receive positive reinforcement from the environment. At this same time, there is a decreased opportunity to learn adaptive behavior. It also may be undesirable to isolate socially withdrawn clients (Kazdin,

1980b) and those who exhibit high rates of self-stimulatory or self-injurious behaviors. Although the procedure was somewhat unorthodoxed, Caynor & Kiland (1974) reduced self-mutilating behavior in a chronic schizophrenic by using brief time-out.

Problems for Which Time-Out Is Applicable

Time-out has been empirically validated as an efficacious approach in perhaps more empirical studies, for more populations, and more problem behaviors than any other punishment procedure. The populations were listed in the preceding section. Some of the problem behaviors now will be addressed, in six different populations.

A variety of behaviors have been targeted in children in a classroom setting. Time-out has been used successfully to reduce inappropriate classroom behaviors (Drabman, Spitalnik, & O'Leary, 1973; Roberts, McMahon, Forehand, & Humphreys, 1978; Sachs, 1973; Walker, Mattson, & Buckley, 1968), inappropriate social behaviors (Birnbrauer, Wolf, Kidder, & Tague, 1965; Sibley et al., 1969), and disruptive classroom behaviors (Clark et al., 1973; Cotler, Applegate, King, & Kristal, 1972; Foxx & Shapiro, 1978; Porterfield et al., 1976; Ramp et al., 1971). Other behaviors that have been decreased include crying (Stark, Meisel, & Wright, 1969; Zimmerman & Zimmerman, 1962), inappropriate speech (Lahey et al., 1973; McReynolds, 1969), resisting authority and criticizing (Wasik et al., 1969), and out-of-seat behavior on a bus (Ritschl et al., 1972).

Time-out also has been used in the home with very specific problems in normal children. Some of the targeted behaviors include tantrum or aggressive behavior (Hawkins et al., 1966; LeBlanc et al., 1974; Wahler & Fox, 1980; Wahler et al., 1965; Zeilberger et al., 1968) and noncompliance (Hobbs et al., 1978), bowel control (Barrett, 1969), elective mutism (Wulbert, Nyman, Snow, & Owen, 1973), thumbsucking (Baer, 1962; Ross, 1975), stomach complaints (Miller & Kratochwill, 1979), and hyperactivity and tics (Varni, Boyd, & Cataldo, 1978; Wulbert & Dries, 1977).

Another population often cited in the time-out literature includes mentally retarded, autistic, or psychotic children. Problem behaviors targeted include tantrum or noncompliant behavior (Doleys et al., 1976; Pendergrass, 1972; Solnick et al., 1977; Wiesen & Watson, 1967; Wolf et al., 1964), perseverative or inappropriate speech (Hewitt, 1965; Reichle, Brubakken, & Tetreault, 1976; Risley & Wolf, 1967; Spitalnik & Drabman, 1976), inappropriate eating behavior (Barton et al., 1970; Martin et al., 1971; O'Brien, Bugle, & Azrin,

1972), self-stimulatory behavior (Hamilton & Stephens, 1967; Koegel, Firestone, Kramme, & Dunlap, 1974), self-injurious behavior (Adams et al., 1973; Anderson, Herrmann, Alpert, & Dancis, 1975; Brawley et al., 1969; Husted et al., 1971; Myers & Deibert, 1971; Solnick et al., 1977; Tate & Baroff, 1966; Wolf et al., 1967), and aggressive/disruptive behavior (Calhoun & Matherne, 1975; Hamilton, Stephens, & Allen, 1967; White et al., 1972).

Delinquent populations also have been amenable to time-out strategies. Several researchers (Burchard & Tyler, 1965; Detrich, 1982; Kendall et al., 1975; Linkenhoker, 1974; Tyler & Brown, 1967) have used various forms of time-out for verbal and physical aggression and noncompliance.

Two problem behaviors that have been targeted in adult normal populations are alcohol consumption and stuttering. Several studies (Bigelow, Liebson, & Griffiths, 1974; Griffiths, Bigelow, & Liebson, 1974; Murray & Hobbs, 1977) have employed time-out successfully to reduce alcohol consumption, and one study (Adams & Popelka, 1971) used time-out to treat stuttering behavior.

The final population that has been targeted for intervention is mentally retarded and/or institutionalized adults. Specific problems have included tantrums or disruptive behavior (Calhoun & Lima, 1977; Cayner & Kiland, 1974; Winkler, 1971), noncompliance and aggressive behavior (Bostow & Bailey, 1969; Mansdorf, 1977; Vukelich & Hake, 1971), and self-mutilation (Cayner & Kiland, 1974). More specific behaviors have included delusions and hallucinations (Davis, Wallace, Liberman, & Finch, 1976; Hayes & Geddy, 1973), toileting (Azrin & Foxx, 1971), inappropriate eating behavior (O'Brien & Azrin, 1972a), noncompliance to self-bathing (Mansdorf, 1977), and "seizure-like" behavior (Iwata & Lorentzson, 1976).

It should not be assumed that time-out was the sole intervention in all of the preceding studies. Very often, either a differential reinforcement schedule or an enriched environmental program initially had been started or was running concomitantly with the time-out program.

Table 4–1 provides a quick reference to a number of behaviors for which time-out is applicable. In addition to providing this list, we will review some procedures in detail to demonstrate the type of problems addressed and the types of time-out that proved to be effective. Varni et al. (1978) used a combination of self-monitoring, external reinforcement, and time-out to control a hyperactive child's multiple tics. This seven-year-old boy was treated successfully for facial grimaces, shoulder shrugging, vocal tics, and rump protru-

Table 4–1. Sample Studies Using Time-Out.

Behavior	Population	Author(s) and Date
Spitting and self-injurious behavior	16-yr.-old retarded male	Solnick, Rincover, & Peterson, 1977
Loud and abusive verbal behavior	58-yr.-old retarded female	Bostow & Bailey, 1969
Aggressive behavior	8-yr.-old female retardate	Clark, Rowbury, Baer, & Baer, 1973
Nonresponsive-elective mutism	6-yr.-old female	Wulbert, Nyman, Snow, & Owen, 1973
Inappropriate eating behavior	6-yr.-old profoundly retarded female	O'Brien, Bugle, & Azrin, 1972
Disruptive behavior	15 boys & 11 girls, ages 12-36 months, normal children in daycare program	Porterfield, Herbert-Jackson, & Risley, 1976
Aggressive behavior	18-yr.-old mentally retarded female	Vukelich & Hake, 1971
Obscene vocalizations with facial twitches	10-yr.-old boy	Lahey, McNees, & McNees, 1973
Inappropriate verbal behavior	5-yr.-old boy	McReynolds, 1969
Incontinence	9 mentally retarded residents, ages 20-62	Azrin & Foxx, 1971
Bizarre and autistic behavior following teacher's instructions	5-yr.-old autistic female	Plummer, Baer, & LeBlanc, 1977
Hyperactivity and ritualistic behavior	8-yr.-old boy	Wulbert & Dries, 1977
Inappropriate mealtime behavior	16 male residents at hospital cottage for retardates, ages 9-23 yrs.	Barton, Guess, Garcia, & Baer, 1970
Noncompliance and uncooperative behavior	8-yr.-old female & two 10-yr.-old males	Doleys, Wells, Hobbs, Roberts, & Cartelli, 1976
Stuttering	7 male & 1 female stutterers, ages 18-27	Adams & Popelka, 1971

(continued)

Table 4–1　(continued)

Behavior	Population	Author(s) and Date
Undesirable behaviors	3 patients in a 66-bed ward for schizo-phrenic and mentally retarded females	Winkler, 1971
Disruptive behavior in classroom	14 boys, average ages 13.1; range 11.8 to 15.8 yrs.	Cotler, Applegate, King, & Kristal, 1972
Hallucinations	45-yr.-old female schizophrenic in state hospital	Hayes & Geddy, 1973
Verbal and physical ag-gression	30 male residents in college for delinquent adoles-cents, ages 9-11	Kendall, Nay, & Jeffers, 1975
"Seizurelike" behavior	41-yr.-old institution-alized retarded male	Iwata & Lorentz-son, 1976
Noncompliance	28 children, ages 4-6.6 yrs., and their mothers	Hobbs, Forehand, & Murray, 1978
Noncompliant behavior	27 children, ages 3-7 years., and their mothers	Roberts, McMahon, Forehand, & Hum-phreys, 1978
Stomach pain complaints	10-yr.-old female	Miller & Kratochwill, 1979

sions (i.e., bending both knees, resulting in the extension of the rump outward from the plane of the body). After several baseline sessions, treatment began on facial tics, at the outpatient clinic. Spe-cifically, the therapist would record each time the child displayed a facial tic: if the child emitted fewer than 10 facial tics in five minutes, he could go out in the corridor and play. However, if he exhibited the behavior more than 10 times, he would be placed in a barren room for 5 minutes (time-out). Also, the child was given a large, table-model stopwatch and instructed how to monitor five-minute intervals.

As facial grimaces decreased in intensity, they were redefined as unilaterial eye squinting, nose wrinkling, and mouth twitching. In addition, feedback was given for appropriate facial mannerisms (e.g., eyeblinks), to help the child to increase his discrimination and self-observation of his tics by having him label such facial movements as were permissible.

Additionally, all categories of inappropriate behavior were monitored by the mother in the home. Two weeks after treatment began in the clinic, the child's mother was instructed to implement treatment for facial grimaces at home using the procedures just described. On the tenth week of home treatment, similar contingencies also were imposed on vocal tics. The directly treated behaviors rapidly declined in frequency. In addition, two important types of generalization were noted: Behaviors in the home setting were suppressed rapidly, as were untreated tics. The authors considered the treatment package cost-efficient, since time requirements were brief and the procedures were readily trained to the child's family.

Another successful application of time-out was reported by Cayner and Kiland (1974). Three hospitalized psychiatric patients (diagnosed chronic schizophrenic) served as subjects. Contingent time-out was used to eliminate disruptive verbal behaviors, tantrum behavior, and self-mutilation (a constant picking and digging at teeth and gums). Treatment consisted of placing the offender in a time-out room similar to the one described earlier in this chapter and depicted earlier in Figure 4–1. The authors noted that, despite the fact that the patients could engage readily in the target behaviors while in the time-out room, they did not. This finding seems somewhat atypical, since in many such cases the client could be expected to exhibit the target behavior in the time-out room. Therefore, a careful evaluation of baseline data respective to antecedents and consequences should be taken in any case where the client is likely to exhibit the behavior selected for treatment in the time-out room.

In another example of the diverse applications of time-out, Barton et al. (1970) treated 16 severely to profoundly mentally retarded institutionalized persons from 9 to 23 years of age. The mealtime behaviors treated included stealing, eating foods with the hands when it was deemed socially inappropriate (e.g., mashed potatoes, green beans), using utensils inappropriately by spilling food or using the wrong utensil for a certain food (e.g., knife to eat peas), and spilling food out of the mouth while eating. Additional behaviors that were positive and incompatible with the previous behaviors also were identified. This latter behavior group was not consequated with time-out. The type of time-out and its length were varied with the behavior treated; thus, for example, stealing food resulted in the offender being removed from the dining area and being placed in a time-out

room for the remainder of the meal, whereas eating foods inappropriately with the hands resulted in removal of the person's food tray
for 15 seconds. Treatment proved to be rapidly effective for all the
inappropriate behaviors. It should be cautioned, however, that methods such as the removal of a person from a meal may not be practical
with the increasing move toward protecting clients' rights. Barton et
al. (1970) should be commended for monitoring the weights of the 16
subjects throughout the course of the study. They indicated that the
mean weight of the group remained unchanged.

Ross (1975) has proposed a variant of time-out for the treatment
of thumbsucking by a nine-year-old boy. The problem was so severe
that a noticeable malocclusion of the front teeth had developed, as
well as a severe lisp that was believed to be at least partially related to
this denture problem.

Two treatments had been attempted previously, both unsuccess-
fully. These included frequent reminders and applying a nonharm-
ful but aversive substance to the thumb. The first task of the successful treatment described in this study was the establishment of a
systematic recording system of inappropriate behaviors. The mother
made three "spot checks" daily to determine if the child was sucking
his thumb while watching television.

After two weeks of observation, "Charlie" was told that the TV
would be turned off for five minutes each time he was found sucking his thumb. After five weeks of treatment, the contingency was
removed for three weeks and then reinstated indefinitely, with data
collected for six weeks. Thumbsucking rapidly decreased when the
time-out contingency was in effect but rapidly returned to pretreatment levels (reversal phase) when treatment was discontinued. This
design served two practical functions. It demonstrated that the time-
out procedure was producing the effect, and it made it clear that
treatment would need to be administered for a long period of time
to insure sustained change.

Linkenhoker (1974) provided a description of a particularly
novel approach to the use of time-out. In his therapeutic learning-
based setting for adolescents who had displayed problems with the
juvenile court system, a major problem was the loss of time from
learning settings engendered by the frequency of time-outs. He
noted that, although the time-out procedure was effective, it not
only removed the individual from the opportunity to learn desirable
behavior, but also increased the cost of valuable therapeutic program time. Therefore, when one of the boys from this all-male program was placed in the time-out room, he was given a cassette tape

recorder and asked to record his description of what had provoked the time-out, his feelings toward the person involved, and solutions that might have kept him from the time-out situation. Prior to making the recording, the individual was required to listen to a prerecorded tape that would describe in a positive manner the reasoning and requirements for this procedure. On completion of the tasks described and after the time-out period was concluded, the child returned the tape player to the designated person.

At the end of the day, all "time-out audiotapes" were reviewed and discussed in the context of a small problem-solving group composed of a staff member and other residents from the offending youth's living cottage. The group's task was to discuss the individual's problem situation and to evaluate the feasibility of alternative solutions proposed by the client. Since staff were responsible for providing the time-out, it was possible to compare staff and offender perceptions of incidents. If the group consensus was that the possible alternatives were realistic, then the group rewarded the client with tokens for effective problem solving. The group also was encouraged to give the offender feedback and assist him in developing alternative treatment strategies.

While the empirical data presented were not particularly strong, they did suggest that the treatment was effective. This procedure is important, since it provides a novel way of evaluating treatment effectiveness and demonstrates one way of maximizing therapeutic aspects of the treatment plan.

By observing the procedural concerns in developing a time-out program and performing a thorough functional analysis of the targeted behavior and the environment, the researcher and clinician can formulate an effective and efficient time-out program. As noted, many behaviors and populations have been treated with this procedure. Furthermore, by following the guidelines and safeguards presented, a humane program can be developed as well.

Physical Restraint:
A Special Case of Time-Out

This section outlines a more restrictive type of time-out procedure, physical restraint, which is a form of punishment that results in the client being removed from a set of highly reinforcing conditions. Little research has been done on this procedure; however, it has been a frequent means of treatment in most psychiatric hospitals and large facilities for the mentally retarded. Despite the view that it is a "barbaric" form of care (Linn, 1975; Winston, 1977), many professionals still endorse its use (Bursten, 1975). To our knowledge, this is one of the few times that physical restraint will be considered a special case of time-out formally, although this has been the case in practice for some time.

Definition

A distinction is drawn first between the traditional definition of physical restraint and a behavior-analytic definition.

Traditionally, physical restraint has referred to the employment of leather or cloth bracelets to restict the movement of a client's limbs. In cases where bracelets are attached, they are used in conjunction with a belt to the bedframe so that the client can be maintained in a supine position. (Sometimes a client may be strapped to a chair; however, in this case the chair must be fastened to the floor so that the client cannot turn it over.) The bracelets must never be so tight that circulation is impaired, and foam rubber padding should be placed between the cuff (if cuffs are used) and the skin. Once in restraint, the client should be placed in a quiet, private room near a nursing station and bedrails (if available) should be maintained in an upright position to prevent injury (Rosen & DiGiacomo, 1978).

The primary indication for the use of this type of physical restraint is to control violent behavior, occurring during the course of a psychotic illness, that cannot be controlled adequately with medications or psychological interventions (Abroms, 1968; Bursten, 1975; Wells, 1972). As stated earlier, this definition in no way resembles time-out, which was defined as the removal of the opportunity to receive reinforcement contingent upon the emission of a specific behavior for the expressed purpose of decreasing the future probability of that response. Physical restraint may be adapted to fit this definition.

Therefore, the behavior-analytic definition of physical restraint would be the physical restriction of the movement of a person's limbs (e.g., holding the limbs behind the person's back) or some other part of the body for a specified brief period of time, contingent upon the emission of a specific behavior funtionally related to limb involvement as a source of reinforcement for the expressed purpose of decreasing the future probability of the targeted behavior. Consequently, it should be used only after consideration has been made of the procedures, rules, guidelines, and safeguards ascribed to time-out. This type of procedure may prove to be an efficacious method in cases of self-injury where placement in a time-out room may exacerbate the behavior.

Advantages, Disadvantages, and Treatment Considerations of Physical Restraint

Most of the advantages and disadvantages delineated with the general form of time-out also apply to physical restraint; however, the major advantage of physical restraint is that it prevents the possibility of self-injury or injury to others. In a time-out room, a person could continue self-abuse (e.g., head-banging, biting limbs). Likewise, when using overcorrection, a struggle could occur during the administration of manual guidance, leading to self-injury and/or injury of the staff member.

A second advantage of physical restraint is that it is a very portable procedure. A person can be restrained physically in most settings, whether it be a picnic, in the day room of a ward, or elsewhere. This aspect of the treatment has major positive implications for decreasing the likelihood of physical harm to clients.

Certainly, a number of drawbacks in the use of physical restraint are readily apparent also. These include the possibilities of physical harm that may result any time an aversive method is employed. Other problems or potential problems include adverse emotional side-effects, such as screaming, crying, and the like, and the resistance that is likely to be present among many advocacy groups toward the use of such methods. This latter point has resulted in the curtailment and in some cases the cessation of the use of such procedures in some settings.

Problems for Which Physical Restraint Is Applicable

Unfortunately, few studies exist that empirically validate the use of this procedure in the behavior-analytic sense (as opposed to the medical/psychiatric use). Although rarely documented, physical restraint has been a widely used technique in dealing with self-injurious behavior (Baumeister & Rollings, 1976). Rapoff, Altman, and Christophersen (1980) recently used brief restraint to successfully reduce the incidence of self-hitting of a mentally retarded blind child. The target behavior was defined as biting and scratching arms and hitting himself in the head with his hands. During the treatment phase, contingent on each incidence of the target behavior, "the teacher said, 'no hitting,' had him sit in a nearby chair, and held both hands behind his back for approximately 30 seconds" (p. 234). Using an ABAB design, the behavior was observed to be functionally controlled by the treatment phases.

Several other studies have documented the effectiveness of brief restraint. Problem behaviors that were reduced successfully included inappropriate eating behavior (Henricksen & Doughty, 1967), crawling behavior (O'Brien, Azrin, & Bugle, 1972), self-destructive behavior (Saposnek & Watson, 1974), and soiling accidents (Giles & Wolf, 1966).

Although this type of time-out procedure has not been researched extensively, it deserves attention in the future. From the preceding evidence, the typically resilient self-injurious behaviors may be amenable to this type of treatment.

Extinction

Definition

The second type of procedure that impacts the schedule and frequency of reinforcement on the targeted behavior is extinction.[3] Harris & Ersner-Hershfield (1978) define extinction as the "withholding of previously given positive reinforcement following the emission of the target behavior. No discriminative cues, such as environmental changes or verbal warnings, are given. For example, in using an extinction procedure to treat tantrums, the therapist simply ignores the tantrum behavior and proceeds as though nothing has happened" (pp. 1355–1356). Extinction is probably one of the most widely *attempted* procedures by the lay community (e.g., "Oh—just ignore him and he'll stop hitting you.") and likewise the most widely misunderstood. Very clear and serious associated effects accompany and probably outweigh its use in most circumstances. However, most individuals who advise others to "simply ignore" certain behaviors are not aware of the contraindications and probably are inflicting a serious injustice by offering advice. Due to excellent recent chapters devoted solely to extinction (Kazdin, 1980b; Rimm & Masters, 1979), we simply will delineate the major points in using extinction procedures.

[3]Technically, extinction is not considered a punishment procedure, since a specific stimulus is not applied (Azrin & Holz, 1966). However, a discussion of extinction is included in this book because a second criterion for defining a procedure as punishment is met (i.e., a reduction in the future probability of a response is observed).

Treatment Considerations

After reviewing the laboratory and applied studies exploring the parameters of extinction, the simplistic, naive, and dangerous advice of "ignore the behavior" has been expanded to include 12 treatment considerations. Some of the following considerations should be extrapolated for every study using extinction. Other points are general statements and conclusions to use when deciding if extinction is the treatment of choice for a particular problem behavior.

Kazdin (1980b) suggests that the efficacy of extinction, as well as the speed at which the problem behavior decreases, is due to the schedule of reinforcement maintaining the problematic response. Several researchers (Herrnstein, 1966; Morse, 1966) have noted that behavior is acquired quickly and lost slowly. Zeiler (1977) advances that a behavior that is reinforced one time will be exhibited repeatedly without another presentation of the reinforcer. He cites several studies (Neuringer, 1970; Skinner, 1938) that demonstrate this effect.

Therefore, the first treatment consideration is that the ease of extinction of a response appears to be related directly to the frequency of the response–reinforcement relationship. A continuously reinforced response is much easier to extinguish than an intermittently reinforced response (Kazdin, 1980b). As a matter of fact, the most highly resistant responses to extinction are those maintained on a very lean or thin intermittent schedule (Bellack & Hersen, 1977). This point cannot be overstated, since most behaviors are maintained on intermittent schedules of reinforcement (Kazdin, 1980b).

This point leads to the second consideration. A critical aspect of the success of the program is the ability to consequent *every* occurrence of the behavior. If the behavior is reinforced occasionally (e.g., with attention), this creates a very thin, intermittent reinforcement schedule that should maintain the behavior indefinitely. Accidental reinforcement (Kazdin, 1980b) is always a problem with extinction procedures.

The next three points also deal with resistance to extinction (Kimble, 1961; Reynolds, 1968). The greater the magnitude of the reinforcer maintaining the behavior, the greater the resistance to extinction. Also, a direct relationship exists between the lengths of time that the behavior has been reinforced and the resistance to extinction. Finally, the decrease in frequency of the response is accelerated if there are numerous exposures to extinction (Zeiler, 1977).

The sixth consideration focuses on the identification and control of reinforcers that are maintaining the adaptive behavior (Kazdin, 1980b). If the reinforcers are defined inadequately, the experimenter or clinician will readily note in the treatment phase that no changes in the behavior will be recognized.

After the reinforcers have been defined adequately and concretely, the experimenter or clinician will have to manipulate the behavior of the agents who deliver the reinforcement such that they never exhibit that reinforcement after the client emits the target behavior. The eighth parameter is a realization that extinction is a gradual process. An immediate decrement is usually uncommon, and a total elimination of the behavior appears to "take forever."

If this is not enough, "extinction bursts" often are observed, usually during the initial stages of extinction, where the frequency of the response increases to above baseline levels. This *should be expected*, and the clinician should not become alarmed. The client suddenly has learned that reinforcement is not forthcoming as it once was, thus an attempt is made (by increasing the frequency) to obtain the old effect. If the reinforcer is withheld, the response ultimately will decrease. If, however, the increased responding is reinforced accidentally, then (1) the client realizes that sometimes increased responding is necessary to obtain the reinforcer, (2) a lean intermittent schedule is reintroduced, and (3) the behavior becomes more resistant to extinction. For this reason, as well as the length of time necessary for eliminating the behavior, extinction may be contraindicated for self-injurious behavior.

The tenth consideration has been termed "spontaneous recovery" (Kimble, 1961), a temporary recurrence of the nonreinforced response during extinction (Kazdin, 1980b). Usually the response rate will be less than baseline levels; however, the same three points made under an extinction burst also are applicable here if during this increased frequency the behavior is reinforced accidentally.

The eleventh consideration is the expectation of other effects sometimes termed emotional responses. Some responses that have been defined include aggression, agitation, frustration, crying, and feelings of failure (Hutchinson, Azrin, & Hunt, 1968; Kazdin, 1980b; Lawson, 1965; Rekers & Lovaas, 1974; Rilling, 1977; Skinner, 1953). This appears to indicate that the procedure is "not liked" or aversive. We would suspect this reaction when someone does not get the reinforcement that they are accustomed to receiving.

A final consideration is the simultaneous differential reinforcement of other adaptive behavior. The individual should be receiving some input on what is a correct way to respond if other, previously reinforced, behavior is being extinguished (Bellack & Hersen, 1977; Kazdin, 1980b; Rimm & Masters, 1979). Such an approach greatly increases the likelihood that behaviors substituted for the response that is suppressed will increase.

The twelve considerations we have outlined here for use when contemplating the use of extinction are critical in terms of a program success. A simple "ignore it" no longer will suffice.

Advantages and Disadvantages of Extinction

Extinction may be considered the least restrictive alternative to most punishment procedures.[4] No additional equipment is necessary, and the technique appears to be easily taught. However, the aforementioned 12 considerations must be dealt with for extinction to be effective.

In addition, it is difficult to ignore extremely aversive behavior (e.g., endless tantrums) for long periods of time (Bellack & Hersen, 1977). As mentioned earlier, every instance of the behavior *must* be consequated or the schedule-induced effects make it extremely difficult to extinguish the behavior. Also, if a high rate of self-injurious behavior is being exhibited, this procedure will take too long and burst too often for it to be recommended.

Problems for Which Extinction Is Applicable

A host of studies have been done that exhibit the suppressive effects of extintion and/or the inclusion of differential reinforcement of other behavior. Some of the treated problematic behaviors have included tantrum behavior (Williams, 1959), self-injurious behavior (Allen & Harris, 1966; Duker, 1975; Peterson & Peterson, 1968), vomiting (Alford, Blanchard, & Buckley, 1972; Wolf, Birnbrauer, Williams, & Lawler, 1965), and disruptive classroom behavior (Madsen, Becker, & Thomas, 1968). Other successfully treated behaviors were persistent scratching (Walton, 1960), crying (Hart, Allen, Buell, Harris, & Wolf, 1964), visits to a nurses' station (Ayllon & Michael, 1959), and excessive or delusional speech (Ayllon & Haughton, 1964; Liberman, Teigen, Patterson, & Baker, 1973; Sajwaj, Twardosz, & Burke, 1972). Finally, the following behaviors decreased after extinction was administered: aggressive behavior (Mar-

---

[4]This would be debated, justifiably, in the case of self-abuse, where the least restrictive alternative probably would be that procedure which eliminated the behavior as quickly as possible.

tin & Foxx, 1973; Pinkston, Reese, LeBlanc, & Baer, 1973), obses-sive–compulsive behaviors (Hallam, 1974; Silverman, 1977), and hysterical fits (Singh, 1975).

Time-Out Versus Seclusion

There has been a great deal of confusion in distinguishing time-out from seclusion. The reader will remember from our definition of time-out that the same type of learning principles advocated with other behavior modification procedures also are applied here. The method is seen strictly as a means of reducing well-defined un-wanted behaviors and is given consistently and contingently on the behavior that has been identified for suppression. In addition, time-out periods are generally quite short, usually lasting only 10 to 15 minutes and rarely more than one hour. Seclusion differs from this method on a number of dimensions, which are detailed below.

The purpose for seclusion and when it is to be used are at best unclear and at worst contradictory and confusing. Seclusion has been defined as "the process whereby a psychiatric inpatient volun-tarily or involuntarily is placed for a specific time in a seclusion room, which is generally a securely built, small room, either unfur-nished or minimally furnished in a way designed to minimize injury to self or others . . . " (Gutheil, 1978, pp. 325–326). The author goes on to assert that the three reasons for seclusion are contain-ment, isolation, and a decrease in sensory input. This definition clearly is confusing since the *behavior* that results in seclusion is not described.

Plutchik, Karasu, Conte, Siegel, and Jerrett (1978) attempted to define seclusion retrospectively by reviewing 431 incidences of seclu-sion recorded in nursing notes. They write "almost all of the reasons for seclusion were forms of aggression toward persons or property, or undirected, agitated behavior" (p. 573). Clearly, the theoretical and conceptual reasons for time-out and seclusion are different.

Similarly, there is considerable confusion as to how the client reacts to seclusion. Greenblatt, York, and Brown (1955) state that clients almost always see this procedure as punishment. Wells (1972), however, states that she would like to think that this is not always the case. To further confuse the issue, Gutheil (1978) has stated that seclusion is not punishment and that it has been given a bad name because it is confused with solitary confinement and time-out.

Finally, reports by those who use seclusion note that the average length of time in the seclusion room was four hours. However, those seclusions lasting four hours or longer usually occurred because the clients fell asleep and were left undisturbed (Plutchik et al., 1978).

In addition to the general lack of support for a rationale of seclusion use, there is also insufficient support for the effectiveness of the procedure. A number of authors state that the method is effective or that direct-care staff think it works, but there is no research to support these claims.

Time-out is a treatment procedure with a clear empirically based rationale and a wealth of empirical data to support its effectiveness. These data are in stark contrast to the seclusion literature. It is our contention, therefore, that time-out is a credible treatment and that efforts should be made to distinguish between these two methods, since many state mental health and mental retardation governing agencies confuse the two procedures. Rimm & Masters (1979) cogently sum, "The point to be gleaned from this is that there are seldom specific operations (such as seclusion or ignoring) that automatically accomplish a desired behavior therapy technique such as time-out, and *procedures,* such as seclusion, must be distinguished from general *principles* or *techniques,* such as time-out, which may be accomplished by certain procedures in some instances but not in others" (p. 347).

It is noted that seclusion may have beneficial aspects; however, until there is consensus as to the rationale of why and when this treatment is used, and until the effectiveness of the treatment can be demonstrated through well-controlled treatment outcome studies, such claims should be avoided.

Conclusions

In this chapter, we have reviewed procedures primarily aimed at the modification of reinforcement contingencies; however, an important point, relative to this issue, is the *a priori* documentation of a reinforcing environment from which the modifications are made. Therefore, pairing a reinforcement program with such methods not only has the advantage of training new alternative behaviors but also of enhancing the effectiveness (positive quality) of the time-out and/or extinction procedures.

We suggest a careful analysis of the time-out and extinction procedures and considerations before any program is initiated. Again, a thorough functional analysis will dictate the critical variables, relationships, and interactions. The thoughtful clinician should be ready at all times to balance the time and effort involved in designing a program of this type from providing no treatment at all. Furthermore, the rights of other clients and staff also need to be considered in the complex equation that results in the development of a treatment program. The reader is directed to the chapter on ethical considerations for a more in-depth review of these issues.

5

The Role of
Positive Control
in Punishment
Programs

INTRODUCTION

The purpose of this book is to present methods to reduce maladaptive behavior. Marholin, Luiselli, and Townsend (1980) suggest that to achieve this goal, we must "increase opportunities for positive reinforcement, reduce aversive and social ostracism, and allow for the development of adaptive and functional skills" (p. 50). When practical considerations are enumerated, this ideal often becomes a nightmare.

However, several component parts of a reduction procedure are essential. We have expressed explicitly in each of the first four chapters that a reinforcement program should be started before or at least concomitantly with a punishment program. Because of this serious and important guideline, great care has been taken to include a chapter on positive control. Often, positive techniques are referred to as "alternatives" to punishment procedures. We feel that this line of reasoning implies an "either/or" decision regarding punishment and reinforcement. We do not support an either/or decision but rather submit that each time a punishment program is considered, a reinforcement component should be included. This position is in line with recent court decisions (Braun, 1975; Repp & Brulle, 1980; Roos, 1974) regarding the use of the least restrictive alternative first.

In addition, there is a great deal of theoretical and conceptual evidence that would suggest the use of reinforcement in all programs (Ferster & Culbertson, 1982; Rachman & Teasdale, 1969). Several points will be outlined. In general, reinforcement is lacking in society and punishment often is substituted for reinforcement as a means to control behavior (Skinner, 1980). One needs only to think of their own personal experiences. We are often corrected for doing something wrong but are seldom "reinforced" for good behavior. Similarly, our interactions with children and students follow the same pattern.

Second, there is a long history exemplifying the power of reinforcement (Ferster & Culbertson, 1982; Ferster & Skinner, 1957). Schedules of reinforcement have been researched extensively and have been shown to have profound effects on performance. There is a lag, however, between when a reinforcement program is started and subsequent behavior change. This "pause in effect" appears to be one reason why control of behavior by positive reinforcement, rather than punishment, is not usually practiced in the natural environment (Ferster & Culbertson, 1982).

Third, there is no reason to expect that an adaptive behavior, which is not being emitted at the present time, will increase unless reinforcement for the desired response occurs (Axelrod et al., 1978). This statement is a simple principle of learning and yet it often is ignored.

A fourth point involves schedules of reinforcement. A great deal of human behavior, adaptive and maladaptive, in the natural environment is maintained on intermittent reinforcement schedules (Ferster & Culbertson, 1982). [In addition, the factors maintaining behavior often are complex and misunderstood (Carr, Newsom, & Binkoff, 1980).] A thorough understanding of the intricacies of scheduling is essential for two reasons. First, since maladaptive behavior is maintained on such schedules, timelines and patterns of reducing behavior can be observed and reasonably projected. Second, because of the resiliency of behaviors maintained on of such schedules, it would be to the clinician's advantage to devise a program that would incorporate schedules of reinforcement on which the adaptive behaviors could be maintained after the problematic behaviors were reduced.

A fifth reason suggesting the use of reinforcement in reductive procedures is that a number of definitions of aberrant behavior include the action (or lack of action) of reinforcement in the maintenance of the behavior (Forehand & Baumeister, 1976). The functional relationship of reinforcement, therefore, is essential to successfully eliminating the problematic behavior.

Finally, positive effects of treatment programs should be expected only in settings where similar contingencies are programmed (Marholin, Luiselli, & Townsend, 1980). To maintain and generalize zero or near-zero levels of maladaptive responding in the natural environment, it has been recommended that stimulus similarities between treatment and nontreatment environments be established (Marholin & Touchette, 1979; Stokes & Baer, 1977). At zero levels of responding, the punishment contingency may be faded out. However, the reinforcement contingency, employed for adaptive behavior (high rates of responding) should remain salient.

In this chapter, we will outline definitions, methods, and treatment considerations in the use of positive control procedures in punishment programs.

Reinforcement Terminology, Parameters, and Types of Reinforcers

Terminology

"Positive reinforcement is the intervention of choice wherever it promises to be effective" (Bellack & Hersen, 1977, p. 176). This position has been stated repeatedly in the behavioral literature and we concur.

It is often the case that when maladaptive behaviors increase or are maintained at high levels of responding, adaptive behaviors are occurring at low rates. At least three factors are suggested as reasons for behavioral deficits. "*First,* the environment might not provide adequate prompts (S^Ds) for the [person] to emit a response already in his repertoire. *Second,* a response in the repertoire might be prompted, but fails to appear because its occurrence is not maintained by reinforcement. *Third,* the response simply might not be in the [person's] repertoire (i.e., a skill deficit)" (Bellack & Hersen, 1977, p. 174).

Therefore, reinforcement contingencies must be established so that a program may be designed to define and accelerate positive behaviors.

> The word *reinforcement* refers to the effect of an operation; it does not describe an independent variable but is the interaction of an independent variable with behavior. By *reinforcement* is meant an increase in responding as a function of a stimulus event following the response. The stimuli having these effects are *reinforcing stimuli* or *reinforcers*. *Schedules of reinforcement* are the rules used to present reinforcing stimuli. [Zeiler, 1977, p. 202]

In addition, contingencies of reinforcement have been defined as "the interrelations among [a discriminative stimulus], [a response], and [reinforcement]" (Skinner, 1969, p. 23). Clear indications of the effective control of behavior using contingent reinforcement (as opposed to noncontingent reinforcement using the same stimulus) have been demonstrated (Bandura & Perloff, 1967; Hart, Reynolds, Baer, Brawley, & Harris, 1968; Redd, 1969). Similarly, the contingent application of a stimulus not demonstrated to be a reinforcer is ineffective in increasing the targeted behavior (Ayllon & Azrin, 1968a; Bassett, Blanchard, & Koshland, 1977; Kelleher, 1966).

Parameters

Ten parameters of reinforcement are delineated that increase the probability of effectively using stimuli to increase behavior. First, the selection of effective reinforcers is critical. Bellack and Hersen (1977) suggest that the reinforcing value of a stimulus cannot be " be determined on an ipso facto basis" (p. 177). Observations must be made as a stimulus is presented to assess the reinforcing value, quality, or preference (Kazdin, 1980b) of the individual. Too often, we assume that specific stimuli act as universal reinforcers.

Second, after demonstration of the stimulus' reinforcing value, it should only be given contingently. Third, the greater the amount of a reinforcer delivered for a response, the more frequent the response (Kimble, 1961).

However, limits to the quantity of the stimulus are defined by the fourth parameter. The reinforcer should not be so large that satiation occurs. The effect magnitude has on reinforcement is limited by the point at which the individual becomes satiated (Kazdin, 1980b).

The fifth parameter has been termed the temporal gradient of reinforcement. Immediate presentation of the reinforcing stimulus after the desired response is emitted occasions the greatest effect (Hull, 1952; Terrell & Ware, 1961).

If a response is not exhibited, it cannot be reinforced. The sixth and seventh points involve various aspects of this statement. If the response is in the individual's repertoire, it may need to be prompted. The prompt may involve the verbalization of the specific if–then contingency. (If the desired behavior is performed, then you will receive the reinforcing stimulus.) If the behavior is not in the individual's repertoire, it may need to be shaped. This process involves the reinforcement of successive approximations of the target behavior.

To avoid satiation, different reinforcers should be available to the individual. This is the eight parameter. Effective reinforcers can be outlined by using a reinforcement menu (Homme, 1971; Homme, Csanyi, Gonzales, & Rechs, 1970), which is simply a list of reinforcers and dispensing media.

The ninth and tenth parameters involve the scheduling of reinforcers. The beginning stages of a program should be operating on a continuous-reinforcement schedule (e.g., each time the behavior is emitted, it should be reinforced). However, the tenth parameter suggests that the contingency should be faded into a specific intermittent schedule. As noted in Chapter 4, this schedule is the most resistant to extinction. (A later section details the specific schedules that are most effective in maintaining responding.)

Types of Reinforcers

Many stimuli may serve as effective reinforcers for different individuals. Several classes or types have been delineated in the behavioral literature. Five global categories are material reinforcers, social reinforcers, activity reinforcers, token reinforcers, and covert reinforcers. Brief descriptions are provided.

Material reinforcers include food, drink, money, and toys. This type of reinforcer appears to be most effective for children, although they have their place in adult life (Rimm & Masters, 1979). Several authors (Lovaas, 1968; Lovaas, Freitag, Kinder, Rubenstein, Schaeffer, & Simmons, 1966) have demonstrated a reinforcing valence to an individual who consistently presents material reinforcers. Therefore, this individual's presence (i.e., approval and attention) also provides socially reinforcing qualities.

Rimm and Masters (1979) suggest that most reinforcers in the natural environment are social (e.g., smiles, praise, physical closeness). Therefore, it is suggested often that social reinforcers be incorporated into reinforcement programs from the beginning. If a person is not responsive to typical social reinforcers, a suggestion is made to pair material reinforcers (if effective) with social reinforcers and then gradually fade the material reinforcers.

The third type of reinforcers are preferred activities. Authors and clinicians (Becker, 1971; Homme, 1971) have referred repeatedly to "Grandma's Rule," or "if–then" contingencies. If you do your homework first, then you can watch television.

The fourth type of reinforcer is a token (Ayllon & Azrin, 1968b; Kazdin, 1977). A token reinforcer is presented to the individual, contingent upon performance. The token is redeemable later for other "backup reinforcers," including any of the first three we've defined (i.e., material, social, activity).

Finally, a fifth form of reinforcer, covert stimuli, has been defined and researched extensively in the past 10 to 15 years (Cautela, 1966, 1967, 1970a, 1971, 1977). These thoughts or cognitions take the form of self-evaluations that an individual may engage in contingent upon his own behavior. Some recent work has demonstrated the effectiveness of this approach (Cautela, 1977; Marshall, Boutilier, & Minnes, 1974; Masters, Furman, & Barden, 1977; Masters & Santrock, 1976.)

For all of these different forms of reinforcers, the schedules of reinforcement play a critical role in the maintenance of target behaviors.

Reinforcement Systems

Reinforcement has been defined and categorized and parameters have been suggested to increase the probability that reinforcement will maintain appropriate behavior effectively. We now would like to discuss various reinforcement systems. Typically, these systems have been referred to as differentiation schedules or differential reinforcement of positive and/or neutral behaviors.

Definition of Differentiation Schedules

"In differentiation schedules reinforcers are presented when a response or a group of responses displays a specified property" (Zeiler, 1977, p. 203). In the traditional applied area of the behavioral literature, four schedules have been defined (Deitz, Repp, & Deitz, 1976; Ferster & Skinner, 1957; Luiselli, Colozzi, Helfen, & Pollow, 1980; Young & Wincze, 1974). Repp and Brulle (1980) define them as follows:

(a) *differential reinforcement of other behavior (DRO)*—reinforcement is delivered if the client does not emit the target response for a specified interval; (b) *differential reinforcement of low rates of responding (DRL)*—reinforcement is delivered if the rate of responding is less than or equal to some criterion; (c) *differential reinforcement of incompatible responding (DRI)*—reinforcement is delivered if a response that is topographically incompatible with the target response occurs; (d) *differential reinforcement of alternative behavior (DRA)*—reinforcement is delivered if a particular alternative but no topographically incompatible response occurs. [p. 2]

In the practical application of these positive procedures, behavior, other than the maladaptive behavior, is reinforced on some specific schedule. A hypothetical case will be presented so that each of the four schedules may be demonstrated.

Let's assume Joe is a moderately mentally retarded institutionalized adult aged 23. Joe has been exhibiting a recently learned maladaptive behavior (e.g., hitting staff members). A DRO schedule could be instituted whereby Joe would be reinforced every three minutes if hitting has not occurred during that time period. We also could implement a DRL program. It has been observed that this behavior has been occurring at high rates, and Joe does not go for three minutes without a "hit." Therefore, he could be reinforced every three minutes if the behavior occurs less than or equal to two times.

Additionally, a DRI program could be started. Every 10 minutes a staff member would approach Joe and extend his/her hand to prompt Joe to extend his hand appropriately to "shake hands." This would be an incompatible behavior and, if emitted, he would be reinforced.

Finally, a DRA schedule could be instituted whereby Joe would be taught appropriate social skills. In all cases some other neutral or positive behavior would be targeted for reinforcement.

Controversy over Labeling of Differentiation Schedules

The reader shoud be aware of some controversy in the field regarding the labeling of differentiation schedules. Lattal and Poling (1981) suggest that the designations just made (e.g., DRL) are based on prediction of the patterns of behavior likely, but not certain, to occur under each condition. They continue that the labels "inevitably confuse theoretical accounts of the schedule with the conditions for reinforcer delivery. For example, in the case of DRL schedules, the possible cause of low rates include the differential reinforcement of low rates in a molar sense (cf. Baum, 1973), the reinforcement of long IRTS [interresponse time], or the reinforcement of mediating response chains" (p. 149). The authors go on to relabel the schedules. This distinction appears to be a valid one and becomes critical when attempts are made to maintain behaviors, since the actual control or functional assessment of controlling variables is unclear when the traditional labels are used. However, due to the wide usage of the terms, we will continue with the labels for this review.

In a similar vein, differentiation schedules (e.g., DRO) are referred to, incorrectly, as reduction procedures (Homer & Peterson, 1980). Many of the studies reviewed made mention of the power (or lack of power) of DRO schedules to reduce behavior. This position is antithetical to the definition of reinforcement. Reinforcement, by definition, increases the probability of a response. How, then, can differential *reinforcement* of other behavior reduce the frequency of a response? It is our contention that the reinforcement schedule does not reduce behavior; rather, the removal of this contingency (i.e., if neutral or positive behavior, then reinforcement) sets up a time-out procedure that then reduces the frequency of the maladaptive behavior. This is a critically important reformulation of the controlling variables in DRO procedures. This position, therefore, reinforces the notion that, for punishment procedures to be effective, reinforcement contingencies must be in effect before beginning the actual punishment contingency. A considerable amount of research has been conducted to support this hypothesis. The basic premise has been that greater amounts of reinforcement in an environment enhance the effects of punishment procedures.

Application of Reinforcement Methods

This section is aimed at describing briefly the application of differential reinforcement methods. DRO, DRL, and DRI will be covered in this section, while DRA will be mentioned later.

As mentioned earlier, a reinforcement component should be incorporated in all programs. The following examples represent some interesting, and at times novel, attempts to devise reinforcement contingencies. The reader and interested clinician need be constrained only by her/his imagination in devising other programs.

The DRO versus DRI distinction is at times rather arbitrary due to a lack of exact explanations of the method in some studies. The

Table 5-1. DRO and DRI Studies Including Problem Behavior and Reinforced Behavior.

Study	Problem Behavior	Reinforced Behavior
Allen & Harris (1966)	Persistent scratching	Other desirable behavior
Aragona, Cassady, & Drabman (1975)	Eating behavior	Exercise and weight loss
Ayllon & Haughton (1964)	Psychotic talk	Normal verbalization
Ayllon, Layman, & Kandel (1975)	Hyperactive behavior	Incompatible behaviors
Ayllon & Michael (1959)	Psychotic talk	Normal verbalizations
Azrin, Besalel, & Wisotzek (1982)	Self-injurious behavior	Incompatible functional behavior
Azrin, Kaplan, & Foxx (1973)	Stereotypic behavior	Appropriate behavior
Bach & Moylan (1975)	Incontinence	Appropriate toileting
Barkley & Zupnick (1976)	Stereotyped body contortions	Appropriate body movements
Barton & Madsen (1980)	Drooling	No drooling
Bennett (1980)	Habitual vomiting	No vomiting
Corte, Wolf, & Locke (1971)	Self-injurious behavior	Other adaptive behavior
Dobes (1977)	Nervous scratching	Decreased scratching
Dougherty & Lane (1976)	Self-injurious behavior	Other adaptive behavior
Knight & McKenzie (1974)	Thumbsucking	No thumbsucking
Leitenberg, Burchard, & Burchard (1977)	Sibling conflict	Alternative behaviors to conflict situations
Lovaas, Litrownick, & Mann (1971)	Self-injurious behavior	Appropriate handclapping
Lowitz & Suib (1978)	Thumbsucking	No thumbsucking
Luiselli & Krause (1981)	Stereotypic behavior	Other adaptive behavior
Luiselli & Reisman (1980)	Inappropriate verbalizations and aggression	Quiet behavior and no aggression
Madsen, Becker, Thomas, Koser, & Plager (1968)	Out-of-seat behavior	Sitting down
Mulhern & Baumeister (1969)	Body rocking	Absence of rocking

(continued)

Table 5-1 (continued)

Study	Problem Behavior	Reinforced Behavior
Neisworth, Madle, & Goeke (1975)	Separation anxiety	Nonanxious behavior
Neisworth & Moore (1972)	Asthma attacks	No asthma attacks
Nordquist & Wahler (1973)	Stereotypic behavior	Correct movements
Peterson & Peterson (1968)	Self-injurious behavior	Other adaptive behavior
Repp & Deitz (1974)	Aggressive and self-injurious behavior	No aggressive or self-injurious responses
Repp, Deitz, & Deitz (1976)	Self-injurious behavior	Other adaptive behavior
Repp, Deitz, & Speir (1974)	Body rocking	Absence of rocking
Shafto & Sulzbacher (1977)	Hyperactive behaviors	Incompatible behavior
Twardosz & Sajwaj (1972)	Hyperactive behaviors	Sitting behavior
Weiher & Harman (1975)	Self-injurious behavior	Other adaptive behavior
Weisberg, Passman, & Russell (1973)	Stereotypic behavior	Appropriate motor behavior

distinction between the two is not critical; therefore, sample studies of the two types are presented together in Table 5–1.

A number of other contingencies (e.g., time-out, response cost) may have been involved in each of the studies. Also, given the controversy on the controlling variables in any differential reinforcement program, we are not suggesting that the DRO/DRL/DRI schedules in the studies presented in Table 5–1 completely controlled the targeted behavior. We are presenting these studies merely as examples of how differential reinforcement programs may be designed. A study representing each type of schedule is presented.

Lowitz and Suib (1978) present a nice example of a DRO program designed to aid in the reduction of thumbsucking in an eight-year-old girl. The child received pennies during the treatment sessions, contingent on one-minute intervals of no thumbsucking. Within five sessions, thumbsucking was eliminated and the program was maintained successfuly at home utilizing a token system.

Nunes, Murphy, and Ruprecht (1977) present a DRI program in the modification of self-injurious behavior (i.e., hitting head and objects with fists). A reinforcer (back massager) was presented to the client contingent on an appropriate use of her hands (e.g., working on a puzzle) that was topographically incompatible with hitting her head. If the self-injurious behavior occurred, the massager was turned off for a set amount of time. The procedure was quite effective within a short period of time. This study demonstrates the prior conceptual note. The reduction in self-injurious behavior appears to be attributed more aptly to time-out from positive reinforcement (the massager) rather than to the DRI schedule. This is not minimizing the effect of the reinforcement program, since the differential effect of no reinforcement probably could be obtained only after a reinforcement program had been started.

Finally, Deitz and Repp (1974) present three studies demonstrating the efficacy of a DRL schedule. Furthermore, the authors make a cogent argument for the modified DRO procedure. By constructing a schedule such that a reinforcer is delivered if fewer than a specified number of responses occur within a present time interval, the procedure is made more amenable to classroom use.

In each of the three studies, talking-out behavior was chosen for modification. The authors presented nonexchangeable gold stars to the children contingent on two or fewer "talk-outs" per session. In all three studies, the procedure was readily effective in reinforcing low rates of disruptive behavior and was manageable by the classroom teacher. Several other studies utilizing DRL schedules are presented in Table 5–2. From the mere number of studies presented in

Table 5-2. DRL Studies Including Problem Behavior and Reinforced Behavior.

Study	Problem Behavior	Reinforced Behavior
Deitz (1977)	Talking-out behavior	Three or less "talk-outs"
Deitz & Repp (1973)	"Talk-outs"	Low rates of "talk-outs"
Deitz & Repp (1974)	"Talk-outs"	Low rates of "talk-outs"
Deitz, Slack, Schwarzmueller, Wilander, Weatherly, & Hilliard (1978)	"Talk-outs"	Low rates of "talk-outs"
Hollis (1963)	Body-rocking	Low rates of rocking

Tables 5–1 and 5–2, and from the explanations of a few studies, the number of method permutations may seem unlimited. We will present some general treatment considerations to help delineate the choices and increase effectiveness of such programs.

General Treatment Considerations

Guidelines for Implementing a Differential Reinforcement Program

When attempting to increase responding, Sulzer-Azaroff and Mayer (1977) cogently summarize four principles by stating, "Reinforce the response immediately and as often as possible with an appropriate amount and type of reinforcer" (p. 179). Also, as mentioned earlier, *be consistent.* The clinician should remember to select reinforcers effective for the individual, use a variety of reinforcers, and select reinforcers found in the natural environment.

In each differential reinforcement program, intervals of time need to be specified (Luiselli, 1981) and reinforcement delivered at the end of the interval if maladaptive responding did not occur within the interval (i.e., DRO and DRI) or at low rates (i.e., DRL). If high rates of maladaptive behavior are occurring, very brief intervals (e.g., 10 seconds) may need to be specified at the beginning of the program (Hobbs & Goswick, 1977; Luiselli, 1981). Once responding has been controlled, the ratio or interval requirements may (and should) be increased gradually and progressively (Sulzer-Azaroff & Mayer, 1977). However, extreme care should be taken to prevent possible contrast effects (i.e., increase in the maladaptive behavior after the contingency has been removed) (Luiselli, 1981).

Finally, the practical application of a differential reinforcement program may necessitate, first, implementing of a DRL schedule, and, second, gradually increasing the requirement for reinforcement until the behavior is eliminated.

General Considerations

Several authors (Carr, 1982; Repp & Deitz, 1974; Zeiler, 1970) have suggested the possibility of other inappropriate behaviors being reinforced successfully on a DRO schedule. If a maladaptive behavior not targeted for intervention occurred near the end of the interval, then reinforcement delivered for the nonoccurrence of the original behavior may become associated with the maladaptive response. This has been the only potential problem with differential reinforcement schedules noted in the literature.

Conversely, it is difficult to conceive a problem from the overuse of DRO procedures (Homer & Peterson, 1980). Additionally, approach behavior on the part of the client has been observed (Favell, McGimsey, & Jones, 1978; Frankel, Moss, Schofield, & Simmons, 1976; Garcia & DeHaven, 1976; Weiher & Harman, 1975), as has increased staff participation (Deitz et al., 1976; Sewell, McCoy, & Sewell, 1973) from the use of such procedures. Harris and Ersner-Hershfield (1978) make a final point. They suggest that, when used alone, DRO may be ineffective. We support the view that differential reinforcement schedules are not reductive procedures but that the therapeutic goal is to increase rates of adaptive responding (Johnson, Baumeister, Penland, & Inwald, 1982). Therefore, the practicing clinician should be aware that a punishment component (e.g., time-out) is built into an effective differential reinforcement procedure (i.e., removal of reinforcement contingent on maladaptive behavior), which causes the reduction in the targeted maladaptive behavior. Differential reinforcement of alternative behaviors (DRA) provides a slightly different emphasis in the treatment of maladaptive behaviors. The following section addresses the relevant issues.

Training Adaptive Skills

Definition of DRA

Differential reinforcement of alternative (DRA) behavior, more recently termed differential reinforcement of compatible (DRC) behavior (Johnson et al., 1982), was defined earlier as "reinforcement . . . delivered if a particular alternative but not topographically incompatible response occurs" (Repp & Brulle, 1980, p. 2). The conceptual rationale for using DRA is slightly different than the use of DRO, DRI, and DRL. Kazdin (1980b) reports that, by reinforcing alternative adaptive behavior, the undesirable behavior is displaced in the individual's repertoire of responses. Carr (1982) labels the process of providing reinforcement for alternative behaviors as a competition. The newly exhibited adaptive behaviors would compete with the maladaptive behaviors for reinforcement. Favell, McGimsey, & Schell (1982) suggest that the provision of alternative activities would set the occasion for the naturally reinforced more appropriate behavior. All of these authors are noting that some maladaptive behavior may be on different schedules of reinforcement than adaptive behaviors. If alternative adaptive behavior can be put on a schedule of reinforcement such that the probability of the frequency of adaptive behavior would increase, then the adaptive behavior would compete with the maladaptive behavior.

Several authors have noted an important consideration in the use of DRA schedules of reinforcement. Since the targeted adaptive behavior is not topographically incompatible with the maladaptive behavior, the individual may continue to engage in the maladaptive response while concurrently engaging in the adaptive response and thus may receive reinforcement for the inappropriate behavior. To remedy this situation, Repp and Brulle (1980) suggest that the amount of work required by the alternative behavior be increased. Another strategy would be to institute a DRO or DRL (with time-out) program until the maladaptive behavior is eliminated or reduced to an appropriate level.

Application of DRA

Few studies have been reported using DRA procedures (Repp & Brulle, 1980); however, the efficacy has been demonstrated of using behavioral principles to increase adaptive responding while not necessarily aimed at the reduction of maladaptive behavior. A number of studies have demonstrated the successful acquisition of leisure skills (Johnson & Bailey, 1977; Matson & Adkins, 1980; Matson & Marchetti, 1980; Schleien, Kiernan, & Wehman, 1981; Schleien, Wehman, & Kiernan, 1981; Wehman, 1978, 1979; Wehman, Renzaglia, Berry, Schutz, & Karan, 1978), vocational skills (Matson & Martin, 1979), and social interaction skills (Barton, 1973; Brodsky, 1967; Deutsch & Parks, 1978; Doljanac, Schrader, & Christian, 1977; Luiselli, Colozzi, Donellon, Helfen, & Pemberton, 1978; Paloutzian, Hasazi, Streifel, & Edgar, 1971; Wehman, Karan, & Rettie, 1976). Additionally, Matson and his colleagues (Matson, 1978; Matson & Stephens, 1978; Matson & Zeiss, 1978, 1979; Matson, Zeiss, Zeiss, & Bowman, 1980) have demonstrated the efficacy of social skills treatment packages in increasing socially appropriate skills and decreasing maladaptive verbalizations. Although not reported as such, their programs could be defined as modified DRA procedures.

For example Matson & Stephens (1978) treated psychiatric inpatients for frequent arguing and fighting. Target behaviors within training sessions were tailored for each subject on the basis of pretreatment observations and included interruptions, irrelevant comments, inappropriate laughter, inappropriate requests, and frequent inattention. Social skills training sessions ranged from 10 to 40 minutes. Feedback concerning appearance was given at the beginning of each session and consisted of praise for appropriate grooming and dress.

Feedback on appearance was followed by role-played social scenes presented by a narrator. Based on the response by the client, the narrator would provide feedback and instructions concerning the appropriateness of the response. This was followed by modeling of the response by the trainer. Reinforcement was provided upon noted improvement. These trained skills generalized to the ward setting, and arguing and fighting were reduced markedly.

Several other studies, presented in Table 5–3, have demonstrated the efficacy of DRA schedules in increasing response rates of adaptive behaviors with other maladaptive behaviors targeted simultaneously for reduction. These inappropriate behaviors included screaming (O'Brien & Azrin, 1972b), disruptive behaviors (Ayllon, Layman, & Burke, 1972), self-injurious behaviors (Johnson et al., 1982; Lovaas, Freitag, Gold, & Kassorla, 1965; Schneider, Ross, & Drubin, 1979), depressive behavior (Hersen, Eisler, Alford, & Agras, 1973), and stereotyped behavior (Johnson et al., 1982).

Table 5-3. DRA Studies Including Problem Behavior and Reinforced Behavior.

Study	Problem Behavior	Reinforced Behavior
Ayllon, Layman, & Burke (1972)	Disruptive behavior	Appropriate academic behavior
Hersen, Eisler, Alford, & Agras (1973)	Depressive behavior	Personal hygiene and work behavior
Johnson, Baumeister, Penland, & Inwald (1982)	Self-injurious and stereotyped behavior	Appropriate compatible behavior
Lovaas, Freitag, Gold, & Kassorla (1965)	Self-injurious (hand-to-object) behavior	Appropriate musical activity
Matson & Stephens (1978)	Arguing and fighting behavior	Social skills
O'Brien & Azrin (1972b)	Screaming	Appropriate social behavior and housekeeping tasks
Schneider, Ross, & Drubin (1979)	Self-injurious behavior	Responding to commands

As can be seen from these studies, DRA programs can be extremely effective in increasing appropriate responding. The mechanisms are unclear by which the secondary effect of decreasing inappropriate behavior is achieved. The maladaptive behavior may be "forced out" because of increased reinforcement of appropriate behavior or perhaps because of a covert time-out contingency. Future research, we hope, will supply some answers.

In addition, as mentioned earlier, the differences among DRO, DRI, DRL, and DRA are sometimes arbitrary and unclear. Some of the studies included under one heading could have been reconceptualized and placed elsewhere.

Sensory Reinforcement

A number of learning hypotheses have been used to account for self-stimulatory and self-injurious behavior. One theory suggests that the behavior is maintained by different forms of positive reinforcement. A second theory suggests the behavior is maintained through negative reinforcement or the escape and/or avoidance of aversive stimulation. If, through a functional analysis, one or both of these hypotheses appeared to be relevant for a given individual, then one of the previously defined reinforcement programs could be started and then a punishment procedure implemented if necessary. However, in the last few years, a new hypothesis has been put forth. It has been suggested that these forms of behavior may be compensating for an insufficiency of environmental stimuli or producing some form of intrinsic reinforcement (e.g., sensory stimulation) (Carr, 1982). The behavior also may maintain as a multiple controlled operant (Iwata, Dorsey, Slifer, Bauman, & Richman, 1982), which may indicate the need for multiple treatments. In any case, since some support has been generated for the sensory stimulation stance, it will be reviewed briefly.

Definition of terms

Devany and Rincover (1982) suggest that self-stimulation may be maintained by the sensory feedback it produces; therefore, it may act as a powerful natural reinforcer. Several authors (Carr, 1982; Devany & Rincover, 1982; Rincover, 1978; Rincover, Cook, Peoples, & Packard, 1979) have suggested that, if self-stimulation/self-injurious behavior is found to be maintained through sensory stimulation, sensory extinction and sensory reinforcement can be used to eliminate maladaptive behavior and increase appropriate responding.

Sensory extinction is a procedure designed to eliminate maladaptive behavior by removing its auditory, visual, or proprioceptive sensory consequences (Rincover et al., 1979). Conversely, sensory reinforcement would involve the application of the same sensory consequences to increase or maintain behavior.

Application of Sensory Reinforcement

Since the concept of sensory reinforcement is new, not many reports of its efficacy are available in the literature; however, one form of sensory reinforcement, contingent vibratory stimulation, was shown to be effective over 20 years ago (Schaefer, 1960). Since that time other forms of sensory stimulation (e.g., tickling, music) have been shown to increase adaptive responding (Fineman, 1968a, 1968b; Fineman & Ferjo, 1969; Hewitt, 1965; Lovaas, 1966). More recently, sensory reinforcement has been used to increase adaptive toy play (Rincover et al., 1979), bar pressing (Rincover, Newsom, Lovaas, & Koegel, 1977), and adaptive nonself-injurious behavior (Barmann, 1980).

Devany and Rincover (1982) point out the complexity of observing the multiple controlling variables in self-stimulatory and self-injurious behavior. They note, that

> failure to conduct a thorough assessment may lead to implementation of a treatment that may be useless or even harmful. For example, if attention is assumed to be the maintaining factor when the behavior is actually maintained by the negative reinforcement of escape from the therapy task, time-out would let the child out of the task and inadvertently reinforce [self-stimulatory behavior] (Carr, Newsom, & Binkoff, 1976). Or, if sensory consequences are maintaining [self-stimulatory behavior], a treatment based on the withdrawal of adult attention, such as time-out or extinction, would be ineffective. (p. 139)

Ecobehavioral Programming

Definition of the Concept

One final technique potentially applicable as a positive control procedure is ecobehavioral programming (Hart & Risley, 1976), also referred to as environmental psychology (VanHorn, Mein, Rich, Tison, Trout, Watterson, & Wilfong, 1981), environmental enrichment (Horner, 1980), and socioecological programming (Jones, Favell, & Risley, 1982). This technique "stresses the physical and human environmental arrangements that set the occasion for the occurrence of desired behavior" (VanBiervliet, Spangler, & Marshall, 1981, p. 296). For example, educational environments are constructed such that skills may be learned easily (Gump, 1974; Krantz & Risley, 1977; Lott & Sommer, 1967; Montes & Risley, 1975).

The environmental arrangement is related directly to the concept of habilitative programming for the mentally retarded (Landesman-Dwyer & Sackett, 1978); however, it has been reported repeatedly (Jones et al., 1982; Repp & Barton, 1980) that there is little correspondence between the guidelines set forth by accreditation governing bodies (Accreditation Council, 1978; U.S. DHEW, 1974) and the actual practice of habilitative programming through ecobehavioral management.

The lack of appropriate habilitative environments has produced recent research defining the goals and variables necessary to promoting skills acquisition. Jones et al. (1982) define four socioecological variables that reflect the quality of the habilitative environment. They define the first variable as material/activity availability. "This variable is concerned with the extent to which appropriate entertainment materials (e.g., toys, games, instructional materials, T.V.) and/ or structured activities (e.g., training, recreation, health care) are provided for clients. This measure varies depending upon the developmental level and extent of physical/sensory handicaps of the clients in a given location" (p. 10).

The second variable is termed client engagement with materials/activities. They define this variable as measuring the amount and appropriateness of use of available materials and participation in structured activities. The third variable is staff behavior with clients. The interactions would be characterized as social, and it is postulated that increases in this variable would enrich the environment.

The final variable is defined as staff behavior in nonclient activities. Good habilitative programming would streamline nonclinical activities (e.g., housekeeping) to increase efficiency, thoroughness, and safety.

Canter and Canter (1979) have designed four models from

which the preceding variables could be viewed and assessed, depending upon the population in question. These are:

1. The prosthetic model—the programming and environment are arranged to compensate for the individual's disabilities.
2. The normalization model—the individual's habilitative program is designed to be as similar as possible to the natural environment to which he/she will be going.
3. The enhancement model—a maximum amount of stimulation and support are provided.
4. The personal model—programming is designed to help the individual reach his/her full potential.

To sum up, Risley and Cataldo (1974) emphasize "the duration and extent of engagement with the physical and social environment appears to be an almost universal indication of the quality of a setting for people" (p. 3).

Application of Ecobehavioral Programming

The applications of ecobehavioral programming have not been as formal as the theories just presented (i.e., there is no specific model that is being attempted). However, the results of a number of studies present some interesting and important data.

The application of ecobehavioral programming has incorporated a number of problem behaviors and populations. Many of the variables presented previously have been manipulated to control hyperactivity in children (Whalen & Henker, 1977; Whalen, Henker, Collins, Finck, & Dotemoto, 1979; Willems, 1977), to shape supervisory involvement to improve work performance (Martin & Pallotta-Cornick, 1979; Martin, Pallotta-Cornick, Johnstone, & Goyos, 1980), to train elderly clients' social behavior (Melin & Gotestam, 1981), to control eating behavior in institutions (VanBiervliet et al., 1981), to encourage participatory behavior (Porterfield, Blunden, & Blewitt, 1980), to reduce child abuse (Lutzker, Frame, & Rice, 1982), and to shape various classroom behaviors of children (Altman & Wohlwill, 1978; VanHorn et al., 1981). The concept of ecobehavioral programming is formulated such that active habilitation is achieved. The environment is designed (or redesigned, as the case may be) to increase the probability of adaptive functional behaviors and minimize the occurrence of maladaptive behaviors.

Summary

In this chapter, we have presented and discussed a number of differentiation schedules of reinforcement, including differential reinforcement of other behavior (DRO), differential reinforcement of low rates of behavior (DRL), differential reinforcement of incompatible behavior (DRI), and differential reinforcement of alternative behavior (DRA). Additionally, sensory reinforcement and ecobehavioral programming were discussed. All of these procedures were presented in the context of positive control procedures to increase and maintain positive performance.

The typical notion that DRO (as well as the other differentiation schedules) is a reductive procedure was refuted on the grounds that, by definition, reinforcement increases the probability of responding. Conceptually, it was noted that the controlling factor in the reduction or elimination when using DRO schedules was the removal of the reinforcement contingency when the maladaptive behavior occurred, thus creating a time-out paradigm.

As mentioned repeatedly, all punishment programs should begin with some sort of reinforcement contingency. Several reasons were posited for this statement and should be considered in the application of these procedures.

6

Issues in Implementing Punishment Programs

Introduction

Schiefelbusch (1981), in an article on the philosophy of intervention, notes that "what is needed for each interventionist is knowledge of validated scientific methodology and a real world philosophy based on personal involvement. The interventionist must be able to transact with the complex set of issues presented by the client, his family, and his friends, which implies that social and humanistic issues are part of a viable philosophy" (p. 373). Several important issues are raised: (1) validated scientific methodology, (2) personal involvement, and (3) a complex set of variables including not only the client, family, and friends but also clinical and staff demands, institutional policies, and administrative issues.

We have attempted to present validated scientific methodology in the first five chapters. Personal involvement may be emphasized but can be realized only if the clinician or consultant is committed to each project. This chapter, therefore, was designed to point out a number of pragmatic variables that are frequently important in the success of punishment programs. We will begin with clinical, staff, and administrative issues.

Clinical Demands and Staff and Administrative Issues

In any instance where punishment is applied, numerous clinical demands must be met for treatment to be successful (Matson & Kazdin, 1981). These demands refer to important practical concerns such as (1) the proficiency of staff in applying the punishment programs and (2) sufficient staff (e.g., teachers, parents, professionals, paraprofessionals, and other behavior change agents) to employ the procedures. Considerable variability may exist in staff ability to execute the contingencies, depending upon the type and frequency of the target behavior, the environment in which assessment and training occur, and the characteristics of the client (e.g., age, weight, sex).

The frequency and intensity of the problem behavior certainly affect the staff requirements. For example, two mentally retarded residents hospitalized in a large institution might demonstrate severe head-banging. One resident's behavior might be of low frequency and high intensity, while the other resident's behavior may be of high frequency and low intensity. The second resident's behavior would be much easier to treat from a staff point of view, since one direct care worker could be assigned during a specific period of time. Since the behavior was of high frequency, the staff would be certain that the undesirable response would occur during that time period. Since an effective punishment contingency often requires several trials (Azrin & Holz, 1966), the staff would recognize that suppression of the undesirable response would be likely to occur in a short period of time during the training session. Systematic and immediate applications of punishment would be more problematic in the case of the first resident, since the behavior was of low frequency or rate. The procedure would require monitoring over a much greater period of time, and probably a more intensive punisher would be needed.

Another example might contrast ages and weights (i.e., strength) of clients. A 30-year-old, 250-pound client exhibiting self-abusive behavior probably would be harder to manage in a procedure than a three-year-old, 40-pound child exhibiting the same behavior.

A second component related to clinical demands is to insure that staff are well trained. Without sufficient training, treatment failure would be predicted and expected. Considerable research has been conducted on how much and what kind of training is needed to execute behavioral programs (Watson & Uzzell, 1980; Yen & McIntire, 1976). Generally, it is agreed that in addition to didactic training, also required are supervised hands-on instruction, role-playing, and feedback. This point should not be taken lightly, since, as mentioned, the entire success of the program may be reliant on this pivotal issue. However, training of this nature frequently is time consuming and difficult to implement and requires continued supervision (Kazdin & Moyer, 1976; Matson & Ollendick, 1977). This training is necessary, though, since most staff and parents who will be required to provide such treatment do not have the skills prior to the development of the program.

A third important clinical demand involves client, staff, family, institution, and community acceptance of the intervention. This variable is particularly important where the introduction of a punishment procedure is at issue. To date, most of the literature concerning acceptability of various punishment procedures is based on clinical impressions; however, more research in this area is beginning to appear (Kazdin, 1980a, 1981).

Kazdin (1980b) suggests that the major contribution of behavior modification programs is to "ensure that consequences are delivered systematically and consistently so that they produce the desired results" (p. 57). We have stressed that consistency is a major concern. Staffing patterns should be adequate to provide consistent intervention (Romanczyk, Colletti, & Lockshin, 1981). If this is not possible, any proposed intervention should be questioned in terms of actual implemention until this criterion can be achieved.

Furthermore, the manner in which a consequence is delivered is as important as the type of consequence (Schreibman & Koegel, 1981). Measures should be taken to insure that staff fulfill the following guidelines:

1. *The consequence must be contingent upon the behavior.* This means that to be effective a consequence must follow *only* the specific target behavior and be present *immediately* upon the behavior's occurrence. . . .
2. *The consequence delivery must be consistent.* If a consequence is to be effective, it must be presented in the same manner and contingent upon the same behavior across trials. . . .
3. *The consequence must be delivered in an unambiguous manner.* The nature of the consequence must always be clear to the [client]. . . .
4. *The consequence should be easily discriminable.* The therapist must make the consequence obvious to the [client]. The best way to do this is to present the stimulus strongly and to minimize extraneous cues at the time. [Schreibman & Koegel, 1981, pp. 520–521]

These guidelines were followed in one of our recent case consultations. An overcorrection procedure of the contingent exercise type had been instituted for self-abusive behavior of a 14-year-old blind retarded girl. The guidelines had been stressed, and the staff carried out the procedure contingent upon the incidence of the targeted behavior, even in a downtown area and after pulling off a highway. With such consistency, the program was readily effective and treatment gains continued after at least two years.

There are several other considerations that must be addressed by the persons who develop punishment programs. The primary requirement is gaining staff involvement. Staff support and acceptance of the program and their willingness to continue treatment under difficult and/or protracted conditions (e.g., extinction bursts) are critical to treatment success (Kemper & Hall, 1977; Miller, 1978). In addition, skill levels of staff, their cohesiveness, and number of staff with advanced training in behavior modification are all critical variables. Finally, the size of staff and the availability of outside consultants and other resources are important. These factors are dictated by financial constraints and geographical positioning respective to large population centers and/or universities where the greatest number of behavior modification consultants work (Matson & Kazdin, 1981).

Institutional Policies

The number of policies regarding the use of behavior modification procedures in institutional treatment settings may vary greatly; however, with the increased emphasis on legal and ethical issues on a national level regarding the use of punishment procedures, two trends have emerged. There has been a concerted effort to establish guidelines for treatment use (May, Risley, Twardosz, Friedman, Bijou, & Wexler, 1976), and litigation has had a nationwide impact on institutional policies regarding the implementation of punishment procedures (R. Martin, 1975).

There are several general institutional policies that have already emerged. Several of these include the frequent prohibition or at least the rare use of contingent electric shock as a treatment, the establishment of in-house review committees, and an effort to obtain informed consent from the client or her/his advocate in situations where clients are incapable of providing informed consent. All of these policies have been established to insure a greater degree of quality care and to protect client rights. However, several difficulties have been noted around these policies as they apply to the use of punishment procedures. As noted in an earlier chapter, punishment procedures are not used often because of an emotional reaction on the part of decision makers, a reaction that lacks an empirical basis. Consider the case of a total ban of contingent electric shock from many facilities. Certainly, less aversive methods or those perceived as less intrusive by the lay public should be attempted first, including reinforcement. Yet, in cases where the behavior may be extremely physically harmful to the client or to others and where there is demonstration and documentation of the failure of other procedures, withholding of such treatment may be not only impractical but also unethical (Repp & Dietz, 1978). This point must be dealt with in institutional policy planning.

The second policy mentioned has involved the establishment of in-house review committees, generally consisting of experts from various disciplines, to review behavioral programs generated by ward or unit-level staff. Thus, the committee serves as a quality control mechanism for punishment-related programs. This policy seems to have been well accepted in many institutions; however, one major problem has been the time involved between program development, committee review, and subsequent program implementation. This appears to be a logistics problem that can be solved adequately, but it can be serious particularly in large institutions where many programs need to be reviewed. With committee members assuming other duties, reviews may occur monthly or even less frequently. This situation, at best, is difficult and, at worst, intolerable from the standpoint of developing optimal treatments. One solution might be to have unit committees review routine programs. However, establishment of such a system is difficult, since it requires good working relationships and knowledge of staff's ability to make important decisions.

A third pragmatic point in the establishment of institutional policies involves obtaining informed consent for the use of punishment procedures. A major problem is deciding what to do when a client will not give informed consent but an interdisciplinary committee strongly feels that treatment is necessary. Also, what should be done when the client is incompetent to make an informed-consent decision and relatives cannot be located? As mentioned, these problems can be ameliorated; however, the primary problem is one of time. By the time the legal system is accessed by petitioning the courts to prove that the client is incompetent legally, his/her hospital stay might be completed, rendering the treatment unusable. This situation may apply also to a seemingly unintrusive treatment such as a reinforcement program. Delays in obtaining approval for treatment certainly do not occur in most cases, but in instances where they do arise, appropriate workable solutions have yet to be devised.

After the initial pragmatic problems have been observed and conquered, more specific practical issues may arise. We now will address how to select the appropriate procedures.

Selecting procedures

General Guidelines

Kazdin (1980b) suggests some general considerations for selecting procedures, including "severity of behavior, the danger of the behavior to the client or the others, the ease of implementing the technique in a particular setting, and the training required of the person(s) who will administer the program" (p. 179). He also suggests consideration should be given to legal issues, the specific events that are used, and possible long-range consequences.

However, a number of formal steps should be taken before selecting which punishment procedure will be used. Romanczyk, Colleti, and Plotkin (1980) suggest a thorough individual behavioral analysis requirement for each client. Romanczyk and Lockshin (1982) have incorporated the elements of a good behavioral analysis which are presented in Table 6–1. Notice the amount and diversity of data obtained even before the procedure is selected.

After the behavior of interest is targeted, Schreibman and Koegel (1981) suggest three steps in a good behavioral assessment. First, the individual behavior(s) must be defined operationally. They note that the behavior must be "spelled out" so that it can be observed and reliably recorded. These objective data are crucial in justifying the use of punishment procedures. [Sulzer-Azaroff and Mayer (1977) present excellent practical observational and recording systems in their units five and six of their book.]

The second step in a thorough behavioral assessment involves identifying the variables that control the behavior (Schreibman & Koegel, 1981). This procedure is referred to as a functional analysis and is probably the single most important step in any program. In many instances, more than one controlling variable or maintaining factor is involved in the maintenance of the maladaptive behavior.

Table 6-1. Elements of a Behavior Analysis.

I. History
   A. Parent interview
      1. Developmental history
      2. Social history
      3. Educational history
      4. Medical history
      5. Family/living environment history
   B. Review existing records
   C. Prior behavior change history
      1. Specific behaviors
      2. Specific procedures
      3. Who implemented program?
      4. Degree of success
      5. Unplanned positive effects
      6. Unplanned negative effects
II. Behavior parameters
   A. Behavior excesses
      1. Frequency
      2. Intensity
      3. Duration
      4. Latency
      5. Controlling stimuli
      6. Correlated behaviors
   B. Behavior deficits
      1. Observed vs. required
         a. Frequency
         b. Intensity
         c. Duration
         d. Latency
         e. Controlling stimuli
         f. Correlated behaviors
   C. Behavior assets
      1. Relation to behavior excesses and/or deficits
      2. Relative strength
      3. Degree of stimulus control
   D. Behavior constraints
      1. Situational opportunity
      2. Orthopedic
      3. Muscular
      4. Sensory
      5. Perceptual *(continued)*

Table 6–1 (continued)

III. Contingency survey
- 6. Fatigue
- 7. Medication

III. Contingency survey
- A. Behavior accelerators
  - 1. Tangible
  - 2. Social
  - 3. Symbolic/conditioned
- B. Behavior decelerators
  - 1. Tangible
  - 2. Social
  - 3. Symbolic/conditioned

IV. Ecological analysis
- A. Will child[a] benefit if change occurs?
- B. Will significant others benefit if change occurs?
- C. Will demands upon child increase/decrease?
- D. Will demands upon significant others increase/decrease?
- E. Who supports change?
- F. Who will not support change?

V. Behavior change responsibility
- A. Does child indicate desire for change?
- B. Do the parents/guardian indicate desire for change?
- C. Is there an objective advocate?
- D. Is there a consensus for change?
- E. Can the child give consent?
- F. Can the child assist in developing the behavior change program?
- G. Can the parents/guardians assist in developing the behavior change program?
- H. What, if any, ethical issues exist?
- I. If there are, has peer review been sought?

Source: Romanczyk, R. G., & Lockshin, S. *The individualized goal selection curriculum.* Vestal, NY: Clinical Behavior Therapy Associates, 1982. Reprinted with permission from authors and publisher.
[a]Child is interchangeable with client or patient.

These data will be critical in the selection of the treatment program. Table 6–2 presents a nice example of a three-step process, adapted from Carr (1982), to assess the controlling variables in the maintenance of self-injurious behavior.

Schreibman and Koegel's (1981) third step in a behavioral assessment is to group the behaviors according to common controlling vari-

Table 6-2. A Screening Sequence to Determine the Controlling Variables of Self-Injurious Behavior.

Step 1
- Screening for genetic abnormalities (e.g., Lesch-Nyhan and de Lange syndromes), particularly if lip-, finger-, or tongue-biting is present.
- Screen for nongenetic abnormalities (e.g., otitis media), particularly if head-banging is present.
- If screening is positive, controlling variable may be organic.
- If Step 1 is negative, proceed to Step 2.

Step 2
- Does self-injurious behavior increase under one or more of the following circumstances:
  - (a) When the behavior is attended to?
  - (b) When reinforcers are withdrawn for behaviors other than self-injurious behavior?
  - (c) When the child is in the company of adults (rather than alone)?
- If yes, controlling variable may be positive reinforcement.
- Does self-injurious behavior occur primarily when demands or other aversive stimuli are presented?
- If yes, controlling variable may be negative reinforcement.
- If Step 2 is negative, proceed to Step 3.

Step 3
- Does self-injurious behavior occur primarily when there are no activities available and/or the environment is barren?
- If yes, controlling variable may be self-stimulation.

Source: Adapted from Carr, E. The motivation of self-injurious behavior. In R. L. Koegel, A. Rincover, & A. L. Egel (Eds.), *Educating and understanding autistic children.* San Diego: College-Hill Press, Inc., 1982. Originally published as Carr, E. G. The motivation of self-injurious behavior: A review of some hypotheses. *Psychological Bulletin,* 1977, *84,* 812. Copyright 1977 by the American Psychological Association. Reprinted/adapted with permission from authors and publishers.

ables. In this way, as with every functional assessment performed, the treatment is specified automatically. A procedure should be selected that would manipulate the controlling variables in the most efficacious way to change the behavior in a desirable and predictable direction (Schreibman & Koegel, 1981). [Sulzer-Azaroff and Mayer, 1977, present a more thorough step-by-step procedure for this process in their unit seven of their book.] In practical terms, consideration must be given first to which types of procedures are possible, taking into account institutional, staff, and clinical demands. Then

the procedure selected should be the one most specific to the controlling variables. After selection of the procedure, other considerations become important.

Azrin and Holz's 14 Considerations

In Chapter 1, we gave a brief list of Azrin and Holz's (1966) 14
considerations that are used to maximize the potential effectiveness
of punishment procedures. These conditions now will be reviewed as
to their adaptability to practical application.

1. *The punishing stimulus should be arranged in such a manner that no
unauthorized escape is possible.* If a contingency (e.g., if screaming, then
time-out) has been devised, the client should not be able to remove
or reduce the intensity of the application of the contingency. At
times, a child may be able to avoid time-out or overcorrection either
by saying, "Give me another chance" or "I won't let it happen again."
The staff member or parent should not back down from carrying
through with the contingency. (An old Western saying comes to
mind: "Don't draw your gun unless you plan to use it.")

2. *The punishing stimulus should be as intense as possible.* Some controversy exists in the applied literature as to the meaning of the term
"intense." Initial experimental work utilized shock as a punishing
stimulus and found that the greater the intensity of the punishing
stimulus, the greater the reduction of the targeted response (Appel,
1963; Azrin, 1959, 1960b; Azrin, Holz, & Hake, 1963; Brethower &
Reynolds, 1962; Dinsmoor, 1952; Estes, 1944). Kazdin (1980b) ob-
serves that, although this relationship has been established for shock,
it may not apply to other punishing stimuli in applied settings. We
take the position that intensity is a relative term. Remember that,
based on the functional analysis of the controlling variables of a
maladaptive behavior, a punishment program is instituted. Therefore, the degree of intensity at which suppression of the response is
noted would be considered "most intense." For example, research
indicates that short periods of time-out can be (and most often are)
effective. If time-out were chosen as the punishment program and
the specific reinforcement maintaining the maladaptive behavior was
targeted (so that the reinforcement could be removed when the
time-out contingency was in effect) *and* 10 minutes of time-out was
producing suppression of the response, then 10 minutes of time-out
would be considered intense for this client.

3. *The punishing stimulus should be delivered after every occurrence of
the targeted behavior.* Logistically, this consideration is extremely hard

to implement, since it would be expensive to have behavior-change agents for 24 hours each day. However, program developers need to attempt to fulfill this point, because we do not want to create an intermittent reinforcement schedule for the maladaptive behavior. Perhaps the program should be implemented only at certain times of the day so that maximal control may be realized.

4. *The punishing stimulus should be introduced immediately after the maladaptive response.* A strong relationship must be observed between response and consequence. The longer the delay, the less likely the targeted behavior is being consequated, since many other behaviors occur in the interim. The lack of response suppression when a delay is encountered is the reason why the old adage "wait till your father gets home" was usually ineffective. At best, the father assumed conditioned punishing properties and, at worst, the behavior often went unconsequated.

5. *The punishing stimulus should not be increased gradually but should be introduced at maximum intensity.* A temporary reduction of behaviors may be noticed with a weak punishing stimulus, but an adaptation to the stimulus occurs so that the stimulus loses its punishing properties (Kazdin, 1971; Phillips, 1968). A good example is the parent telling a child, "Now, don't run around," while in a supermarket. There are always kids running around in supermarkets, which says something about the effectiveness of this procedure.

6. *The punishing stimulus should be given in brief periods of time.* The point of punishment is to consequate the behavior immediately and quickly, then allow the client to return to the natural environment to potentiate the occurrence of positive reinforcement for adaptive behavior. A time-out procedure for 10 minutes instead of 30 minutes (assuming it is effective) places the individual back in the natural environment for 20 extra minutes, twice the time of the procedure.

7. *The punishing stimulus should not be differentially associated with the delivery of reinforcement.* If it is, the punishing stimulus may acquire conditioned reinforcing properties (Azrin & Holz, 1966). An example of the confusion generated by nonadherence to this consideration would be the "mixed message" received by a child who gets punished for a response then "hugged" by the parent, who feels guilty for punishing him. The child learns to misbehave to receive affection.

8. *The punishing stimulus should be a discriminative stimulus for extinction.* Azrin and Holz (1966) point out the distinction between aversive and discriminative properties of a punishing stimulus. Throughout this book, the aversive properties of a punishing stimulus have been described; however, Azrin and Holz (1966) note how

punishment also can be a discriminative stimulus for (1) another punishing stimulus, (2) absence of reinforcement, or (3) the presence of reinforcement. The goal of punishment procedures is to design the contingency such that the punishing stimulus is a discriminative cue for the absence of reinforcement or extinction. An example of an incorrect discrimination would be talking to a client about the day's events while performing an overcorrection procedure. The punishment program becomes a discriminative stimulus for "a social event" (i.e., a potentially enjoyable activity) instead of a discriminative stimulus for extinction.

9. *The degree of motivation to emit the punished response should be reduced.* Motivation might be defined as those contingencies controlling a response such that the response is reinforced when emitted. If the conditions are such that it is very reinforcing to emit the maladaptive response, the punishment may be less effective (Azrin, 1960a; Azrin & Holz, 1966; Azrin et al., 1963; Morse & Kelleher, 1977). To reduce "motivation," reinforcement for the maladaptive response should be addressed and removed, while reinforcement for other adaptive behaviors should be provided.

10. *An alternative response to the punished response should be available and reinforced such that it will produce the same or greater reinforcement as the punished response.* This point was covered extensively in Chapter 5. In general, the natural environment should become a more reinforcing place to live.

11. *If an alternative response is not available, a different situation should be available to receive reinforcement.* As an example, let's select out-of-seat gross motor behavior in the classroom as the target behavior. Since the goal may be in-seat work in this situation, out-of-seat behavior cannot be reinforced. However, other situations (e.g., recess or playtime) may be provided several times throughout the day in which out-of-seat gross motor behavior is reinforced.

12. *If the punishing stimulus cannot be delivered, then a conditioned aversive stimulus should be presented.* This point will be discussed in a later section, so only a brief overview will be presented here. Many times, it may be difficult to follow through with a punishment program because of extraneous variables. However, if a neutral stimulus has been paired with the punishing stimulus such that it has acquired conditioned punishing properties, then, upon administration of the conditioned punisher, a subsequent reduction in the target behavior will be observed. For example, if a verbalization such as "no" has been paired with a punishment procedure, then subsequently the verbalization may acquire condi-

tioned punishing properties and be effective in reducing the targeted response.

13. *If a punishing stimulus cannot be administered, then a reduction in positive reinforcement may be used as punishment (e.g., time-out and response cost).* Azrin and Holz (1966) point out several critical points that somehow have been forgotten in the application of this consideration. "Both methods [time-out and response cost] require that the subject have a high level of reinforcement to begin with; otherwise, no withdrawal of reinforcement is possible. If non-physical punishment is to be used, it appears desirable to provide the subject with a substantial history of reinforcement in order to provide the opportunity for withdrawing the reinforcement as punishment for the undesired response" (p. 427). This point is detailed in Chapter 5.

14. *The punished response should not be positively reinforced.* Again, this consideration emphasizes the necessity for consistency. An attempt should be made to monitor and reduce the differential reinforcement and punishment of the same response (e.g., Joey gets punished at home for taking cookies and gets reinforced at Grandmother's home for the same behavior).

Azrin and Holz's (1966) 14 considerations have been outlined and examples presented as to how they apply in practice. Assuming that the reader is is not overwhelmed at this point, we will outline a few more pragmatic variables.

Schedules of Reinforcement

As noted in Chapter 1, Dinsmoor (1952) observed that behavior does not occur in a vacuum. Adaptive behaviors, as well as maladaptive behaviors, are maintained through some form of reinforcement. An identification of the reinforcement maintaining maladaptive behavior would be, in effect, an observation of the controlling variables. This process was termed a "functional analysis."

Azrin and Holz (1966) suggested the importance of identifying not only the reinforcement that maintains the problematic behavior but also the schedule. These authors noted that the "type of response reduction that is induced by punishment has been found to depend on the type of schedule of reinforcement that is maintaining the punished response" (p. 400). We have already mentioned how some authors (Morse & Kelleher, 1977) have noted that schedule control is the single most important property of operant conditioning. Pragmatically, this information could be useful in at least two ways. First, if the schedule of reinforcement could be identified, these data could provide additional input into the behavioral assessment and, therefore, the intervention. Second, since the schedule would define the type of response reduction, changes in responding after the program was started could be monitored to assess their congruence with previous research results. Several reinforcement schedules are discussed in relation to subsequent reduction effects with punishment.

A *variable-interval reinforcement schedule* produces responses at a fairly uniform rate (Ferster & Skinner, 1957). When punishment is applied for every response, the rate is reduced but the basic uniformity does not change (Azrin, 1960a, 1960b; Brethower & Reynolds, 1962; Dinsmoor, 1952, Holz & Azrin, 1961).

Responses maintained on a *fixed-interval reinforcement schedule* positively accelerate between reinforcements (Ferster & Skinner, 1957). The degree of this response acceleration can be considered to be a type of temporal discrimination or patterning (Azrin & Holz, 1966). With continuous punishment of the behavior, the number of responses may be reduced (Azrin, 1958; Estes, 1944; Skinner, 1938) but the degree of temporal discrimination remains unchanged (Azrin & Holz, 1961).

Azrin and Holz (1966) define responding under *fixed-ratio reinforcement* as bivalued: a period of zero responding immediately after reinforcement is followed by a very high response rate. When punishment is delivered for every response during this reinforcement schedule, the postreinforcement pause is lengthened but the high response rate is reduced only slightly (Azrin, 1959). They go on to point out that the use of punishment under this schedule does not manifest itself in a lower rate, as would be expected. The terminal response rate remains fairly constant with the overall rate of response reduced.

Taking into account these simple schedules of reinforcement that may be maintaining a maladaptive response, we see several forms of response reduction. Consider, as well, other possible complex schedules (e.g., concurrent, tandem, etc.) operating on behavior and our concept of typical response reduction rates may be simplistic. Additionally, the concept of schedule-induced behavior (Staddon, 1977) is being applied to self-stimulatory and self-injurious behavior, which raises other practical implications. (An explanation of schedule-induced behavior is beyond the scope of this discussion. The reader is referred to Staddon, 1977, for a more in-depth review.) If it were observed that maladaptive behavior was a function of several schedules operating at the same time, modifications in the schedules would be called for instead of more traditional punishment programs. Much of this discussion on schedule-induced behavior has been complex, and most of the research so far has been on animals. However, schedules of reinforcement operating on maladaptive behavior may be critically important and should, at least, be mentioned.

Azrin and Holz (1966) conclude, "We have seen that the choice of a particular reinforcement schedule to maintain the punished response will determine the temporal patterning of responses during punishment. In order to specify the nature of the response reduction by punishment, it is necessary to specify the schedule of reinforcement that is maintaining the responses. The simple statement that punishment reduces the punished responses is inadequate and occasionally inaccurate" (p. 401).

Conditioned Punishment

Over 20 years ago, several researchers (Barlow, 1952; Baron, 1959; Evans, 1962; Hake & Azrin, 1965; Mowrer & Aiken, 1954; Mowrer & Solomon, 1954) demonstrated a phenomenon known as conditioned punishment, in which a neutral stimulus acts as a punisher as a result of pairings with an already demonstrated punisher. Hake and Azrin (1965) defined conditioned punishment as the following three-step process: "(1) there is little or no punishment effect before the stimulus is paired with an unconditioned punisher, but (2) a punishment effect occurs after (3) the stimulus has been paired, or is being paired, with an unconditioned punisher" (p. 279).

If effective, conditioned punishment has wide-ranging implications in the practical application of punishment procedures in the natural environment. When originally conceived, doubt had been raised concerning the maintenance of conditioned punishing effects; however, the Hake and Azrin (1965) experiment demonstrated that the response-produced conditioned punishing effects could be maintained as long as the pairings of the conditioned stimulus and unconditioned stimulus were continued. Azrin and Holz (1966) concluded "it appears that conditioned punishment need not be a transitory phenomenon; a previously neutral stimulus will continue to suppress the responses that it follows if that neutral stimulus is occasionally associated with the unconditioned stimulus" (p. 389).

The conditioning of otherwise neutral stimuli (e.g., specific verbalizations such as "no" or if–then contingencies) as punishers could be very helpful in the natural environment. If a punishing stimulus could not be administered due to practical complexities, the conditioned punisher could be utilized and similar reductive effects could be noted. However, if the conditioned punisher were no longer paired with the original punishing stimulus, as demonstrated by Hake and Azrin (1965), which is typically the case in the natural environment, the effects of the conditioned punisher would be weakened. An example of this condition is presented. Parents, as well as other potential behavior-change agents, often will remark, "My child won't do as he is told unless I get angry and raise my voice." Ferster and Culbertson (1982) note:

> . . . when we observe someone who frequently makes threats without actually achieving the intended control, it is likely that the threat is not followed by the aversive stimulus often enough. If the threat is never followed by the aversive consequences, it ceases to serve [as] an aversive stimulus at all. . . . Most often, threats are emitted in anger or under other strong emotional states, but this correlation is not a necessary condition for the effective function of the threat. . . . Parents who are indisposed to punish a child may even consciously goad themselves into escalating their emotional state to make it possible to deliver the aversive stimulus that is intended to generate the avoidance or escape performances by which the child is controlled. From the child's point of view, the parent's extreme emotional state sets the occasion for when to act. [p. 77]

In summary, conditioned punishment can be (1) effective and (2) extremely useful practically *if* administered as presented here.

One final related issue is that punishment tends to be more effective the earlier it is delivered in a response chain (Aronfreed & Reber, 1965). Kazdin (1980b) notes that a maladaptive response is not a single behavior but a chain or sequence of behaviors that culminates in the undesirable response. If the punishing stimulus can be employed early in the chain, the final reinforcing effect of the actual maladaptive behavior will be minimized. Additionally, if a reprimand is used early in the chain and this response is programmed to take on conditioned punishing effects, then the following through of the punishing stimulus must be initiated early, as well, if the conditioned punisher does not produce the reductive effects. In practice, only *one* warning should be given before taking action.

Conditioned punishment, although not mentioned as such, has

been incorporated into many programs. Numerous studies have included a negative verbal statement (e.g., "no, don't scream") just before employing time-out, overcorrection, or some other form of punishment program. In essence, the verbalization could have been tested for conditioned punishing effects. One such study (Bittle & Hake, 1977), observed the effects of this type of negative statement after first pairing the statement with a punisher (i.e., a manual task). The authors noted that the single most effective procedure in reducing self-stimulatory behavior was intructions (i.e., negative statements). They stated that "the effects of instructions appeared more dependent upon the child's history of pairings between punishers and instructions than redirection to an incompatible response, because negative instructions were nearly as effective alone as when they were combined with positive instructions and the incompatible response" (p. 913).

Side-Effects Relabeled

We have outlined in previous chapters the positive and negative side-effects that have been noted in the punishment literature. The occurrence of these side-effects during punishment programs may pose practical problems. The topic of side-effects will be discussed briefly.

Lichstein and Schreibman (1976, p. 171) note that "the model of man in which a rigidly delineated, autonomous response is tied to a similarly defined stimulus is simplistic and questionable. It appears that classes of responses covary with the application of single or multiple stimuli. . . . Thus, an effect may be termed a *side effect* only as long as our ignorance delimits our ability to anticipate more than one direct effect (Willems, 1974)."

Therefore, when observed effects that are different from those intended are termed side-effects, we are exemplifying a notion that something "extra" has occurred when, indeed, multiple effects should be expected and preparation should be made for their occurrence. Osborne (1976) has stated that "the practitioner needs to know what effects will result and when, and the applied analyst needs to supply this information" (pp. 22–23). Therefore, discussions of the pros and cons of side-effects when using punishment programs are a moot point to the practitioner. Instead, we should discuss and outline potential "additional effects" of punishment programs so that effectiveness may be made optimal.

Osborne (1976) continues that the valence (i.e., positive or negative) of side-effects will vary based on the values of the observer. Additionally, even if the negative effects are observed with a program, it still may be the technique of choice. "For example, some negative side effects could be considerably less serious to the welfare of the patient than was the original undesirable behavior. If a technique decreased self-mutilation at the cost of increasing autistic rocking, clinical gains may have occurred" (p. 22). As this example points out, another maladaptive behavior could increase while the targeted behavior decreases.

This discussion brings up the point of symptom substitution. After reviewing the literature on this topic, Gordon and Zax (1981) summarized," . . . the behavioral literature on symptom substitution falls far short of proving empirically that symptom substitution is, at best, a nonexistent and, at worst, a negligible phenomenon" (p. 44). The punishment literature certainly is not exempt from this finding. When punishment programs have been initiated and control of adaptive behavior with reinforcement programs is not demonstrated, other maladaptive behaviors often occur when the targeted behavior decreases. Kazdin and Wilson (1978) offer a behavioral definition of symptom substitution:

> Rather than substitute symptoms, these emergent responses can be explained more parsimoniously. Behaviors are not necessarily discrete and independent units of an individual's response repertoire. Evidence suggests that behaviors may cluster or covary in larger units than single responses (Wahler, 1975). Changes in one behavior may be expected to result in changes in other behaviors. Also, behavior change does not occur in a social vacuum. Given the reciprocal interaction of behavior and the environment, one would expect that behavior changes will influence the social environment in which the individual functions (Bandura, 1977; Goldiamond & Dyrud, 1968). Changes in the social environment in turn are likely to alter further responses of the individual outside these focused upon in treatment. [pp. 101–102]

A number of possible reasons have been suggested for the occurrence of "additional effects" or "emergent responses." These factors should be considered by each practitioner to prepare for and adjust to the possible occurrence of these effects. First, if treatment fails to alter the "major conditions controlling emission of the deviant behavior" (Bandura, 1969, p. 101), emergent responses may occur. A thorough functional analysis should help target these conditions. Second, Bandura (1969) also suggests the occurrence of additional responses if the target behavior is extinguished but no adaptive response is developed to replace it. Ullmann and Krasner (1965) suggest that, when the emission of a maladaptive response no longer sets the occasion for reinforcement, another maladaptive response may be created to attempt to gain this lost reinforcement. Third, if the target behavior is an avoidance response, when reduced or eliminated, another response logically should succeed it (Cahoon, 1968). If it is determined that the person is attempting to avoid a situation, additional information should be sought to delineate the reasons for the avoidance. These reasons then should be modified as opposed to the specific avoidance response. Fourth, as mentioned earlier, clusters or classes of responses may covary and be maintained by the same reinforcement contingencies, or they may be under the control of the same stimulus conditions (Cahoon, 1968; Yates, 1970). Schreibman and Koegel (1981) suggest grouping these behaviors in the behavioral assessment stage of programming. Finally, Wolpe (1958) suggests that anxiety may be implicated as a controlling factor in maladaptive behaviors and, if not identified when a response is eliminated, another maladaptive response will take its place. This condition also suggests the need for a thorough functional analysis.

No matter how we term the phenomenon of "extra effects" (i.e., side effects, additional effects, symptom substitution, or emergent responses), they do occur in some instances. The goal in helping the practitioner program an effective punishment procedure is not to deny occurrence or minimize their influence but to (1) expect their emergence, (2) define their cause, and (3) program their elimination, if necessary.

Response Maintenance and Programming Generalization

Throughout this book, we have delineated behavior-change methods and demonstrated their efficacy, limitations, and practical considerations. However, of equal importance is maintainance of treatment gains. Stokes and Baer (1977) in a seminal paper on generalization noted:

> Traditionally, many theorists have considered generalization to be a *passive* phenomenon. Generalization was not seen as an operant response that could be programmed, but as a description of a "natural" outcome of any behavior-change process. . . . Even though the litera-

ture shows many instances of generalization, it is still frequently observed that when a change in behavior has been accomplished through experimental contingencies, then that change is manifest where and when those contingencies operate, and is often seen in only transitory forms in other places and at other times. The frequent need for generalization of therapeutic behavior change is widely accepted, but it is not always realized that generalization does not automatically occur simply because a behavior change is accomplished. Thus, the need actively to *program* generalization, rather than passively to expect it as an outcome of certain training procedures, is a point requiring both emphasis and effective techniques. [pp. 349–350]

Kazdin (1980b) refers to two types of generalization: (1) response maintenance—the degree to which behaviors are maintained after the program has been terminated and (2) transfer of training—the degree to which behaviors transfer to situations and settings other than the training situation. He suggests eight pragmatic techniques to help insure maintenance and transfer. We will discuss them briefly.

The first procedure is to bring the changed behavior under the control of natural contingencies. During training the target behavior should be reinforced or punished with naturally occurring consequences (e.g., praise or reprimands). Also, behaviors should be chosen that are naturally consequated (e.g., grooming). Second, naturally occurring reinforcers should be utilized. This procedure consists of developing a program that takes advantage of events and resources in the natural environment. Third, the programmed contingencies should be removed or faded gradually. An abrupt withdrawal will produce the baseline condition too quickly and can be discriminated easily by the client. Fourth, stimulus control should be expanded. Stimulus control refers to control obtained by associating certain stimuli with programmed contingencies or conditions. If a narrow range of cues is programmed, the desired behavior will occur only when the circumscribed cues are presented. With a broader range of cues, the behavior will occur in a greater number of situations.

The fifth technique to aid in generalization involves schedules of reinforcement. After the targeted behavior is well established, it should be reinforced intermittently, since behavior controlled under this schedule is most resistant to extinction. The sixth procedure involves delaying reinforcement. Since most reinforcers in the natural environment are delayed (e.g., a paycheck at the end of the month), it is important to fade from immediate reinforcement. One caution is to be sure the behavior is well established before instituting a delay.

The seventh technique is to use peers or other behavior-change agents in the program, since they may have contact with the client across a variety of situations. Several excellent reviews outline a number of potential sources: parents (Atkeson & Forehand, 1979; Harris & Milch, 1981), teachers (Koegel, Rincover, & Russo, 1982; Koegel, Russo, Rincover, & Schreibman, 1982), and paraprofessionals and staff (Bellack & Hersen, 1977; Kazdin, 1980b). The final technique is the designing of self-control procedures. Kazdin (1980b) notes that performance might not be restricted to a narrow set of stimulus conditions (i.e., involving external behavior-change agents) if clients could be trained to control their own behavior.

Response maintenance and programming generalization should be critical aspects of every punishment program. Some of the practical considerations and procedures we have presented exemplify methods that should insure response maintenance and transfer of training.

Summary and Conclusions

This chapter was designed to provide the reader with an understanding of pragmatic issues in the development and implementation of punishment programs. As observed, the practicalities, at best, are complex and, at worst, overwhelming. It is hoped that not all of the presented issues will be encountered in every program, although the practitioner will need to be aware of what is important and what potentially may occur. Johnston (1972) cogently summarizes:

> It must be stressed that the successful use of the punishment paradigm cannot be reduced simply to such a concise summary of principles; these basic principles must be expanded in application to a variety of procedural details, the importance of any one of which will vary with each situation. Ignoring any one of these variables certainly does not doom necessarily any particular manipulation or therapeutic endeavor; rather, the probability of maximally effective results from any punishment paradigm is increased to the extent that such factors are carefully considered in the design and execution of the study or therapeutic attempt. [p. 1034]

7

Ethical and Legal Issues

Introduction

Psychologists respect the dignity and worth of the individual and honor the perservation and protection of fundamental human rights. They are committed to increasing knowledge of human behavior and of people's understanding of themselves and others and to the ultilization of such knowledge for the promotion of human welfare. While pursuing these endeavors, they make every effort to protect the welfare of those who seek their services or of any human being or animal that may be the object of study. They use their skills only for purposes consistent with these values and do not knowingly permit their misuse by others. While demanding for themselves freedom of inquiry and communication, psychologists accept the responsibility this freedom requires: competence, objectivity in the application of skills and concern for the best interest of clients, colleagues, and society in general. In the pursuit of these ideals, psychologists subscribe to principles in the following areas: 1. Responsibility, 2. Competence, 3. Moral and Legal Standards, 4. Public Statements, 5. Confidentiality, 6. Welfare of the Consumer, 7. Professional Relationships, 8. Utilization of Assessment Techniques, and 9. Pursuit of Research Activities. [American Psychological Association, 1979]

This paragraph is the preamble to the *Ethical Standards of Psychologists* (APA, 1979). Other professions have similar ethical standards by which members are to adhere. As Stuart (1981) has suggested, this code of ethics attempts to specify practice. Many other excellent articles, chapters, and books have been written recently attempting to define the ethical and legal practice of behavior modification and the psychological treatment of clients (Budd & Baer, 1976; Friedman, 1975; Golann & Fremouw, 1976; Hannah, Christian, & Clark, 1981; Kazdin, 1980b; Krapfl & Vargas, 1977; Martin, R., 1975; Matson & Kazdin, 1981; Morris & Brown, 1983; Schwitzgebel & Schwitzgebel, 1980; Stuart, 1981; Wexler, 1975). Obviously, since entire books have been written on this topic, it is beyond the scope of this chapter to study in depth the philosophical and moral issues involved; therefore, the reader is referred to the sources just listed. This chapter has been designed to offer a somewhat different perspective related to ethical and legal issues.

This entire book has been devoted to the documentation of empirical research regarding the application of punishment procedures. This chapter will be no different. Although it would be difficult to define ethical behavior empirically, we seek here to provide the reader with the issues and tools for administering ethically and legally sound procedures and techniques. Therefore, through our examination of the literature on this topic, we will bring together in this chapter examples of guidelines and procedures in the practical application of the many ethical and legal issues involved in utilizing punishment programs.

Ethical Issues

In addition to the general ethical guidelines set forth by the American Psychological Association, another important bit of information was provided by a committee appointed by the Association for Advancement of Behavior Therapy (1977), who developed a set of questions that address ethical issues, which each practitioner may ask of himself/herself when developing a program. This simple evaluation (reprinted in Table 7–1 in the appendix in this chapter) is an excellent checklist that should be considered not only when an ethical concern is raised reactive to some incident but also in the planning of any type of therapeutic program. Each of the questions contained in this evaluation (Table 7–1) will be addressed and practical applications of most of the issues will be presented. However, one additional note is in order. A number of individuals (e.g., Sajwaj, 1977; Stolz, 1977) have been discussing recently the arguments for (or against) guidelines for behavior modification. The Commission on Behavior Modification of the American Psychological Association has taken the position that "it would be unwise for the American Psychological Association to enunciate guidelines for the practice of behavior modification. The procedures of behavior modification appear to be no more or less subject to abuse and no more or less in need of ethical regulation than intervention procedures derived from any other set of principles and called by other terms" (Stolz & Associates, 1978, p. 104). Stuart (1981) cogently summarizes,

> In short, the commission shied away from the practice of imposing special controls on behavior therapy simply because of its effectiveness (see: Holland, 1973), recognized that behavior therapy is neither more nor less value governed nor aimed at interpersonal influence than other psychological approaches (Bandura, 1969; Benjamin, 1974; Frank, 1961), and heeded Agras' (1973) admonition that the imposition of special controls could have a chilling effect on innovation both within and beyond behavior modification. [p. 716]

It is our contention that the presentation of specific outlines addressing each ethical guideline in this chapter is for the purpose of supplying examples of how others have resolved ethical concerns and is not a concession that guidelines should exist for behavior modification.

Adequacy of Treatment Goals

Have the goals of treatment been adequately considered? A number of considerations must be made in establishing adequate goals. R. Martin (1975) lists a few questions that should be addressed in deciding the goals of treatment.

1. Does your program have a concrete, objectively stated goal?
2. Is it directly related to the reason the individual was brought to your attention?
3. When it is achieved, can your involvement with the client be terminated?
4. Will the change benefit the individual more than the institution?
5. Can the goal be achieved?
6. Is the goal a positive behavior change rather than a negative behavior suppression?
7. Does the goal involve changing a behavior that is actually constitutionally permissible? [Martin, R., 1975, pp. 69–70]

In addition to answering these questions, procedural safeguards insuring proper goals should be observed. Romanczyk, Coletti, and

Lockshin (1981) have presented an excellent guideline that they use in their institutional setting (see Table 7–2 in the chapter appendix) when deciding whether punishment procedures are appropriate.

Also inherent in all programs is the need for a formal treatment plan. The case of *Wyatt v. Stickney* (1972) formalized this requirement and called for the following criteria to be met:

1. A statement of the nature of the specific limitations and specific needs of the client.
2. A description of intermediate and long-range treatment goals, with a projected timetable for their attainment.
3. A statement of, and an explanation for, the plan of treatment for achieving these intermediate and long-range goals.
4. A statement of the least restrictive setting for treatment necessary to achieve the treatment goals of the client.
5. A specification of the professionals and other staff members who are responsible for the particular resident's attaining these treatment goals.
6. Criteria for release to less restrictive settings for treatment, including criteria for discharge. and a projected date for discharge.

One way to make this process quite explicit is for the therapist to construct a contract detailing the goals, procedures, and so on of the ensuing therapy. Ayllon and Skuban (1973) have presented an excellent example of this type of contract, which is presented in the chapter appendix in Table 7-3. The ethical questions, criteria for treatment plans, and contractural agreements are a few of the ways the practitioner can be sure that adequate treatment goals have been delineated.

Adequacy of Treatment Choice

Has the choice of treatment methods been adequately considered? It is hoped that the first six chapters of this book have presented data noting the adequacy of specific punishment programs as treatment for specific problematic behaviors. However, a number of individuals have suggested the need for a formal review process before implementing any punishment program. Morris and Brown (1983) express the need for both an internal review board (i.e., a program review committee) and an external review board (i.e., a human rights and ethics committee). These authors suggest that the decision as to whether the program should be initiated would be made by the program review committee and based on several factors including the recent treatment literature, clarity of the procedure and congruence with the overall plans for the client, the use of the least restrictive alternative, the use of sufficiently trained staff, the use of data collection devices, and whether the program is in the best interests of the client.

The human rights and ethics committee would have a more global function to serve as an advocate for clients' rights. Morris and Brown (1983) suggest that this committee address issues such as client and family involvement in treatment planning, the program's congruence with immediate and long-term goals of the client, client's right to refuse treatment, protection of other client rights, conditions under which this committee should make on-site visits, review of educational or therapeutic procedures, specification of conditions warranting the administration of psychotherapeutic drugs, the procedure for review of allegations of abuse or neglect, and committal of the institution to return clients to the community.

The guidelines presented for both committees provide an excellent source for newly formed or proposed committees to follow. One example of the review process actually implemented is presented in the form of a flowchart in Figure 7–1. One potential problem of the review process, noted in Chapter 6, is that the potentially life-threatening maladaptive behavior may continue during the period between the actual writing of the program and the affirmation of the committees to implement the procedure. This review process may consume "months" of time. A practitioner who needs to implement punishment programs regularly may seek to streamline the process to be able to implement these programs as quickly as possible and at the same time assure clients' rights.

Informed Consent

Is the client's participation voluntary? This guideline has been observed as the most important doctrine of all ethical standards. Stuart (1981) notes, "There is no legal or ethical consideration that comes closer to a universal moral precept than respect for the right to informed consent to participation in therapeutic and research endeavors" (p. 717).

Three components of consent have been delineated: *competence, knowledge,* and *volition* (Friedman, 1975; Katz, 1972; Kazdin, 1980b; Martin, R., 1975). Kazdin (1980b) defines competence as "the indi-

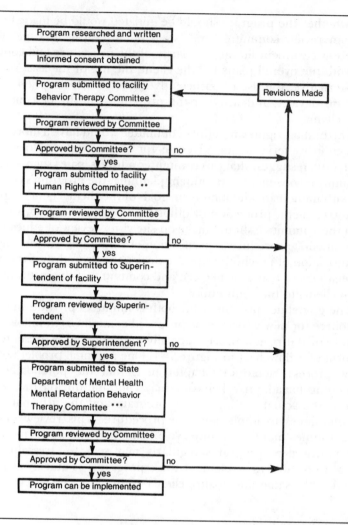

Figure 7-1. Review process for programs utilizing aversive stimulation.

*Committee consists of at least one psychologist, one physician, and one community advocate.

**Committee consists of three agency representatives and two community advocates.

***Committee consists of 14 members from around the state, including but not limited to psychiatrists, psychologists, social workers, and community advocates.

*Source:*Traugott, M. A. & Campbell, C. O. Reduction of self-injurious behaviors through the use of contingent electric shock. Paper presented at the Association for Behavior Analysis, Milwaukee, May 1981. Reprinted with permission from the authors.

vidual's ability to make a well reasoned decision, to understand the nature of the choice presented, and to give consent meaningfully" (p. 318). Roth, Meisel, and Lidz (1977) presented five methods for determining competence: (1) a desire to participate in the procedure; (2) adoption of a reasonable choice; (3) a rational reasoning process used to determine participation; (4) the ability to understand the procedures; and (5) evaluation of actual level of understanding. [See Roth et al. (1977) for complete definitions].

Knowledge, the second component of consent, requires that the client understand the suggested treatment, alternatives, and potential risks and benefits. Kazdin (1980b) notes that this guideline is difficult to meet, since little is known about many treatments; however, two important aspects must be observed. The client must understand that she or he does not have to give consent and that, if consent is given, it may be withdrawn later.

Finally, volition is defined as agreement to participate that is given without coercion or under duress. Involuntary commitments or confinements pose special problems to the accomplishment of informed consent.

Cook, Altman, and Haavik (1978) have expanded these requirements for informed consent into 11 safeguards and incorporated each into an excellent consent form presented in Table 7–4 in the chapter appendix. This section has been a cursory attempt at defining relevant issues involved in obtaining informed consent. It is hoped that the model consent form will help the reader to devise consent forms that will evaluate and document competence, knowledge, and volition on the part of the client or legal guardian.

Who Is the Client?

When another person or an agency is empowered to arrange for therapy, have the interests of the subordinated client been sufficiently considered? Concern for the well-being and quality of life for the client should be the paramount concern of each therapist. This statement appears to be simple and natural; however, when institutions, schools, and parents contract the therapist to aid in changing problematic behaviors of their residents or children, the therapist must ask, "Who would benefit from a change in the targeted individual's behavior?" At times, the therapist may find (s)he is in a situation where a change in behavior is viewed differently by two or more individuals. The therapist is faced with goal conflicts (Sulzer-Azaroff

& Mayer, 1977). The therapist may have to ponder if the intervention is designed to help the individual (e.g., decrease self-abusive behavior) or to establish rules for the institution or parents to increase conformity and convenience (Bellack & Hersen, 1977; Brown, Wienckowski, & Stolz, 1975). If the therapist cannot find a clear reason to implement the intervention for the benefit of the single individual, then (s)he may need to refuse to intervene. Bellack and Hersen (1977) suggest that appropriate requests may be modified by presenting normative information to parents about child development. As a suggestion to schools, they recommend modifying the environment to promote cooperation through increased student enjoyment and success rather than employing punishment procedures to reduce nonconformist behaviors.

Adequacy of Treatment Measurement

Has the adequacy of treatment been evaluated? "[A] hallmark of the behavioral tradition has been measurement and general concern for documentation" (Bellack & Hersen, 1977, p. 257). Adequacy of measurement is probably more important when using punishment procedures for several reasons. First, it must be documented that a maladaptive response is occurring at a sufficient rate to warrant intervention. Second, controlling variables (i.e., antecedent and consequent conditions) must be delineated. Third, a demonstration of the lack of effectiveness of less intrusive techniques must be observed before punishment procedures are attempted. Ethical and legal standards demand reliable and accurate data.

Confidentiality

Has the confidentiality of the treatment relationship been protected? Confidentiality is a general ethical practice that protects a client from unauthorized disclosures of information given, in confidence, without the consent of the client (Schwitzgebel & Schwitzgebel, 1980). Confidentiality is no less of an issue when treating clients with punishment procedures (notably children and the mentally retarded). Since many punishment programs will be performed in institutions, schools, or with parents (i.e., not directly with the client), issues of confidentiality may be forgotten or even ignored, since many individuals could be involved. Policies regarding disclosures of information must be designed by each institution or therapist, but in general the reader should remember that the client or his/her guardian must authorize, in writing, who can see the data that are collected and what information is discussed. This ethical issue is extremely important and should not be taken lightly.

Referral

Does the therapist refer the clients to other therapists when necessary? Two important issues should be addressed under this topic: (1) consultation and (2) what should be done if treatment does not produce the desired effects.

Rimm and Masters (1979) note: "In no case should [punishment procedures] be employed without the direct supervision of doctorally trained therapists who are experts in the use of such techniques" (p. 320). We concur that punishment procedures should not be attempted unless expert supervision is provided, but from observing the numbers of experts in this field, we find Rimm and Masters' statement quite limiting. Consultation may provide the answer to this dilemma. If an institution, school, or individual is considering the use of punishment, and a trained therapist is not on staff, the institution would be bound ethically to seek such an individual through consultation.

If treatment is not effective, what should be done? If a thorough treatment plan and consent form were devised at the onset of treatment, this question would be answered already. The reader is referred back to Table 7–4, under item V, Description of Aversive Treatment Procedure(s). This category includes the statement, "Include Hierarchy of Treatment Procedures." Under this heading the therapist should have included other procedures or modifications that should be attempted in the absence of success with initial treatment. A review of the literature and/or consultation with an expert would provide the answers.

Repp and Deitz (1978) suggest that the program chairperson should presume that the procedure will fail, so alternatives can be explored early. This approach will prevent long delays between phases of treatment, which could exacerbate the problem by producing extinction-induced aggression, behavioral recovery, or behavioral contrast effects.

Qualifications of the Therapist

Is the therapist qualified to provide treatment? *Wyatt v. Stickney* (1972) defined a "qualified mental health professional" as

(1) a psychiatrist with three years of residency training in psychiatry; (2) a psychologist with a doctoral degree from an accredited program; (3) a social worker with a master's degree from an accredited program and two years of clinical experience under the supervision of a Qualified Mental Health Professional; or (4) a registered nurse with a graduate degree in psychiatric nursing and two years of clinical experience under the supervision of a Qualified Mental Health Professional.

Although licensing and certification laws exist within each of these professions, the specificity of the technical approach in the administration of behavioral programs is not covered (Bellack & Hersen, 1977).

May, Risley, Twardosz, Friedman, Bijou, and Wexler (1975) set up guidelines for the qualifications of personnel who administer behavior modification programs. These are presented in Table 7–5 in the chapter appendix. These guidelines help to point out necessary requisite skills; however, there is no formal certification of behavior therapists. Controversy also exists within the field as to whether or not certification is necessary. Considerable debate will be necessary in the future to arrive at some decisions about the need for certification. To aid the reader in assessing the areas of importance in certification, an excellent review of the relevant competencies and performance criteria for individuals using aversive procedures (Thomas & Murphy, 1981) is included in Table 7–6 in the chapter appendix. The reader should note the extensiveness of the categories, emphasizing again the necessity for expert supervision discussed in the previous section on referral.

In addition to the general guidelines proposed by the American Psychological Association and the Association for Advancement of Behavior Therapy, the following guidelines specific to punishment are worthy of review. These should be considered of particular import, since extreme caution and the most conservative guidelines should be followed in the application of punishment methods.

Deprivation as a Treatment Factor

Deprivation involves the withholding of the delivery of specific forms of noncontingent reinforcement, substituting instead a schedule of reinforcement that is designed such that delivery is contingently provided upon the emission of adaptive behavior. This component of a treatment package becomes an ethical issue when primary reinforcers (e.g., food and water) are withheld, constituting a violation of basic human rights. However, primary reinforcers infrequently are withheld, as deprivation usually involves secondary reinforcers.

Kazdin (1980b) cogently summarized an interesting conceptual twist to therapeutically designed deprivation. He suggests that deprivation plays a major role in ordinary social existence. For example, individuals feel deprived of sexual expression and free speech. Likewise, "the majority of individuals for whom behavior modification techniques are used are deprived in some significant way by virtue of their failure to perform certain behaviors" (p. 325). For example, institutionalized clients are deprived of normal community living, students with academic problems may be deprived of access to employment, and delinquents may be deprived of some feature of social living. The deprivation incurred as a function of behavioral problems must be weighed against the temporary deprivation resulting from treatment. This decision process often is difficult but surely is where the answer lies as to the ethics of therapeutic deprivation.

The Painful Nature of the Stimulus

Painful is an emotionally laden and often-confused term. Even among behavioral psychologists there is confusion about what constitutes painful procedures. Rimm and Masters (1979) note that "aversive control will always involve the infliction of pain" (p. 320). On the other hand, Johnston (1972), in discussing a punishing stimulus, states that "it should be noted that there is neither stated nor intended any implication that the consequent stimulus must be in any way painful to the subject or experimenter" (p. 1034). Kazdin (1980b) asserts that "aversive events are not necessarily painful or demeaning. They do not require a violation of rights or deprivation of essential human needs" (p. 324).

With such divergent views, the definition of what constitutes a painful procedure probably is not negotiable. Begelman (1975) takes a different position. He suggests that aversive procedures should not be labeled as unethical because of the potential of pain.

> The argument that aversive procedures per se are unethical because they involve pain or discomfort to clients or patients is totally without validity. Indeed, if the absence of pain were a necessary condition of any treatment procedure, we all would have succumbed to one or another variety of infections, conditions we have been immunized from by *painful* inoculations. . . . Obviously, the conscientious adminis-

tration of an aversive procedure is hardly undertaken with the sole aim of inflicting pain on clients. It is undertaken with the ultimate goal of ameliorating a behavioral problem, and in this sense, the pain involved is incidental. The relevant point is that no treatment procedure involving pain as a direct or indirect consequence of the methods employed can be declared unethical on the abstract base alone. [pp. 184–185].

. As this statement, as well as the discussion on deprivation, imply, an analysis of short-term consequences versus long-term benefits to the client is essential. However, long-term risks and benefits can be assessed only through follow-up of empirical research projects. In the interim, the practitioner will have to (1) make a judgment that the present maladaptive behaviors are so disruptive that future adjustment is impossible without intervention, (2) intervene, and (3) set up contingencies such that the probability of the client emitting adaptive behaviors is increased (i.e., program maintenance and generalization).

Legal Issues

As mentioned in the introduction to this chapter, the amount of information written about ethical behavior and judicial decisions regarding therapeutic interventions is so vast that only a brief sampling of the literature is possible. Again, we will provide an overview of relevant topics and some guidelines regarding important issues.

Constitutional Protections

Eight basic rights will be outlined in this section:

1. Right to treatment
2. Informed consent
3. Right to refuse treatment
4. Protection from cruel and unusual punishment
5. Due process
6. Least restrictive alternative
7. Protection against harm
8. Individualized treatment

Brief overviews now will be presented as to the definitions and legal ramifications.

Right to Treatment. "Treatment may be defined as a course of planned intervention designed to change behaviors that are considered (by some standard) aberrant, disordered, or dangerous" (Schwitzgebel & Schwitzgebel, 1980). The right to treatment refers to the right of an individual to receive adequate treatment when her/his freedom is denied due to an involuntary commitment. This right applies to both the mentally ill and the mentally retarded. Morris (1970) notes, "If society confines a man for the benevolent purpose of helping him—'for his own good,' in the standard phrase—then its right to do so withhold his freedom depends entirely upon whether help is in fact provided" (p. 102).

Informed Consent. This has been reviewed earlier. One recent legal case is important regarding this issue, namely, *Kaimowitz v. Michigan Department of Mental Health* (1973), which indicated that "informed" consent may not be possible within an institutional setting. This ruling points to the importance of securing consent from relatives or guardians of the client.

Right to Refuse Treatment. Schwitzgebel & Schwitzgebel (1980) point to the fact that the right to obtain treatment does not impose obligation upon the client to accept treatment. Recently, court decisions (*Rennie v. Klein,* 1979) have indicated that clients have the right to refuse treatment. R. Martin (1980) notes that it appears paradoxical that the same body of constitutional law gives both the right to treatment and the right to refuse treatment.

Protection from Cruel and Unusual Punishment. "Excessive bail shall not be required, nor excessive fines imposed, nor cruel and unusual punishment inflicted." This statement is the Eighth Amendment to the U.S. Constitution. Although originally written to protect criminal offenders, this amendment has been cited in court cases with the mentally ill. Much controversy exists in attempting to define the meaning of this amendment with regard to treatment. We note one interesting legal decision that is incongruent with empirical research. A recent Supreme Court decision (*Ingraham v. Wright,* 1977) has upheld the ruling that corporal punishment in public schools does not violate the constitutional safeguard against cruel and unusual punishment. Therefore, corporal punishment has returned to the forefront of educational controversy with *no* empirical evidence that it is effective (Rose, 1981).

Due Process. This refers to the provision of a hearing at which the client is represented by counsel when his/her liberty is restricted (Romanczyk, Kistner, & Crimmins, 1980). "To deprive any citizen of his or her liberty upon the altruistic theory that the confinement is for humane therapeutic reasons and then fail to provide adequate treatment violates the very fundamentals of due process" (*Wyatt v. Stickney*, 1972). Therefore, the treatment should be related to the rehabilitation of the person, should not unduly restrict his/her liberty, and should not be incompatible with freedom of choice (Schwitzgebel & Schwitzgebel, 1980).

Least Restrictive Alternative. This concept was formulated from an old Supreme Court decision. "In a series of decisions this Court has held that even though the government purpose be legitimate and substantial, that purpose cannot be pursued by means that broadly stifle fundamental personal liberties where the end can be more narrowly achieved. The breadth of legislative abridgement must be viewed in light of less drastic means by achieving the same basic purpose" (*Shelton v. Tucker*, 1960). Additionally, the least restrictive alternative applies to the alternatives for treatment within an institution as well as the alternatives to commitment (*New York Association for Retarded Citizens v. Carey*, 1975). The *Wyatt* decision provided the following:

1. No person shall be admitted to the institution unless a prior determination shall have been made that residence in the institution is the least restrictive habilitation setting feasible for that person.
2. No mentally retarded person shall be admitted to the institution if services and programs in the community can afford adequate habilitation to such persons.
3. Residents shall have a right to the least restrictive conditions necessary to achieve the purposes of habilitation. To this end, the institution shall make every attempt to move residents from (1) more to less structured living, (2) larger to smaller facilities, (3) larger to smaller living units, (4) group to individual residence, (5) segregated from the community to integrated into the community, (6) dependent to independent living.

Protection against Harm. Clients are also protected against additional harm from "therapeutic institutionalization" (*New York Association for Retarded Citizens v. Rockefeller*, 1973). Martin (1981) notes that an individual may lose functional behaviors and acquire maladaptive behaviors just by living in large institutions. Other alternatives must be explored to control for this potential problem.

Individualized Treatment. A number of court decisions have led to the formation of the right to individual treatment. Individual treatment plans must be written specifying goals, short-term objectives, and the person responsible for program implementation (Martin, 1981). Examples and guidelines were presented in the ethics section of this chapter.

Client Rights after Institutionalization

The *Wyatt v. Stickney* litigation is considered to have put forth landmark decisions in the area of client rights (Braun, 1975). A list of some of these rights are summarized as follows:

1. Clients have a right to privacy and dignity.
2. Clients have a right to the least restrictive conditions necessary to achieve the purposes of commitment.
3. No person shall be deemed incompetent to manage his/her affairs solely by reason of his/her admission or commitment to a hospital.
4. Clients have the rights to have visitors, to have telephone communication, and to send and receive sealed mail.
5. Clients have a right to be free from unnecessary or excessive medication.
6. Clients have a right to be free from physical restraint and isolation.
7. Clients have a right not to be subjected to experimental research without express and informed consent from them and their guardians after consultation with legal counsel.
8. Clients have a right not to be subjected to treatment procedures such a lobotomy, electroconvulsive treatment, aversive conditioning, or other unusual or hazardous treatment procedures without their express and informed consent after consultation with legal counsel.
9. Clients have a right to receive prompt and adequate medical treatment for any physical ailments.
10. Clients have a right to wear their own clothes and to keep and use their own personal possessions.
11. Clients have a right to regular physical exercise several times a week.
12. Clients have a right to be outdoors at regular and frequent intervals.
13. The institution shall provide, with adequate supervision, suitable opportunities for the client's interaction with members of the opposite sex.

14. No client shall be required to perform labor that involves the operation and maintenance of the hospital or for which the hospital is under contract with an outside organization.
15. Clients may engage voluntarily in therapeutic labor for which the hospital would otherwise have to pay an employee, provided the specific labor or any change in labor assignment is:
    a. an integrated part of the client's treatment plan and
    b. supervised by a staff member to oversee the therapeutic aspects of the activity and
    c. compensated in accordance with the minimum wage laws of the Fair Labor Standards Act.
16. A client has a right to a humane psychological and physical environment within the hospital facilities.
17. Clients shall eat in dining rooms. The diet for clients will provide at a minimum the Recommended Daily Dietary Allowances as developed by the National Academy of Sciences.
18. Each client shall have a comprehensive physical and mental examination and review of behavioral status within 48 hours after admission.
19. Each client shall have an individualized treatment plan.
20. In addition to complying with all the other standards, a hospital shall make special provisions for the treatment of clients who are children or young adults.

A number of other rights were delineated in the Wyatt case in addition to the provision that some restrictions may be imposed by the qualified mental health professional. These rights have had a significant impact on the legalities of institutional care in Alabama, as well as across the nation.

Conclusions

There are no guarantees that a program will always uphold clients' rights or that with new legal decisions the program will not need modification (Martin, 1981). Program developers and administrative personnel will have to review their programs periodically to help determine if client rights are being preserved. A number of sources (Hasazi, Surles, & Hannah, 1981; Martin, 1981; Schwitzgebel & Schwitzgebel, 1980) may be consulted for information regarding the protection of clients' rights in treatment and educational programming.

The reader may feel somewhat overwhelmed at this point with the many issues and questions presented regarding ethical and legal issues. The majority of punishment procedures reviewed in this book, however, have not come under scrutiny by the courts. Many of the procedures used in behavioral research are probably less intrusive and severe from the public's point of view than punishment tolerated in everyday life. For example, response cost (loss of tokens), wearing a time-out ribbon, or sitting on the periphery of the classroom for a minute are probably less severe than corporal punishment or shouting at and shaking a child, which are alternatives often used in everyday life. The courts have ruled on the acceptability of procedures that are much more extreme than proponents of behavior modification normally would endorse (teacher use of corporal punishment, for example). Thus, court decisions do not always represent the most sensitive or empirically validated methods of protecting individuals against aversive procedures.

Another reason that punishment procedures typically used in behavior modification have not come under scrutiny is that selected procedures are those normally used in everyday life. Part of the contribution of behavioral research has been to emphasize the systematic application of selected consequences (e.g., reprimands) and the conditions under which naturally occurring events are likely to be effective (e.g., when used as part of reinforcement programs for prosocial behavior).

The present chapter was not designed to overwhelm the potential practitioner of punishment programs with all the ethical and legal issues presented but to note that the establishment and maintenance of such procedures enhance the protection of both the client and therapist and increase the viability of punishment procedures by demonstrating care and sensitivity in their application. By viewing as "too much work" the guidelines by which ethically and legally safe procedures are developed, and thereby making an excuse for not developing punishment programs when appropriate, a great injustice is done to the client. "Not to rescue a person from an unhappy organization of his behavior is to punish him in that it leaves him in a state of recurrent punishment" (Baer, 1970, p. 246).

Appendix to Chapter 7

Table 7-1. Ethical Issues for Human Services.

In 1975, the Board of Directors of the Association for Advancement of Behavior Therapy appointed a committee to consider the development of a statement on ethical practice for the organization. The committee consisted of Nathan H. Azrin (Anna Mental Health and Developmental Center, Anna, Illinois) and Richard B. Stuart (University of Utah, Salt Lake City), co-chairpersons; Todd R. Risley (University of Kansas, Lawrence); and Stephanie B. Stolz (National Institute of Mental Health, Rockville, Maryland). The Board of Directors adopted this statement at its May 22, 1977 meeting.

Rather than recommending a list of prescriptions and proscriptions, the committee agreed to focus on critical ethical issues of central importance to human services.

On each of the issues described below, ideal interventions would have maximum involvement by the person whose behavior is to be changed, and the fullest possible consideration of societal pressures on that person, the therapist, and the therapist's employer. The committee recognizes that the practicalities of actual settings sometimes require exceptions, and that there certainly are occasions when exceptions can be consistent with ethical practice. Even though some exceptions may eventually be necessary, the committee feels that each of these issues should be explicitly considered.

The questions related to each issue have deliberately been cast in a general manner that applies to all types of interventions, and not solely or specifically to the practice of behavior therapy. The committee felt strongly that issues directed specifically to behavior therapists might imply erroneously that behavior therapy was in some way more in need of ethical concern than non-behaviorally-oriented therapies.

In the list of issues, the term "client" is used to describe the person whose behavior is to be changed; "therapist" is used to describe the professional in charge of the intervention: "treatment" and "problem," although used in the singular, refer to any and all treatments and problems being formulated with this checklist. The issues are formulated so as to be relevant across as many settings and populations as possible. Thus, they need to be qualified when someone other than the person whose behavior is to be changed is paying the

(continued)

Table 7-1 (continued)

therapist, or when that person's competence or the voluntary nature of that person's consent is questioned. For example, if the therapist has found that the client does not understand the goals or methods being considered, the therapist should substitute the client's guardian or other responsible person for "client," when reviewing the issues below.

A. Have the goals of treatment been adequately considered?
  1. To insure that the goals are explicit, are they written?
  2. Has the client's understanding of the goals been assured by having the client restate them orally or in writing?
  3. Have the therapist and client agreed on the goals of therapy?
  4. Will serving the client's interests be contrary to the interests of other persons?
  5. Will serving the client's immediate interest be contrary to the client's long term interest?
B. Has the choice of treatment methods been adequately considered?
  1. Does the published literature show the procedure to be the best one available for that problem?
  2. If no literature exists regarding the treatment method, is the method consistent with generally accepted practice?
  3. Has the client been told of alternative procedures that might be preferred by the client on the basis of significant differences in discomfort, treatment time, cost, or degree of demonstrated effectiveness?
  4. If a treatment procedure is publicly, legally, or professionally controversial, has formal professional consultation been obtained, has the reaction of the affected segment of the public been adequately considered, and have the alternative treatment methods been more closely reexamined and reconsidered?
C. Is the client's participation voluntary?
  1. Have possible sources of coercion of the client's participation been considered?
  2. If treatment is legally mandated, has the available range of treatments and therapists been offered?
  3. Can the client withdraw from treatment without a penalty of financial loss that exceeds actual clinical costs?
D. When another person or an agency is empowered to arrange for therapy, have the interests of the subordinated client been sufficiently considered?
  1. Has the subordinated client been informed of the treatment objectives and participated in the choice of treatment procedures?

(continued)

Table 7-1 (continued)

    2. Where the subordinated client's competence to decide is limited, have the client as well as the guardian participated in the treatment discussions to the extent that the client's abilities permit?

    3. If the interests of the subordinated person and the superordinate persons or agency conflict, have attempts been made to reduce the conflict by dealing with both interests?

E. Has the adequacy of treatment been evaluated?

    1. Have quantitative measures of the problem and its progress been obtained?

    2. Have the measures of the problem and its progress been made available to the client during treatment?

F. Has the confidentiality of the treatment relationship been protected?

    1. Has the client been told who has access to the records?

    2. Are records available only to authorized persons?

G. Does the therapist refer the clients to other therapists when necessary?

    1. If the treatment is unsuccessful, is the client referred to other therapists?

    2. Has the client been told that if dissatisfied with the treatment, referral will be made?

H. Is the therapist qualified to provide treatment?

    1. Has the therapist had training or experience in treating problems like the client's?

    2. If deficits exist in the therapist's qualifications, has the client been informed?

    3. If the therapist is not adequately qualified, is the client referred to other therapists, or has supervision by a qualified therapist been provided? Is the client informed of the supervisory relation?

    4. If the treatment is administered by mediators, have the mediators been adequately supervised by a qualified therapist?

Source: Association for Advancement of Behavior Therapy. Ethical issues for human service. *Behavior Therapy*, 1977, *8*, 763-764. Reprinted with permission from the publisher.

Table 7–2. Procedural Safeguards for Aversive Interventions.

1. Approval for the use of aversive procedures may only be given by the Director.
2. At the beginning of each school year, during the I.E.P. process and in the initial parent meeting, the philosophy and utilization of aversive procedures are discussed. At that time, based on the information available to the staff from the parents and referring agencies, concerning any severe behavioral problems, the probability of the necessity of utilizing aversive procedures is discussed when applicable. However, this is meant to be a discussion point and is not considered an affirmation on the part of the parents for the utilization of aversive procedures.
3. There are limited classes of behavior that are considered appropriate to indicate the possible need for the use of aversive procedures. These behaviors are limited to the following:
   a. self-injurious behavior
   b. aggression
   c. acting-out
   d. self-stimulatory behavior
   e. "psychotic" behavior
   In general, the criteria used to decide whether a problematic behavior is severe enough to merit consideration of aversive intervention is the question of whether or not this behavior pattern is significantly impeding the educational and/or sociobehavioral development of the child (it is certainly possible for such behaviors to be non-problematic at certain low levels of frequency and intensity). The intensity or severity of the behavior is a critical variable, as it relates to the type and intensity of the aversive procedure to be employed. Also of prime importance is the consideration of whether or not the expression of this behavior results in the child being placed in a more restrictive educational and treatment environment than would be the case if the behavior were not emitted. It is considered inappropriate to use aversive procedures for the purpose of attempting to teach positive adaptive skills. Rather, it is to be used solely for the purpose of eliminating maladaptive behavior patterns.
4. Prior to discussion of the utilization of an aversive procedure, the results of an objective analysis of the antecedents, rate, intensity and distribution of the problematic behavior pattern must be presented at a staff meeting.
5. After staff discussion of the objective information concerning the behavior pattern and whether or not it is considered serious enough to indicate the need for aversive procedures, the following must result:

(continued)

Table 7-2 (continued)

For a reasonable time period, typically 2-3 weeks, other attempts must be made to deal with the behavior pattern in a non-intrusive, non-aversive manner. Typical in these procedures are the following:

a. alter task type
b. alter task difficulty
c. alter proportion of on-task vs. off-task time
d. alter task temporal structure
e. alter staffing patterns
f. increase positive motivation
g. alter physical environment
h. reinforce incompatible behaviors
i. utilize extinction procedures
j. alter staff interaction/teaching patterns

While the minimum specified time for such procedures is usually 2 weeks, on the average, staff typically spend 2-3 months in attempting to ameliorate these behavior patterns in the manner herein described.

6. Should attempts at non-aversive intervention prove unsuccessful, and the behavior remains problematic and continues to meet criteria for consideration of aversive procedures, the next step is consultation with the parents and/or guardians of the child, to discuss the child's current status. At this meeting, the information gathered is transmitted to the parents and/or guardians. They are asked to consider the information before either granting or not granting their permission for the staff to utilize an aversive procedure.

7. If the parents' and/or guardians' decision is to grant permission, an aversive program is delineated. The procedure is as follows:

   a. A formal and rigorous recording system is instituted at the Unit for the particular target behaviors as well as other related behavior patterns and a baseline is collected of at least one week duration prior to intervention. This baseline is in addition to the information collected previous to this decision point. Thus, there are typically at least 6-8 weeks of baseline data available prior to intervention.

   b. Next, discussion takes place at the staff meeting concerning the various procedures that are considered appropriate for intervention. All procedures discussed are examined from both ethical and clinical perspectives, with information from the professional literature central to these discussions. That is, examination of the professional literature is made, along with the clinical experience of the staff, so as to estimate probability of successful outcome and the appropriateness of the procedure presented.

(continued) 175

Table 7-2 (continued)

   c. The procedures must be integrated within the framework of the child's existing programs and must be matched by programs of a positive nature to simultaneously increase the possibility of occurrence of adaptive behavior patterns that are at least potentially incompatible with the maladaptive behavior patterns to be reduced.

   d. The entire treatment intervention program is discussed and consensus sought from the staff. However, the final decision and authority rests solely with the Director with respect to implementing or not implementing the specifics of the aversive program, given parental permission.

   e. Evaluation points are specified as to how often the program will be reviewed. The minimum evaluation point is daily and in some cases may be as frequent as each half-hour. In addition, all aversive programs that are in effect are discussed each week by the entire staff at the staff meeting. This is in addition to the daily evaluation by the individual staff members responsible for the child and the discussions between those staff members and the Assistant Director.

8. Parents are kept informed as to the child's progress, so as to allow them to continuously re-evaluate their initial decision to grant permission.

9. In addition to the evaluation of procedures made by the Director and the staff, it is also policy of the Unit to periodically have consultants from other facilities visit the Unit to observe and provide feedback concerning the general conduct of the Unit, in the areas of special education, language development, basic learning processes and sociobehavioral development, and also to provide specific feedback concerning aversive procedures and policy.

10. The Unit utilizes as its ethical guidelines the standards employed by the Association for the Advancement of Behavior Therapy and the American Psychological Association.

Source: Romanczyk, R. G., Colletti, G. & Lockshin, S. Developing a policy concerning the use of aversive procedures: Ethical, legal, and empirical issues. Paper presented at the Association for Behavior Analysis, Milwaukee, May 1981. Reprinted with permission from the authors.

Table 7-3. Sample Therapeutic Contract.

I. Overview of problem and therapeutic program

The overall objective of this therapeutic program is to develop and stabilize Mike's behavior patterns so that he may be considered for admission to school this fall. In general, this will involve strengthening some requisite behaviors such as following commands from an adult, and eliminating others, such as the screaming and tantrumming that accompany most of his refusals to follow instructions.

Mike has a discouraging behavior history for most teachers to consider working with. Because his characteristic reaction to requests is to throw tantrums, he is considered "untestable" by standard psychological means. This does not necessarily mean that he cannot do the items on a test, but rather that he has little or no control over his own behavior. His uncooperativeness quickly discourages most people from making much of an effort to work with him. What is clearly needed is an intensive rehabilitation program designed to enable Mike to build patterns of self-control that would lead to the elimination or drastic reduction of his disruptive behavior. This, in turn, would open other possibilities for developing Mike's potential, that is, the avenues which are blocked by his unmanageable behavior.

The overall goal of this 8-week program will be the development of self-control with its reciprocal outcome of decreasing or eliminating tantrums and disruptive behaviors. Implementation of this program will require that the child and his trainer engage in such activities as trips to the zoo, museums, parks, movies, swimming pools, shopping centers, supermarkets, and so on as well as having lunch and snacks together. These settings are included to expose Mike to a maximal number of normal situations where expectations of a standard of conduct are imposed by the setting itself.

As much as possible, the techniques used in the day program will be designed with the ultimate objective of utilization in the home. An attempt will be made to see that procedures used in the program are transferred to home management at the termination of treatment. The therapist will give instructions weekly to the parents by phone to insure that efforts both at home and in rehabilitation do not conflict.

II. Behavioral objectives of therapy

1. The objective of the therapeutic program is to teach Mike to comply with between 80-100 per cent of the verbal commands given to him by an adult(s). Compliance will be defined as Mike's beginning to perform the behavior specified by the command within 15 sec after it has been stated and then completing the specified task.

(continued)

Table 7-3 (continued)

2. In addition, we intend to eliminate or drastically reduce Mike's excessive screaming and tantrumming. The goal is not to tantrum more frequently than once out of 30 commands and for no longer than 1 min at a time.

3. Evaluation of treatment outcome: The decision as to the attainment of these specific objectives will rest upon Mike's performance during a 30 min test session to be conducted in a classroom situation. At this session the therapist, the parents, and an additional person will make 10 verbal requests each of Mike, for a total of 30 verbal requests. Mike must comply with 80-100 per cent of these requests for the program to be considered a success. In addition, he must have tantrummed not more than once, and not more than 1 min during this final evaluation.

III. Time and Place of therapeutic intervention

1. The therapeutic program will start on _____ and terminate on _____ . Evaluation of the effectiveness of treatment will be held on or about the termination date of the therapeutic program.

2. Location: The meeting place will be at the _____ . Session activities, however, will involve time spent elsewhere, for example, having lunch trips to shopping centers, amusements, and other special events. If the facility is not available, some other place agreeable can be designated as meeting and base center.

3. Days of training: Therapy sessions will be scheduled 5 days per week. The specific days may vary from week to week to comply with the objectives of the program. The family will be advised of the therapy schedule 1 week in advance.

4. Hours per day: Therapeutic sessions will be scheduled for 7 hr a day. Session time may be extended when therapeutically necessary as decided by the therapist.

5. Absences: There will be 4 notified absences allowed. The mother is expected to notify the therapist at least 1 hr before the scheduled therapy session. Any additional absences will require an additional fee of $10 per absence.

IV. Fees

Achievement of the behavioral objectives is expected to take 7 weeks of training from _____ . This training will cost a total of _____ . The monies will be disbursed in the following manner:

1. A check for 2/3 of the total amount will be given to the therapist at the beginning of therapy.

(continued)

Table 7-3 (continued)

2. The balance of 1/3 will be paid to the therapist upon the achievement of the program objectives as specified above on about the date of termination of the program. In the event that the above objectives are not reached by this date, therapy will be discontinued and the balance will be forfeited by the therapist.

3. All expenses incurred during training will be defrayed by the therapist. This will include admission to baseball games, the city zoo, swimming pools, and so on as well as the cost of field trips, lunch, and snacks.

By my signature I do hereby attest that I have read the above proposal and agree to the conditions stated therein.

_____
(Parent)

_____
(Supervising Therapist)

_____
(Co-Therapist)

_____
(Date)

Source: Ayllon, T., & Skuban, W. Accountability in psychotherapy: A test case. *Journal of Behavior Therapy and Experimental Psychiatry*, 1973, *4*, 19-30. Reprinted with permission from the authors and publisher.

Table 7-4. Model Informed Consent Form for Aversive Treatment Procedures.

Name: ·Sam Smith
Birth Date: 5-13-73
Hospital No.: 660-128
Date: 12-8-76
Supervisor: Karl Altman, Ph.D.
Therapists: Bill Cook, M.A.
Ann Maskarinec, Ph.D.

I. *Description of Behavior to be Modified*: The primary behavior to be modified will be hand-biting, defined as occurring whenever any part of Sam's hand passes the lips or enters any part of the oral cavity. Also being monitored are head-slapping and eye gouging. If these latter behaviors appear to be causing harm they may be targeted for modification at a later date. These behaviors are defined as follows: Eye-gouging is defined as occurring whenever the fingers of either hand come in direct contact with the sclera. Head-slapping is defined as occurring whenever either hand comes in contact with any part of the head, exclusive of pats or strokes. For the latter two behaviors each hand counts as one response.

II. *Description of Treatment Procedures That Have Already Been Implemented* (give outcome): 1. Ignoring—tried.and found ineffective. 2. Differential Reinforcement of Other (DRO) behavior—in Sam's pre-school setting this strategy has been in effect for nearly 4 months without success. 3. Saying "No" and removing his hand from his mouth—this strategy has been combined with DRO in Sam's pre-school program. For a time it decreased the behavior to approximately 3–5 times/90 min. session. However, the behavior was not eliminated and has now increased to a median of 20 times/90 minute session for the past 5 days. 4. Physical punishment (spanking)—this procedure models a behavior that Sam already emits and which may later be a target for deceleration. Sam's parents have tried spanking his hand contingent upon biting responses, but his mother reports that this procedure did not decrease the frequency of the response.

III. *Description of Other Treatment Alternatives*: 1. Heavy sedation—not desirable by parents or therapists. 2. Time-out—the behavior could not be precluded. Also, time-out has not been successful with other behaviors of Sam's in the past. 3. Overcorrection—this procedure would require too great a time investment by the parents to implement practically at home. Also, physical guidance seems to accelerate the target behaviors.

(continued)

Table 7-4 (continued)

IV. *Justification for Use of Aversive Treatment Procedure*: Thus far, none of the procedures described above have been effective in eliminating Sam's self-injurious behavior. A review of the literature (Baumeister & Rollings [1976]) indicates that aversive treatment procedures have been most effective in this regard. At present, Sam's knuckles show actual tissue damage from frequent biting. In addition, these self-injurious behaviors greatly interfere with his performance in acquiring new skills in his preschool program, and will probably make it difficult for Sam to succeed in other preschool settings. Sam's parents are concerned and would like the behavior eliminated. Sam will continue to receive ongoing reinforcement for appropriate behavior during the aversive treatment sessions.

V. *Description of Aversive Treatment Procedure(s)*—Include Hierarchy of Treatment Procedures Where Appropriate: At the onset of the treatment program, only the hand-biting response will be targeted for modification. Contingent upon each hand-biting response, an unused capsule of aromatic ammonia will be broken open and then placed immediately under Sam's nose. The duration of the ammonia presentation will be determined by the duration of the biting response. This procedure was successfully employed by Tanner & Zeiler (1975) for face slapping. If this procedure is not effective, a 3-sec. administration (which was successful in another case) would then be tried.

VI. *Description of Possible Side Effects*: Sam may become more alert and attend better to his environment (i.e., a positive side effect). A pediatrician and a pediatric neurologist were consulted regarding possible negative side effects. Both said that the procedure should be safe medically. Temporary nasal congestion, flushing and tearing may follow ammonia administration. The pediatrician noted that prolonged use in a non-ventilated area could produce vomiting or diarrhea. The therapists and parents will also watch for increased screaming or avoidance of the punishing agents as a result of the aversive treatment procedure. Tanner & Zeiler (1975) reported that the procedure may cause a facial rash, but this finding was not well-established.

VII. *Describe Any Special Precautions to Be Used in Implementing Treatment Procedure*: 1. Direct monitoring will be provided by the supervisor (Dr. Karl Altman). 2. Care will be taken that the ammonia is not ingested and does not come in contact with the eyes or skin. 3. Should side effects show no sign of remission in a brief period of time, a physician will be summoned.

(continued) *181*

Table 7-4 (continued)

VIII. *Data Recording Procedures* (Give Baseline Data): Baseline data is being recorded daily by having observers record the rate of each behavior for a 30 min. time segment during Sam's preschool session, and during 2-3 ten-minute observation periods in the home. Reliability of the recording procedures is also being assessed in both environments by having 2 observers record the time from a digital clock whenever one of the target behaviors occurs. These behaviors show a great deal of variability. In the preschool room for the past month, the frequency of bites/minutes has ranged from .08 to .53, with a median of .19 for the past week. In the home, the frequency of bites/minute after 2 days of data has ranged from .37 to .21. Interobserver agreement ranged from 67% to 100% with a mean of 95%.

IX. *Expected Behavioral Outcome* (Also Give Expected Time for Treatment to be Effective): Short range goal: If the procedure is effective, it should reduce the target behavior to less than 10% of the baseline frequency after 2 days of treatment. Long range goal: Ultimately, the goal of the treatment program will be to reduce Sam's hand-biting to zero responses during both the preschool sessions and during recording at home for seven consecutive days. This long-range goal should be accomplished within 1 month after aversive treatment begins. Intense or prolonged side effects will result in an immediate cessation of treatment.

X. *List Persons Who Will Implement Treatment Procedures*: *Names and Qualifications*:
Bill Cook—Psychology Intern at CRU; M.A., Psychology
Ann Maskarinec—Psychology Intern at CRU; Ph.D., Psychology
*Karl Altman—Ph.D., Clinical Psychology
*Supervisor

XI. *Committee on Legal and Ethical Protection*:
Names   *Signatures*
Karl Altman, Ph.D. _____
Fred Girardeau, Ph.D. _____
Mary Mira, Ph.D. _____
Barbara Blee, J.D., M.S.W. _____
John Spaulding, M.D. _____
Ms. Smith _____

XII. *Sample Post-test Questions*:
1. I can stop this treatment procedure at any time (check one)
_____ yes
_____ no

(continued)

Table 7-4 (continued)

2. Possible side effects of this treatment procedure include the following (check those that apply);
   _____ a. facial flush
   _____ b. Sam may try to hide from his mother so that she cannot punish him
   _____ c. bleeding from the nose
   _____ d. runny nose
   _____ e. crying or screaming
   _____ f. vomiting or diarrhea
3. In order to see if this treatment procedure is working it will probably take: (check one)
   _____ a. several weeks or months
   _____ b. about 2 days
   _____ c. about a year

XIII. *Informed Consent*:
   1. As legal guardian for this patient, I, _____ ,
      (Name of Legal Guardian)
      hereby consent to the use of the treatment procedures described on the previous pages in the treatment of _____Sam_____.
      (Name of Patient)
   2. I acknowledge that no guarantees have been made to me regarding the results of this treatment.
   3. I understand that within the scope of this treatment there is no intent to cause detrimental side effects to the patient.
   4. I also understand that the treatment procedure described above will be closely monitored and supervised and in the event of the observation of any detrimental side effects which might be injurious to the patient (see VI above), the treatment procedures will be immediately terminated. I further understand that the decision to terminate may be made either by myself or by the therapist. However, normally the decision will be made jointly.
   5. This form has been fully explained to me and I certify that I understand its contents.
      Signature of person legally authorized to consent for patient:

_____

Address _____

City & State _____

Relationship _____

(Date) _____   *(continued)* 183

Table 7-4 (continued)

Witness:	
Signature	_____
Address	_____
City & State	_____

Director of Clinical Services: John Spaulding, M.D. (913) 588-5919

Source: Cook, J. W., Altman, K., & Haavik, S. Consent for aversive treatment: A model form. *Mental Retardation,* 1978, *16*, 49–51. Copyright, 1978, The American Association on Mental Deficiency. Reprinted by permission of authors and publisher.

Table 7-5. Guidelines for Staff Qualifications.

Resident Life Assistant

Formal Qualifications: High school graduate or equivalent experience.
Behavioral Criteria: Until meeting the following criteria, a person holding this position is on probationary status. The Supervisor should evaluate performance according to a prespecified set of written criteria. The employee must demonstrate the basic skills of differential reinforcement and extinction in the context of maintaining a minimum level of interaction of one contact per minute with client. Error rate in differential reinforcement and extinction should be no higher than 10%. The Resident Life Assistant should also be able to implement under supervision some of the training procedures appropriate for the population.

Resident Trainer (Trainer–Instructor)

Formal Qualifications: High school graduate or equivalent experience.
Behavioral Criteria: Promotion to this position is based upon successful completion of the requirements of RLA, and demonstrated skill in all of the training procedures appropriate to that population and in keeping records in client progress. Evaluation on a pre-specified set of written criteria should be done by the Director of Residential Training Programs.

Unit Manager or Director

Formal Qualifications: Two years of college or equivalent experience.

(continued)

Table 7-5 (continued)

Behavioral Criteria: This person must have demonstrated competence in the duties of RLA and Resident Trainer, and in addition have successfully supervised RLA's in implementing training procedures. Evaluation on a pre-specified set of written criteria should be done by the Director of Residential Training Programs.

Supervisor

Formal Qualifications: Four years of college and experience.

Behavioral Criteria: The Supervisor must have experience in successfully supervising others in implementing all of the training procedures and health care routines relevant to the population. An extremely important requirement is that the individual be able to give formal feedback on staff performance, particularly inadequate performance, and be able to write the necessary reports on client progress in training programs.

All Units: Director of Residential Training Programs

Formal Qualifications: Master's level specialist.

Behavioral Criteria: This person must have formal training including practicum experience in all behavioral procedures relevant to the population, the ability to locate information and training packages, the ability to organize and implement them, and supervisory skills. He/she should have no additional administrative responsibilities.

Director of Programs and Services or Outside Consultant

Formal Qualifications: Ph.D. or equivalent.

Behavioral Criteria: In addition to the skills of the Director of Residential Training Programs this person must have a broad knowledge of all other programs operating in the institution, i.e., education, music therapy, and recreation therapy, and the ability to integrate them into a coordinated, full-day program.

Source: May, J. G., Risley, T. R., Twardosz, S., Friedman, P., Bijou, S., & Wexler, D. *Guidelines for the use of behavioral procedures in state programs for retarded persons.* Arlington, Tex.: Association for Retarded Children, 1975. Reprinted with permission from the authors and publisher.

Table 7-6. Relevant Competencies and Performance Criteria for Personnel Using Aversive and Deprivation Procedures.

A. *Competency Demonstrations Required to Obtain Initial Certification*

1. COMPETENCY: Identifies target behaviors in relation to antecedent and consequent environmental events which are associated with them and identifies direction of desired behavior change.
CRITERION: (Simulation exercises) Given one video taped example each of inappropriate stimulus control, behavioral deficit, and behavior excess, the candidate identifies the appropriate targets, the associated antecedent and consequent events and specifies the direction of desired behavior change.

2. COMPETENCY: Conducts reliable measurement of targeted behaviors.
CRITERION: (Simulation exercises) Given a video taped presentation of target behavior, a recording procedure, response definition, data sheet and other necessary equipment, the candidate measures with 80% or better reliability using each of the following measurement techniques: (a) frequency count; (b) time sampling; (c) interval recording; (d) duration recording.

3. COMPETENCY: Selects a measure and develops a scoring method (data sheet design, instrument selection, procedure, instructions, etc.) for a specified target behavior, including identification of relevant collateral behaviors.
CRITERION: (Simulation exercises) Given a video taped presentation of a behavior to be targeted for deceleration, the candidate operationally defines the targeted response and at least two relevant collateral behaviors, specifies and defines the type of recording procedure to be used, gives specific directions on how the procedure is to be used, designs a sample data sheet and justifies the selection made.

4. COMPETENCY: Operationally defines and illustrates observational recording techniques.
CRITERION: (Written test) Given five recording techniques (frequency count, interval recording, time-sampling, duration recording and permanent product) the candidate operationally defines each and matches each technique with appropriate examples.

5. COMPETENCY: Identifies variables which may prevent appropriate evaluation of treatment effects.
CRITERION: (Written test) Can explain the effects of at least five of the following: maturation, non-contingent reinforcement, concurrent shifts in multiple independent variables, sensory abnormalities, improper definition of dependent variable, inconsistent

186

(continued)

Table 7-6 (continued)

implementation of treatment procedures. Given two reports of treatment effects, can identify variables which confound the relationship between treatment and outcome.

6. COMPETENCY: Is familiar with ethical issues, standards, and practices.
CRITERION: (Written test) Given bibliography of selected readings, the candidate will score at least 90% on an objective examination.

7. COMPETENCY: Incorporates ethical standards in program design, implementation, communication, and evaluation.
CRITERION: (Simulation exercises) Given an illustrative problem situation, an aversive and/or deprivation program designed by the applicant is rated for consistency with a checklist of ethical standards. The checklist on ethical standards will be derived from the standards recommended by the Association for Advancement of Behavior Therapy to the American Psychological Association.

8. COMPETENCY: Identifies major ethical issues: (a) Whose agent is the therapist? (b) Who decides what is best for the client? On what grounds? (c) Who has responsibility for the client? (d) How does one decide who receives treatment and who doesn't? (e) What are the pros and cons for: Changing behavior? Using aversive consequences? Reporting procedures and results? (f) How much and what type of information is given to the client? (g) How are the human rights of the individual and the family best safeguarded?
CRITERION: (Oral interview) Given an illustrative problem situation, the candidate will relate these major issues to the problem solution.

9. COMPETENCY: Identifies Federal and State laws and legal procedures as they affect the conduct of education-treatment activities.
CRITERION: 1. (Written test) Given a bibliography of appropriate laws and legal precedents, the candidate will pass on an objective examination with 90% accuracy. At a minimum, the bibliography will reference the following principles: (a) treatment with trained staff in adequate numbers; (b) the least restrictive alternative in treatment methods and setting; (c) freedom from deprivation of normal goods and services without due process; (d) freedom from participation in programs without informed consent being given; (e) right to withdraw consent from treatment programs; (f) education regardless of handicap for school aged; (g) minimum wage in non-therapeutic work situations; (h) individu-

Table 7-6 (continued)

alized treatment plan. 2. (Simulation exercise) Given an illustrative problem situation, the candidate will correctly identify violations of legal precedents and/or laws.

10. COMPETENCY: Is familiar with Minnesota Management Guidelines: Conditions for the Utilization of Aversive and Deprivation Procedures.
CRITERION: (Written test) Passes objective exam on the details of Minnesota Behavior Management Guidelines: Conditions for the Utilization of Aversive and Deprivation Procedures.

11. COMPETENCY: Knowledge of current regulations and utilization of FDA approved aversive stimulation devices including types of available instrumentation, knowledge of dangers and side effects and knowledge of dangers associated with the operation of apparatus.
CRITERION: (Written test and simulation exercise) The candidate will pass an objective test over this area and will correctly identify hazards shown in at least three video taped segments.

12. COMPETENCY: Demonstrates familiarity with current literature on application of widely validated aversive and deprivation procedures.
CRITERION: (Written test) Given bibliography of selected readings, the candidate will pass objective test on content. In addition, the candidate will appropriately reference this literature in proposing procedures to alter a problem behavior in the simulation exercises required to demonstrate competencies in designing programs.

13. COMPETENCY: Programming for behavior change: Lists the essential steps in designing and conducting behavior change activities directed toward altering a behavioral excess or deficit.
CRITERION: (Written test) Given a brief narrative description of the problem and its history, the candidate can describe in writing the steps necessary to design a behavior change program based on positive reinforcement. The description must include at least the following: (a) the target behavior stated in objective and quantifiable terms; (b) the objective or goal of the treatment program; (c) the change procedure to be employed, including the stimulus circumstances and environment under which the treatment would take place, the baseline procedures, the positive consequences to be provided, the schedule or other procedures of delivering the consequences contingently; (d) the method of measuring the behavior and consequences throughout the treatment program; (e) control of probe techniques to determine the necessity of continuing treat-

(continued)

Table 7-6 (continued)

ment; (f) a plan for program generalization and maintenance; (g) the conditions under which the program would be changed or terminated.

14. COMPETENCY: Writes a proposal for a behavior change (i.e., habilitative/educational) program.

    CRITERION: (Simulation exercise) Given a brief narrative description of the problem and its history and a video taped demonstration of the problem behavior, the candidate writes a program which incorporates the following: (a) the targeted behavior stated in objective and quantifiable terms; (b) the objective or goal of the treatment program; (c) the change procedure to be employed, including the stimulus circumstances and environment under which the treatment would take place, the baseline procedures, the positive consequences to be provided, the schedule or other procedure of delivering the consequences contingently; (d) the method of measuring the behavior and consequences throughout the treatment program; (e) control or probe techniques to determine the necessity of continuing treatment; (f) a plan for program generalization and maintenance; (g) the conditions under which the program would be changed or terminated.

15. COMPETENCY: Provides a written report of the program effects.

    CRITERION: (Simulation exercise) Given illustrative case study material, the candidate will write a report suitable for submission to a county or state agency at the time of termination of treatment or transfer. The report will include the following elements: (a) client description, name, age, sex, diagnostic and other psychometric information; (b) a brief history leading to the problem which was treated; (c) an objective description of the problem including quantification of the pre-treatment problem intensity and the current levels of behavioral occurrences (frequency, duration, etc.); (d) a description in minimally technical but accurate language of the procedures employed; (e) a quantitative (preferably graphic) summary plus a narrative description of the results; (f) recommendations for methods of increasing the probability of program generality to a new setting.

16. COMPETENCY: Identifies variables which may contraindicate specific treatment procedures.

    CRITERION: (Written test) For each of five procedures, the candidate can identify the possible client or program characteristics which would indicate rejection of these procedures as inappropriate

Table 7-6 (continued)

or unsafe. Examples include: (a) using Gatorade or milk for hydration in the Foxx-Azrin toilet training program; (b) painful shock; (c) physically enforced over-correction; (d) food/candy reinforcement; (e) seclusion time-out.

17. COMPETENCY: Is familiar with important therapeutic concerns regarding procedures which are frequently used in behavior therapy and in educational/habilitative programming.
CRITERION: (Written test) The candidate can identify for each item on a selected list of procedures, the following characteristics: degree of intrusiveness (i.e., not intrusive vs. mild to very intrusive), time to become effective (very short vs. moderate to long), durability and generality of effect (very durable and easily generalized vs. limited durability and generalizability), likelihood of side effects (none or minimal vs. occasional to frequent), and risk of harm to client or staff (none to minimal vs. significant). At a minimum, the list of procedures will include the following: (1) extinction; (2) reinforcement of incompatible behaviors; (3) time-out in room; (4) graduated guidance; (5) restitution; (6) response cost; (7) required relaxation; (8) time-out (separation); (9) restraint; (10) noxious noises, smells, etc.; (11) deprivation of food or water; (12) slapping, spanking; (13) painful skin shock.

18. COMPETENCY: Is familiar with procedures for arranging contingent relationships between targeted responses and consequences which are available in the natural environment.
CRITERION: (Written test) Given examples of three target behaviors which are measured by their duration, intensity, and frequency respectively, the candidate will specify consequences for each which should decrease the behaviors. The consequences identified should already exist in the environment or be available without substantial additional funds or resources. The candidate will also specify the treatment environment (preferably the candidate's work setting).

19. COMPETENCY: Must be able to devise at least two alternative treatment procedures in each of three levels of intrusiveness of intervention.
CRITERION: (Simulation exercise) Given a video taped example of a behavior to be decelerated, the candidate will briefly describe two alternative treatment procedures from each of the three levels of intrusiveness, all of which can be justified as having reasonable likelihood of reducing problem behavior.

20. COMPETENCY: Is familiar with learning principles and the treatment procedures which have been derived from them.

(continued)

Table 7-6 (continued)

CRITERION: (Written test) Given a sample of at least twenty written definitions and/or examples, the candidate will correctly match from a list of phenomena and procedures with at least 90% accuracy. The pool from which the examples will be taken will include at least the following: Definitions: operant conditioning, positive reinforcement, negative reinforcement, differential reinforcement, punishment, avoidance, time-out, respondent conditioning, respondent extinction, covert sensitization, DRO, DRH, DRL, baseline, probe, deprivation, escape, required relaxation, token economy, EST, shock punishment, reliability validity, steady state, restitution. Examples: stimulus control, shaping, chaining, fading, continuous reinforcement, interval schedule, multiple schedule, extinction, response cost, satiation, desensitization, aversion therapy, overcorrection, positive practice, reversal, restraint, graduated guidance, flooding, superstitious reinforcement, Premack Principle. Procedure: (Simulation exercise) When shown video taped samples of the following procedures, the candidate can correctly identify the procedure with 70% accuracy on a multiple choice test: positive reinforcement (social, token), stimulus control, extinction, seclusion time-out, response cost, reinforcement of incompatible behavior, desensitization, aversion therapy, positive practice, over-correction, DRO, contingent observation, restraint, graduated guidance, flooding, superstitious reinforcement, restitution.

21. COMPETENCY: Identifies pool of procedures which may be used in human services settings to alter staff behavior in order to enable implementation of treatment programs.
    CRITERION: (Oral interview) Describes procedures which can be used without violating DPW work rules, union contracts or Department of Personnel policies and procedures.

22. COMPETENCY: Communication: Written and Graphic.
    CRITERION: (Simulation exercise) 1. Written: Explicitly describes treatment program, in writing, so that a naive individual who follows the program does not make errors in demonstrating the procedures. (The task specified in Programming Competency No. 3 is utilized for evaluative purposes). 2. Graphic: Given video taped simulation of data collection situation and the raw data which results from the observation, the candidate will design a graph, plot the data, label the ordinates and otherwise identify the variables shown so as to graphically communicate the behavioral

Table 7-6 (continued)

changes shown in the video taped presentation. (The task specified in Programming Competency No. 4 is utilized for evaluation purposes).

B. *In-Service Competency Demonstrations Required to Retain Certification*

23. COMPETENCY: Conducts reliable measurement of target behaviors.

   CRITERION: Treatment programs submitted for committee review include reliability checks on data required to evaluate effects.

24. COMPETENCY: Incorporates ethical standards in program design, implementation, communication, and evaluation.

   CRITERION: Two aversive and/or deprivation programs designed by the applicant are rated by the review committee for consistency with a checklist of ethical standards.

25. COMPETENCY: Does not violate Federal and State laws and legal precedents as they relate to the conduct of educational–treatment activities.

   CRITERION: The Minnesota Behavior Management review committee evaluates programs designed by the "expert" in terms of their consistency with a checklist of legal issues.

26. COMPETENCY: Does not violate Minnesota Behavior Management Guidelines: Conditions for the Utilization of Aversive and Deprivation Procedures.

   CRITERION: The Minnesota Behavior Management review committee will assess compliance with Minnesota Behavior Management Guidelines: Conditions for the Utilization of Aversive and Deprivation Procedures by comparing the job performance with the requirements of the rule on a standard checklist.

27. COMPETENCY: Writes proposals for behavior change (i.e., habilitative/educational) programs and provides written reports of program effects.

   CRITERION: The Minnesota Behavior Management review committee certifies that treatment plans submitted to them include at least the following: (a) the targeted behavior stated in objective and identifiable terms; (b) the objective or goal of the treatment program; (c) the change procedure to be employed, including the stimulus circumstances and environment under which the treatment would take place, the baseline procedures, the positive contingencies; (d) the method of measuring the behavior and consequences throughout the treatment program; (e) control or probe techniques to determine the necessity of continuing treatment;

(continued)

Table 7–6 (continued)

(f) a plan for program generalization and maintenance; (g) the conditions under which the program would be changed or terminated. In addition, the committee certifies that reports suitable for submission to a county or state agency have been prepared at the time of termination of treatment for transfer. The reports will include the following elements: (a) client description, name, age, sex, diagnostic and other psychometric information; (b) a brief history leading to the problem which was treated; (c) an objective description of the problem including quantification of the pre-treatment problem intensity and the current levels of behavioral occurrences (frequency, duration, etc.); (d) a description in minimally technical but accurate language of the procedures employed; (e) a quantitative (preferably graphic) summary plus a narrative description of the results; (f) recommendations for methods of increasing the probability of program generality to a new setting.

28. COMPETENCY: Identifies variables which may contraindicate specific treatment procedures.
    CRITERION: The regular performance checklist completed by the Minnesota Behavior Management review committee will certify that the therapist obtains appropriate inter-disciplinary consultation (medical, dental, social work, psychodiagnostic, etc.) regarding possible client characteristics which would contraindicate proposed behavior change program procedures prior to implementing the treatment programs.

29. COMPETENCY: Assessment, goal formulation and targeting.
    CRITERION: The Minnesota Behavior Management review committee evaluates the candidate's specification of appropriate and realistic program goals with a checklist. The checklist includes terms such as operationalized target behaviors, the employment of the normalization principle, the availability of trained staff in adequate numbers, etc.

30. COMPETENCY: Can apply and demonstrate the effectiveness of procedures for various types of behavioral change categories.
    CRITERION: The Minnesota Behavior Management review committee certifies that the programmer applies at least one procedure for each of the following categories with a concomitant demonstration of procedural effectiveness: (a) increase in behavior; (b) decrease in behavior; (c) maintenance of behavior; (d) teaching a new behavior; (e) stimulus control.

Table 7-6 (continued)

31. COMPETENCY: Supervision: Coordinates behavior change programs.

    CRITERION: The Minnesota Behavior Management review committee certifies that the candidate monitors program procedures at regular intervals; acts as supervisor for line personnel; and consults with parents as necessary.

32. COMPETENCY: Communication: Written, Oral, and Graphic.

    CRITERION: The Minnesota Behavior Management review committee will rate the effectiveness of the behavioral programmer in two types of oral and written reports: (a) ratings will be given on the clarity of description of program procedures and rationales; (b) ratings will be given on the clarity of the descriptions of program results.

Source: Thomas, D. R., & Murphy, R. J. Practitioner competencies needed for implementing behavior management guidelines. *The Behavior Therapist*, 1981, *4*(1), 7–10. Reprinted with permission from the authors and publishers.

8

Current Status
and Future Trends
in Punishment
Procedures

Introduction

In this book the authors have attempted to present a description of
various treatments which fit under the general rubric of punishment
methods in behavior modification. A discussion of conditions where
these various treatments could be used appropriately has been presented. Furthermore, a description of ethical and legal considerations for using these treatments has been made. An additional factor
not addressed to this point in selecting a punishment procedure
pertains to relative effectiveness of the method compared to other
treatments. The only way of making such an evaluation appropriately is by studies that at the outset are designed to evaluate different procedures. The major thrust of this chapter will be to discuss
evaluative studies on the relative effectiveness of various procedures
(e.g., overcorrection, response cost).

Treatment effectiveness may be evaluated along a number of
variables. These may include the degree to which the undesirable
behavior is suppressed and the effect on other appropriate behaviors both in increasing positive behavior and decreasing inappropriate responses. Similarly, the effect on positive behavior needs to be

195

considered (Maley & Marston, 1973; Maley, Feldman, & Ruskin, 1973). Unfortunately, very few studies to date have taken collateral behaviors (e.g., those not directly treated) into account; therefore, what constitutes "effective" should cover a broad number and type of responses within this complex issue. Beyond measuring multiple behaviors, a number of additional points should be evaluated, as follows:

1. Treatment outcome can be evaluated on the rapidity to which behaviors are changed or how well they are maintained.
2. Rating scales and direct observational systems used together may provide a more complex and better understanding of the ramifications of treatment.
3. Terms such as time-out and overcorrection are general descriptions and thus one must be careful not to make broad generalizations about the minimal comparative research available.
4. Long-term follow-up is needed (one or more years) so that rates on degree of relapse and remission on inappropriate behaviors can be made.
5. Those techniques with discrete components (e.g., ammonia as punishing stimulus) are more easily investigated than those that depend upon more global and nebulous factors (e.g., overcorrection). Along these same lines, comparisons of some procedures may be less useful than others.
6. It must be determined if adequate methodological rigor has been demonstrated to make the results of a particular study reliable and valid, as well as if the studies have been described adequately for replication.
7. The treatments compared should be of equal length and given for long enough intervals to evaluate treatment effectiveness. Establishing a criterion that one of the treatments must reach may be a more appropriate approach than the arbitrary time limits often imposed with treatments.
8. The criteria for terminating treatments should be specified and consistent across experimental conditions within a study.
9. Treatment conditions should be distinct (Marks, Sonoda, & Schalock, 1968). This approach is very difficult in single case experimental designs since effects from preceding conditions may confound other conditions. (Unfortunately,

the reader will note in the comparative research described later in this chapter that most of these studies are of the single case variety.)

10. Effectiveness should be evaluated on clinical as well as statistical significance (Matson & Kazdin, 1981).
11. Ease of applying the procedure should be considered carefully. This consideration may pertain to cost, rapidity, and simplicity of training therapists and related programmatic concerns. The extent to which a technique can be widely disseminated also is a measure of efficiency (Kazdin & Wilson, 1978).

Having noted the preceding, it is important to point out that taking into account all of these factors (and there are probably more) in a given study, is unlikely. Unfortunately, these factors have not approximated the "effectiveness criteria" used in most cases. These data suggest that the results of comparative studies need to be evaluated with caution.

A final point respective to evaluating the research that will be presented in this chapter concerns the tables we have provided for each treatment procedure where comparative studies were found. Each table presents the author(s) and publication date of the study, problem and population treated, treatment method(s) used, the type of observations used, and which of the treatments proved to be most effective. Although, these categories are fairly global, they include the types of information discussed in other evaluative studies and provide some common ground for comparison.

Comparative Treatment Studies

Covert Sensitization

A relatively new area for research on punishment has been covert sensitization. While few studies have been done in this area, those conducted have employed good methodologies. One particularly sound study is described by Sachs, Bean, and Morrow (1970). The authors describe the treatment of 24 adults with a smoking habit. Aspects of the study are presented in Table 8-1. Groups in this study consisted of a covert sensitization group, self-control group, and a no-treatment control group. In the covert sensitization group, muscle relaxation training was trained first. Then the subjects were

Table 8-1. Covert Sensitization: Summary of Comparative
Treatment Studies.

Study	Population and Problem	Treatment Method(s)	Measures	Most Effective Treatment
Sachs, Bean, & Morrow (1970)	Adult smokers	Self-control, covert sensitization	Observations	Covert sensitization

asked to pair the image of pleasurable smoking sensations (the first
item in a hierarchy) with their visualizations of an aversive scene. The
pairings continued until the subject no longer felt the urge to smoke.
When success on this pleasurable scene was achieved, the next scene
in the hierarchy, in terms of pleasure, was treated and so on. With the
self-control procedure, subjects rank-ordered from least to most com-
pelling the situations in which they had the urge to smoke. Subjects
then were instructed to discontinue smoking in the presence of the
easiest situation and to work cumulatively to the hardest. Thus, as
subjects gained control over their smoking behavior in environmental
situations at the bottom of the hierarchy, they graduated progressively to more difficult situations. Covert sensitization was more effective than self-control, although differences were marginal. Both treatments were significantly more effective than no treatment.

Overcorrection

Of the punishment procedures reviewed in this book, overcorrection
has been perhaps the most heavily researched in recent years. As
might be expected, a number of these studies have compared various other treatment procedures to overcorrection (see Table 8-2).
Only one study could be found, however, in which a group design
was employed. In this case the study compared restitution and positive practice overcorrection rather than overcorrection relative to
other methods.

    As noted earlier, a particularly difficult problem in comparative
treatment studies with overcorrection is the marked variability across
overcorrection methods (see Chapter 3). Therefore, while a number
of studies are presented, it must be kept in mind that the overcorrection methods are quite different from each other in a number of
instances.

Table 8-2. Overcorrection: Summary of Comparative Treatment Studies.

Study	Population and problem	Treatment Method(s)	Measures	Most Effective Treatment
Azrin, Nunn, & Frantz (1980a)	37 chronic nailbiting adults	Negative practice, habit reversal overcorrection	Observations	Habit reversal overcorrection
Azrin, Nunn, & Frantz (1980b)	22 adults with tics	Habit reversal overcorrection, negative practice	Observations	Habit reversal overcorrection
Azrin & Wesolowski (1975)	Habitual vomiting in a mentally retarded woman	Time-out, required relaxation, and positive practice	Observations	Positive practice
Bornstein, Hamilton, & Quevillon (1977)	9-yr.-old boy for noncompliance	DRO, overcorrection	Observations	Overcorrection
Doleys, Wells, Hobbs, Roberts, & Cartelli (1976)	Four mentally retarded children for acting out in class	Time-out, positive practice, overcorrection, social punishment	Observations	Social punishment
Foxx (1976b)	Stripping in a mentally retarded woman	Time-out and overcorrection	Observations	Overcorrection
Foxx & Azrin (1973b)	Two mentally retarded children for self-stimulation	DRO, noncontingent reinforcement, distasteful solution, overcorrection, physical punishment	Observations	Overcorrection
Matson & Stephens (1977)	Aggression in a mentally retarded adult	DRI, overcorrection	Observations	Overcorrection

In an early comparative study, Azrin and Wesolowski (1975) eliminated the habitual vomiting of a profoundly mentally retarded woman. The vomiting had been chronic, occurring twice daily for many years. Thus, the positive treatment effects obtained were even more impressive. Several treatments were attempted before a successful method was established. Initially, time-out was tried, given contingently for 30 minutes based on each episode of the inappropriate behavior. Since this method did not work, required relaxation was administered. As the reader may be aware by now, this is an overcorrection procedure based primarily on enforced quiet toward the client while (s)he is lying on a bed. The method is applied contingently when the target behavior occurs and is administered for two hours per disruptive episode.

Finally, positive practice and self-correction were given. Whenever the client vomited, she was required to clean up the mess created by this misbehavior, change her clothes or bed sheets if they had been soiled, and then practice correct vomiting. (This latter method constituted positive practice.) In the case of the last behavior, she was to go to the toilet, bend over with her mouth open, and then flush toilet. She then returned to where the vomiting episode occurred. This sequence constituted one trial and was repeated 15 times. Effects of this latter method were rapid and were sustained for nine months. However, an AB design with only one subject was used and order effects may have contributed to the latter treatment's effectiveness. Thus, the study needs replication under more controlled conditions.

In yet another comparative study, Foxx and Azrin (1973b) treated two severely mentally retarded girls, ages 7 and 8. In the former case, DRO, noncontingent reinforcement, physical punishment (contingent slaps), and overcorrection were compared in treating self-stimulation. With the latter child physical punishment, noncontingent reinforcement, a distasteful solution, and overcorrection were evaluated.

In both cases, overcorrection was the superior treatment. The authors did not speculate as to the reason for these findings; however, data generally were consistent with several other comparative studies that showed the superiority of overcorrection.

Doleys et al. (1976) assessed the effects of social punishment, positive practice, and time-out on the noncompliant behavior of four mentally retarded children. Social punishment consisted of the experimenter walking over to the child, holding the child firmly by the shoulders, and in a loud voice scolding him (e.g., "You did not do as

I asked right away and I don't like it when you disobey me!"). The trainer then released the child, put his/her hands on his/her hips and glared silently at the child for 40 seconds. Conversely, positive practice consisted of the trainer leading the child to the task and manually guiding him/her through appropriate play activities. Manual guidance was carried out by assuming a position behind the child, taking his/her hand, and directing it to the task for 40 seconds.

The third and final procedure, time-out, consisted of the trainer approaching the child, stating to the child his error, and placing him in a corner. The trainer stood by the child during the time-out and ignored him unless he attempted to escape. If the latter situation arose, the trainer returned the child to the corner.

The authors concluded that social punishment was the most effective treatment procedure. Also, they felt that this method had several other practical advantages including the ability to consequate behavior immediately, no need for special facilities, and accomplishing tasks rapidly.

In another comparative study (Matson & Stephens, 1977), overcorrection was compared to differential reinforcement of incompatible behavior (DRI) to treat the aggressive behavior of a 62-year-old schizophrenic woman. With overcorrection, the client was required to apologize after an aggressive episode; if she refused, the trainer verbalized the apology for her. Next, five minutes of training were provided during which time she was to pick up trash in the day room or hallways and place it in a garbage can. DRI consisted of reinforcing behaviors incompatible with disruptions, using edibles and social praise. Behaviors that were reinforced included appropriate hand movements, sitting, walking or appropriately interacting with others. Overcorrection was rapidly effective, while DRI had no appreciable effect.

Another comparative study using differential reinforcement procedures and overcorrection is described by Bornstein, Hamilton, and Quevillon (1977). The subject was a nine-year-old boy of normal intelligence treated for noncompliant and aggressive behavior. Differential reinforcement of other behavior (DRO) consisted of reminding the child that leaving his seat without permission was not allowed and verbally praising his performance on current classroom behavior.

At the beginning of overcorrection the teacher informed the child that leaving his seat without permission was against the rules and would be consequated with overcorrection. This procedure consisted of reciting the classroom rule upon request, raising his hand,

and upon being acknowledged by the teacher, asking permission to leave his seat. This procedure was to be repeated for three minutes. Results of the study showed overcorrection to be highly effective, while DRO was not.

Azrin, Nunn, and Frantz (1980a) recently compared a variant of overcorrection, termed habit reversal, to negative practice in the treatment of 37 adults who were chronic nail-biters. In habit reversal the nail-biters learned to engage in a competing hand-grasping reaction for three minutes whenever nail-biting occurred. They were also taught to identify the situational, social, and postural precursors of nail-biting. By so doing, it was felt that the client would be able to anticipate the behavior and practice the nail-biting response in front of a partner and the counselor to facilitate identification of the response. Subjects were to practice the competing behavior until it could be performed unobtrusively. Positive nail care to reduce frayed nails and cuticles was taught via the use of a nail file and hand lotion, with both items used in conjunction with the competing grasping reaction, contingent upon a nail-biting episode and also as a daily preventive measure.

In negative practice, clients were to simulate their nail-biting in front of each other while telling themselves how ridiculous they appeared. The counselor described the rationale of negative practice, answered questions, and supervised their practice. Nail-biters were to practice these exercises for 30 seconds every hour after the treatment session and were to continue doing so for four days after their problem had been eliminated. Based on the results, it was concluded that habit reversal was more effective than negative practice in reducing nail-biting. Effects were attributed to the specific properties of treatment.

Azrin, Nunn, and Frantz (1980b) made a similar comparison with 22 clients who displayed tics. These included backward head-jerking, sideways head-jerking, shoulder-jerking, head-shaking, wrist tics, neck-stretching, and shoulder contractures. As in the previous study, habit reversal was by far the most effective treatment.

Foxx (1976b) conducted a comparative study with a profoundly mentally retarded woman (Amy) who stripped off her clothes when angered. Treatments included either 30 minutes in the ward time-out room or overcorrection. In the latter procedure, when the maladaptive behavior occurred, Amy was required to pick up the discarded clothing and practice dressing in the ward clothing room. After dressing, Amy was guided throughout the ward where she assisted other residents in improving their appearance by buttoning or zipping any undone clothing, straightening residents' rumpled or twisted clothing, walking to the ward clothing room to secure shoes or slippers for any residents without footwear, and doing other related tasks.

Overcorrection proved to be vastly superior to time-out. This may have been due largely to the fact that many of the principles of time-out were not met when the procedure was being administered. For example, Amy was discovered masturbating on many occasions during her time-out confinement. In fact, the author notes that she may have been stripping so she could be placed in isolation. Therefore, the current study's findings must be largely discounted in terms of comparative treatment effectiveness.

Not unlike the overcorrection literature in general, the current studies are quite unbalanced in terms of methodology, number of subjects tested, and priority given to making a clear comparison between methods. As noted at the outset of this chapter a primary goal of good evaluative research must be the design of comparative studies with this goal as the major precept. Such does not seem to be the case in many of the studies reviewed, particularly in the overcorrection section. Rather, these studies seem to have been geared more toward finding a treatment that was effective, rather than making relative comparisons of methods. This point is quite important, since the dependent variables employed and related methodological considerations are predicated by such issues.

Response Cost

Relative to the total number of treatment studies that have been conducted for a particular punishment procedure, response cost would seem to have by far the greatest percentage of comparative studies. Additionally, research of this nature that has been done is generally methodologically sound. We will give a brief review of these studies and detail some of their implications (see Table 8-3).

Kazdin (1973) studied 48 mentally retarded clients selected from a sheltered workshop. Withdrawing tokens when speech dysfluencies occurred was compared to (1) an aversive stimulus (loud noise) contingent on the aberrant speech or (2) information control in the form of a light when a dysfluency occurred. The two latter treatments proved to be hardly more effective than no treatment at all. Response cost, however, resulted in dramatic reductions in inappropriate responses that Kazdin indicated were not due merely to a few subjects' changing dysfluency rates. The aversive stimulus condition, which proved to be the next most effective method, had three of 10

Table 8-3. Response Cost: Summary of Comparative Treatment Studies.

Study	Population and Problem	Treatment Method(s)	Measures	Most Effective Treatment
Harmatz & Lapuc (1968)	Adult psychiatric patients for weight problems	Response cost, group therapy	Weight in pounds	Response cost
Humphrey, Karoly, & Kirschenbaum (1978)	Reading rate of behaviorally disturbed children	Response cost, self-reward	Standardized reading tests	Self-reward
Kaufman & O'Leary (1972)	16 children in a psychiatric hospital for disruptive behavior	Response cost, rewards	Observations	No difference
Kazdin (1973)	Speech dysfluencies of mentally retarded adults	Response cost, aversive stimulation, information control	Observations	Response cost
McLaughlin & Malaby (1972)	27 sixth-grade children for inappropriate vocalizations	Response cost, rewards	Observations	Rewards
Phillips, Phillips, Fixsen, & Wolf (1971)	6 adolescent boys for following rules such as promptness to meals and cleaning one's room	Response cost, token reinforcement, both combined	Observations	Both combined

(continued)

Table 8-3 (continued)

Study	Population and Problem	Treatment Method(s)	Measures	Most Effective Treatment
Reisinger (1972)	Adult female for anxiety-depression	Token reinforcement plus response cost, extinction	Observations	Token reinforcement, response cost
Schmauk (1970)	Sociopathic and normal adults on learning task	Response cost, contingent electrical shock, social disapproval	Observations	Response cost for sociopaths, no difference for normals
Thompson, Kodluboy, & Heston (1980)	One mildly mentally retarded woman with Prader-Willi Syndrome for obesity	Social isolation plus response cost, response cost	Weight in pounds	Social isolation plus response cost

subjects who decreased aberrant responding by 50 percent or more, while eight of 10 persons with response cost had such decrements. Similarly, generalization of treated responses in this well-controlled group study was greatest for the response cost group.

Several hypotheses were raised for why response cost proved most effective. It was assumed, for example, that providing a tangible reinforcer (token) at the beginning of treatment might elicit affective responses conducive to less dysfluent speech. The subsequent exchange of tokens for backup rewards may enhance further the nonanxiety-provoking cues of treatment. Thus, few dysfluencies may have been due to stress reduction.

Alternately, the greater effectiveness of response cost might be due to reinforcement for fluent speech provided for the response cost group. This is supported by laboratory studies of punishment that have shown that providing reinforcement for an alternative response increases the effectiveness of punishment (Azrin & Holz, 1966). (This has been discussed at length elsewhere in this book.)

A second comparative study took place in a second-grade reading class located in an inner-city school (Humphrey, Karoly, & Kirschenbaum, 1978). Eighteen children with behavior problems as well as deficits in reading rate were selected from this group. Children were assigned to one of two conditions, reinforcement or response cost. In the self-reward group, the child placed tokens from one dispenser prefilled with tokens to a cup that signified reinforcers that could be kept contingent upon accurate performance on the reading tasks.

In the self-imposed response cost group children started with all their tokens in the cup, which signified reinforcers that could be kept. They were to remove tokens from the cup as a penalty for inappropriate behavior. Thus, the conditions for the study were in effect contingent reinforcement versus contingent response cost.

Under both conditions each type of self-management resulted in increased reading rate. The authors noted, however, that self-reward was more effective. Several reasons were hypothesized for this effect. First, self-imposed cost may have been more difficult to use because it required children to subtract rather than add and to adjust the quantity of tokens they fined themselves. Another explanation put forth was fear of failure (Kagen & Kagan, 1970), which basically means in this case that the children would have minimized errors in order to avoid losing reinforcement. It is believed that to eliminate errors children may have worked more slowly.

A study that might be considered comparative in nature, albeit a weak one, was reported by Thompson, Kodluboy, and Heston

(1980). They treated a 22-year-old mildly retarded woman with Prader-Willi syndrome for obesity. Initial treatment consisted of the client either earning points for weight loss or else losing points and being socially isolated if half a pound or more was gained in a given day. Additionally, she was put on a fixed-calorie diet throughout this first and all succeeding conditions.

During the first month of hospitalization, treatment consisted of losing points (response cost) and social isolation for weight gain. This method was compared to response cost and aversive therapy consisting of alternately presenting slides of high- and low-calorie foods. After a high-calorie slide had been presented for 15 seconds, a 25-sec/5-ma/250-volt electric shock was presented across the first and third fingers of the right hand using stainless steel skin electrodes and electrode jelly. No consequences were associated with low-calorie slides. The authors concluded that close supervision with point loss consequences (response cost) for inappropriate eating was the most effective procedure in obtaining weight loss. No rationale for these effects was noted.

Harmatz and Lapuc (1968) also used response cost for the treatment of weight problems. In their study, obese psychiatric patients were treated with either group therapy or response cost after being placed on a calorie-restricted diet during meals. Those receiving response cost lost money if weight was not lost each week, while those in group therapy discussed underlying causes of obesity and received praise for weight loss. While response cost was more effective, differences were not great.

In yet another comparative study, Phillips, Phillips, Fixsen, and Wolf (1971) evaluated the relative efficacy of token reinforcement, response cost, and a combination of these procedures to treat several maladaptive behaviors of adolescent boys. The combined procedure was the most effective, with response cost alone being the second most effective method.

Schmauk (1970) also compared the effectiveness of response cost to other methods in effectiveness. Sociopathic and normal individuals were treated either with physical punishment in the form of contingent shock, loss of money (response cost), or social disapproval for making errors on a learning task. Normals learned equally well under all conditions, but with the sociopaths response cost was the most effective treatment.

McLaughlin and Malaby (1972) treated 27 children in a sixth-grade classroom for inappropriate verbalizations. Initially, response cost was implemented and was correlated with a low but steady rate of verbalizations. Point gain contingent on quiet behavior produced a marked decrease in inappropriate verbalizations. A return to contingent point loss was accompanied by an increasing rate of inappropriate verbalizations which decreased when quiet behavior was reinforced again.

The authors did hypothesize as to what resulted in the differential effectiveness of the treatments. It was assumed that, if adult attention functions as reinforcement for some children, then removal of points at the teacher's request may serve to reinforce and maintain the occurrence of inappropriate verbalizations in the classroom rather than eliminate them. This hypothesis was considered feasible because, under another condition, the teacher had ignored verbalizations and reinforced quiet behavior, resulting in a decreased rate of inappropriate verbalizations.

Kaufman and O'Leary (1972) compared response cost and a reward program for treating disruptive behavior. Treatment was carried out in a psychiatric hospital with 16 children in their classroom setting. The nine categories of behavior for which children were fined or rewarded included (1) out-of-chair, (2) modified out-of-chair (unlike item 1, some portion of the child's body was still in contact with the chair), (3) taking others' property, (4) vocalizations, (5) playing, (6) orienting, (7) noise, (8) aggression, and (9) time-off-task. No appreciable difference in either treatment was noted. Further, the authors did not provide a rationale for these findings.

In one final example, Reisinger (1972) treated a 20-year-old woman residing in a psychiatric hospital for anxiety and depression. Target behaviors were excessive crying and failure to smile. Token reinforcement for smiling and token loss for crying (referred to as token economy) were compared to extinction alone for the inappropriate response, and fading of token reinforcement to social praise for performing an appropriate behavior. Procedures were applied in a single-case fashion consisting of baseline, token economy, extinction, reversal, token plus social reinforcement, and social reinforcement alone. The token economy was effective, whereas extinction was not. A significant aspect of this study was that the token program could be faded so that social praise would be sufficient to maintain change.

Time-Out

As noted earlier, time-out from reinforcement is one of the most widely researched punishment procedures. Thus, as one might expect, several comparative studies have been conducted. O'Brien,

Table 8-4. Time-Out: Summary of Comparative Treatment Studies.

Study	Population and Problem	Treatment Method(s)	Measures	Most Effective Treatment
Lahey, McNees, & McNees (1973)	10-year-old boy for obscene speech	Time-out, instructed repetition	Observations	Time-out
O'Brien, Bugle, & Azrin (1972)	Profoundly retarded female child for proper eating	Time-out, time-out plus manual guidance, manual guidance	Observations	Time-out plus manual guidance
Plummer, Baer, & LeBlanc (1977)	8 preschool children for disruptive behavior	Paced instructions with and without time-out	Observations	Paced instructions alone
Roberts, McMahon, Forehand, & Humphreys (1978)	27 mother-child pairs for compliance with instructions	Command training, time-out plus command training	Observations	Time-out plus command training

Bugle, and Azrin (1972) reported one such study. They trained socially appropriate eating to a six-year-old girl, who was profoundly mentally retarded. They used manual guidance, which could be conceptualized as a nonverbal prompting procedure, and interrupted extinction. This latter method was, in effect, a form of time-out, since it involved removing food from the individual. This conceptualization seems appropriate, since Azrin and his colleagues in later work refer to a similar procedure as time-out (removal of food tray for a brief period based on an error in the self-feeding procedure). Conditions were A (baseline), B (interrupted extinction), A, C (manual guidance), D (B and C), A, B, and A. The manual guidance plus interrupted extinction was the most effective method.

Lahey, McNees, and McNees (1973) modified the rather unusual behavior of a 10-year-old borderline mentally retarded boy who was treated for obscene vocalizations accompanied by facial twitches. Conditions were A (baseline), B (instructed repetition), C (time-out), A, and B. During instructed repetition the child was required to repeat rapidly the most frequent obscene word. Whenever he stopped, the instructions were given again. This procedure continued for 15 minutes. For time-out he was placed in a room designed for time-out (see Chapter 4) for a minimum of five minutes and until he was quiet for at least one minute. Instructed repetition had little effect, but time-out was highly successful.

Yet another comparative study employing time-out is reported by Roberts, McMahon, Forehand, and Humphreys (1978). They investigated the effects of parental instruction-giving and child compliance by studying 27 mother–child pairs randomly assigned to one of three conditions: (1) command training, (2) command plus time-out training, and (3) a no-treatment group. Command training involved having parents issue specific, single instructions followed by a five-second interval in which the parent did not physically interfere or verbally interrupt the child. Those who employed the second active treatment used all aspects of the command training and in addition they employed a four-step time-out program. This consisted of giving feedback on the behavior to be punished, guiding the child to the time-out area, ignoring the child for a two minute period, and employing a back-up penalty for children who left time-out too soon. The latter treatment proved to be the most effective.

Plummer, Baer, and LeBlanc (1977) treated eight preschoolers (four to six years of age) for disruptive behavior. Treatments consisted of paced instructions with and without a time-out contingency. When time-out was used, the teacher was asked to stop interacting with the child for one minute following each disruption. Paced instructions, on the other hand, consisted of giving one instruction to the child per minute on a paced schedule. The paced instructions alone procedure proved to be an effective method while the paced instructions plus time-out method, described here, did not.

Extinction

There are few comparative studies in the research literature for treating aberrant behavior with extinction, especially compared to many of the other methods (see Table 8-5). In one such report, Lovaas and Simmons (1969) treated two severely and one profoundly mentally retarded children for self-injurious behavior. In the case of extinction, two children were treated for self-injurious behavior by ignoring the behavior. Contingent electric shock was employed with all of the children, also for frequently hitting themselves. It was concluded by the authors that: "withdrawing or making potential reinforcers unavailable has an undesirable attribute, in that it is not immediately effective and temporarily exposes the child to the danger of severe damage from his own self-destruction, which is particularly intense during the early stages of the extinction run. In some cases of severe self-destruction, it is ill-advised to place the child on extinction" (p. 159). The authors further concluded that, based on their findings and those of others, contingent electric shock is more rapid in its effects and is to be preferred over extinction.

In another comparative study, Steeves, Martin, and Pear (1970) evaluated time-out and extinction with two mentally retarded boys. In this study, extinction in an ABC design proved to be the more effective method for controlling inattentive behavior.

Physical Restraint

This procedure, unfortunately, has been researched infrequently relative to the frequency of its use. As a result, only one comparative study could be found, and in that case an autistic girl was the subject (see Table 8-6). Treatments for her frequent tantrums and self-stimulation consisted of restraining body parts not involved in self-stimulating (e.g., holding shoulders and knees) or restraining body parts topographically specific to self-stimulation, such as the hands. Topographically specific restraint proved to be the more effective method. This may have been the case, according to the authors, because the procedure minimized the reinforcing attributes of the environment.

Table 8-5. Extinction: Summary of Comparative Treatment Studies.

Study	Population and Problem	Treatment Method(s)	Measures	Most Effective Treatment
Lovaas & Simmons (1969)	Self-injurious behavior of 3 mentally retarded children	Extinction, contingent electric shock	Observations	Contingent electric shock
Steeves, Martin, & Pear (1970)	Inattentive behavior of two mentally retarded boys	Extinction, time-out	Observations	Extinction

Table 8-6. Physical Restraint: Summary of Comparative Treatment Studies.

Study	Population and Problem	Treatment Method(s)	Measures	Most Effective Treatment
Solnick, Rincover, & Peterson (1977)	Autistic girl who self-stimulated	Topographically specific restraint, nontopographically specific restraint	Observations	Topographically specific restraint

Analysis of Comparative
Treatment Studies

Some general conclusions also may be derived from an analysis of the tables and our discussion in the preceding section. For example, in almost every instance, direct observations were the only method of obtaining outcome data. Deviations from this point included response cost studies. Two of the three papers were weight reduction studies where pounds, a conventional dependent variable for this type of work, were assessed.

All the studies reviewed were conducted in the last 15 years and no dramatic trend in a decrease or increase in the number of studies was noted. Covert sensitization, physical restraint, and extinction were the least studied procedures while response cost, overcorrection, and time-out were the most studied. Surprisingly, the number of studies that compared three or more treatments was almost equal to the number that compared two. Pragmatically, it would seem that it is much easier to get the requisite number of subjects and implement the necessary methodological controls with two treatments. However, the reason that the more complex comparisons have been undertaken so frequently is that in many cases the primary purpose was to find an effective treatment rather than to compare treatments for relative effectiveness in a highly controlled number. The overcorrection studies, which in all but one case compared three or more treatments, may exemplify this principle best.

A very general analysis of the tabled data for evaluating treatment effectiveness showed that covert sensitization was most effective in one study, while overcorrection was most effective in seven of eight of the reviewed studies. The picture of least clarity relative to a treatment's effectiveness was noted with response cost. In two instances response cost alone was the most effective treatment, although it was the most effective method when used alone or combined with something else in six of nine cases. In two cases something other than response cost was most effective and in one case no difference was noted. With time-out, this method alone or in combination with something else proved to be the most effective treatment in three of four cases. Extinction was the most effective method in one of two studies compared while topographically specific restraint proved more effective than nontopographically specific restraint in the one instance where it was evaluated in a comparative study.

In this chapter an effort has been made to compare the relative efficacy of punishment procedures where comparative studies have been performed. As noted previously in this chapter, the reported studies rarely met even a few of the points considered important for comparative research by the authors. This is certainly disappointing. However, an encouraging note is that the most recent studies appeared to be the more methodologically sound investigations.

A second point is that authors who have traditionally studied one type of punishment method, such as overcorrection, have typically found that method superior to other approaches. This phenomenon is also evident within the context of other punishment methods. This may imply that the dependent variables selected for particular treatments may have inadvertently been biased toward a particular treatment. Additionally, the authors conducting much of the research on a particular topic are more familiar with specific methods relative to others. As a result, these researchers may be able to apply their preferred approach in a more accurate and efficient manner. In any event, this factor could further confound the obtained results and warrants cross validation via future research.

Conclusions

While we have noted throughout this book that further research is needed, at the same time, we do not wish to appear too critical. Relative to nonbehavioral approaches, the research indicating the effectiveness of punishment methods for the problems discussed is quite good. Additionally, while well-delineated method sections are still the exception rather than the rule, this situation has improved. Many of the best examples of well-detailed methodology sections in the social sciences are typically found in the behavioral journals. More research and better means of determining applicability of certain treatments are needed not only with respect to punishment procedures but also with other methods as well.

It is our view that in many cases, policy makers, administrators, and many professionals have overreacted concerning the use of punishment methods. Part of the problem is a misunderstanding of the methods themselves. Our firm contention and hope is that those who read this book will understand and be better prepared to design punishment methods when justified. If punishment procedures are used judiciously, with proper safety guidelines, and in appropriate situations, such an approach may take into consideration the best interests of the client and all professional personnel concerned.

References

Abel, G., Levis, D., & Clancy, J. Aversion therapy applied to taped sequences of deviant behavior in exhibitionism and other sexual deviation. A preliminary report. *Journal of Behavior Therapy and Experimental Psychiatry*, 1970, *1*, 59–60.

Abroms, G. M. Setting limits. *Archives of General Psychiatry*, 1968, *19*, 113–119.

Accreditation Council for Services for the Mentally Retarded and Other Developmentally Disabled Persons. *Standards for services for developmentally disabled individuals.* Chicago: Joint Commission on Accreditation of Hospitals, 1978.

Adams, K. M., Klinge, V. K., & Keiser, T. W. The extinction of a self-injurious behavior in an epileptic child. *Behaviour Research and Therapy*, 1973, *11*, 351–356.

Adams, M. R., & Popelka, G. The influence of "time-out" on stutterers and their dysfluency. *Behavior Therapy*, 1971, *2*, 334–339.

Adler, A. *The education of children.* (E. Jensen & F. Jensen, trans.) Chicago: Regnery, 1970. (Original publication, 1930.)

Agras, W. S. Toward the certification of behavior therapists. *Journal of Applied Behavior Analysis*, 1973, *6*, 167–171.

Alevizos, K. J., & Alevizos, P. N. The effects of verbalizing contingencies in time-out procedures. *Journal of Behavior Therapy and Experimental Psychiatry*, 1975, *6*, 253–255.

Alexander, R. N., Corbett, T. F., & Smigel, J. The effects of individual and group consequences on school attendance and curfew violations with predelinquent adolescents. *Journal of Applied Behavior Analysis*, 1976, *9*, 221–226.

Alford, G. S., Blanchard, E. B., & Buckley, T. M. Treatment of hysterical vomiting by modification of social contingencies: A case study. *Journal of Behavior Therapy and Experimental Psychiatry*, 1972, *3*, 209–212.

Allen, K. E., & Harris, F. R. Elimination of a child's excessive scratching by training the mother in reinfocement procedures. *Behaviour Research and Therapy*, 1966, *4*, 79–84.

Allison, T. S., & Allison, S. L. Time out from reinforcement: Effect on sibling aggression. *Psychological Record*, 1971, *21*, 81–86.

Altman, I., & Wohlwill, J. F. *Children and the environment.* New York: Plenum Press, 1978.

Altman, K., Haavik, S., & Cook, J. W. Punishment of self-injurious behavior in natural settings using contingent aromatic ammonia. *Behaviour Research and Therapy*, 1978, *16*, 85–96.

Aman, M. G., & Singh, N. The usefulness of thioridazine in childhood disorders—Fact or folklore? *American Journal of Mental Deficiency*, 1979, *84*, 331–338.

American Psychological Association. *Ethical standards of psychologists: 1979 Revision.* Washington, D.C.: American Psychological Association, 1979.

Anant, S. S. The use of verbal aversion (negative conditioning) with an alcoholic: A case report. *Behaviour Research and Therapy*, 1968, *6*, 695–696.

Anderson, L. T., Herrmann, L., Alpert, M., & Dancis, J. Elimination of self-mutilation in Lesch-Nyhan disease. *Pediatric Research*, 1975, *9*, 257.

Apolito, P. M., & Sulzer-Azaroff, B. Lemon-juice therapy: The control of chronic vomiting in a twelve-year-old profoundly retarded female. *Education and Treatment of Children*, 1981, *4*, 339–347.

Appel, J. B. The aversive control of an operant discrimination. *Journal of the Experimental Analysis of Behavior*, 1960, *3*, 35–37.

Appel, J. B. Punishment and shock intensity. *Science*, 1963, *141*, 528–529.

Applezweig, M. H. Response potential as a function of effort. *Journal of Comparative and Physiological Psychology*, 1951, *44*, 225–235.

Aragona, J., Cassady, J., & Drabman, R. S. Treating overweight children through parental training and contingency management. *Journal of Applied Behavior Analysis*, 1975, *8*, 269–278.

Aronfreed, J. Aversive control of socialization. In W. J. Arnold (ed.), *Nebraska symposium on motivation.* Lincoln: University of Nebraska Press, 1968.

Aronfreed, J., & Reber, A. Internalized behavioral suppression and the timing of social punishment. *Journal of Personality and Social Psychology*, 1965, *1*, 3–16.

Ashem, B., & Donner, L. Covert sensitization with alcoholics: A controlled replication. *Behaviour Research and Therapy*, 1968, *6*, 7–12.

Association for Advancement of Behavior Therapy. Ethical issues for human service. *Behavior Therapy*, 1977, *8*, 763–764.

Atkeson, B. M., & Forehand, R. Home-based reinforcement programs designed to modify classroom behavior: A review and methodological evaluation. *Psychological Bulletin*, 1979, *86*, 1298–1308.

Axelrod, S., Brantner, J. P., & Meddock, T. D. Overcorrection: A review and critical analysis. *The Journal of Special Education*, 1978, *12*, 367–391.

Ayllon, T., & Azrin, N. H. Reinforcement sampling: A technique for increasing the behavior of mental patients. *Journal of Applied Behavior Analysis*, 1968, *1*, 13–20. (a)

Ayllon, T., & Azrin, N. H. *The token economy: A motivational system for therapy and rehabilitation.* New York: Appleton-Century-Crofts, 1968. (b)

Ayllon, T., & Haughton, E. Modification of symptomatic verbal behavior of mental patients. *Behaviour Research and Therapy*, 1964, *2*, 84–97.

Ayllon, T., Layman, S., & Burke, S. Disruptive behavior and reinforcement of academic performance. *The Psychological Record*, 1972, *22*, 315–323.

Ayllon, T., Layman, D., & Kandel, H. J. A behavioral–educational alternative to drug control of hyperactive children. *Journal of Applied Behavior Analysis*, 1975, *8*, 137–146.

Ayllon, T., & Michael, J. The psychiatric nurse as a behavioral engineer. *Journal of the Experimental Analysis of Behavior*, 1959, *2*, 323–334.

Ayllon, T., & Skuban, W. Accountability in psychotherapy: A test case. *Journal of Behavior Therapy and Experimental Psychiatry*, 1973, *4*, 19–30.

Azrin, N. H. Some effects of two intermittent schedules of immediate and non-immediate punishment. *Journal of Psychology*, 1956, *42*, 3–21.

Azrin, N. H. Some effects of noise on human behavior. *Journal of the Experimental Analysis of Behavior*, 1958, *1*, 183–200.

Azrin, N. H. Punishment and recovery during fixed-ratio performance. *Journal of the Experimental Analysis of Behavior*, 1959, *2*, 301–305.

Azrin, N. H. Effects of punishment intensity during variable-interval reinforcement. *Journal of the Experimental Analysis of Behavior*, 1960, *3*, 123–142. (a)

Azrin, N. H. Sequential effects of punishment. *Science*, 1960, *131*, 605–606. (b)

Azrin, N. H., & Armstrong, P. M. The "mini-meal"—A method for teaching eating skills to the profoundly retarded. *Mental Retardation*, 1973, *11*, 9–13.

Azrin, N. H., Besalel, V. A., & Wisotezek, I. E. Treatment of self-injury by a reinforcement plus interruption procedure. *Analysis and Intervention in Developmental Disabilities*, 1982, *2*, 105–113.

Azrin, N. H., & Foxx, R. M. A rapid method of toilet training the institutionalized retarded. *Journal of Applied Behavior Analysis*, 1971, *4*, 89–99.

Azrin, N. H., Gottlieb, L., Hughart, L., Wesolowski, M. D., & Rahn, T. Eliminating self-injurious behavior by educative procedures. *Behaviour Research and Therapy*, 1975, *13*, 101–111.

Azrin, N. H., & Holz, W. C. Punishment during fixed-interval reinforcement. *Journal of the Experimental Analysis of Behavior*, 1961, *4*, 343–347.

Azrin, N. H., & Holz, W. C. Punishment. In W. K. Honig (ed.), *Operant behavior: Areas of research and application.* New York: Appleton-Century-Crofts, 1966.

Azrin, N. H., Holz, W. C., & Hake, D. Fixed-ratio punishment. *Journal of the Experimental Analysis of Behavior*, 1963, *6*, 141–148.

Azrin, N. H., & Hutchison, R. R. Conditioning of the aggressive behavior of pigeons by a fixed-interval schedule of reinforcement. *Journal of the Experimental Analysis of Behavior,* 1967, *10,* 395–402.

Azrin, N. H., Kaplan, S. J., & Foxx, R. M. Autism reversal: Eliminating stereotyped self-stimulation of retarded individuals. *American Journal of Mental Deficiency,* 1973, *78,* 241–248.

Azrin, N. H., & Nunn, R. G. Habit reversal: A method of eliminating nervous habits and tics. *Behaviour Research and Therapy,* 1973, *11,* 619–628.

Azrin, N. H., Nunn, R. G., & Frantz, S. E. Habit reversal vs. negative practice treatment of nailbiting. *Behaviour Research and Therapy,* 1980, *18,* 281–285. (a)

Azrin, N. H., Nunn, R. G., & Frantz, S. E. Habit reversal vs. negative practice treatment of nervous tics. *Behavior Therapy,* 1980, *11,* 169–178. (b)

Azrin, N. H., & Powers, M. A. Eliminating classroom disturbances of emotionally disturbed children by positive practice procedures. *Behavior Therapy,* 1975, *6,* 525–534.

Azrin, N. H., Sneed, T. J., & Foxx, R. M. Dry bed: A rapid method of eliminating (enuresis) of the retarded. *Behavior Therapy,* 1973, *11,* 427–434.

Azrin, N. H., Sneed, T. J., & Foxx, R. M. Dry-bed training: Rapid elimination of childhood enuresis. *Behaviour Research and Therapy,* 1974, *12,* 147–156.

Azrin, N. H., & Wesolowski, M. D. Theft reversal: An overcorrection procedure for eliminating stealing by retarded persons. *Journal of Applied Behavior Analysis,* 1974, *7,* 577–582.

Azrin, N. H., & Wesolowski, M. D. Eliminating habitual vomiting in a retarded adult by positive practice and self-correction. *Journal of Behavior Therapy and Experimental Psychiatry,* 1975, *6,* 145–148. (a)

Azrin, N. H., & Wesolowski, M. D. The use of positive practice to eliminate persistent floor sprawling by profoundly retarded persons. *Behavior Therapy,* 1975, *6,* 627–631. (b)

Bach, R., & Moylan, J. H. Parents administered behavior therapy for inappropriate urination and encopresis: A case study. *Journal of Behavior Therapy and Experimental Psychiatry,* 1976, *6,* 239–241.

Bachman, J. A. Self-injurious behavior: A behavioral analysis. *Journal of Abnormal Psychology,* 1972, *80,* 211–224.

Baer, D. M. Laboratory control of thumbsucking by withdrawal and representation of reinforcement. *Journal of the Experimental Analysis of Behavior,* 1962, *5,* 525–528.

Baer, D. M. A case for the selective reinforcement of punishment. In C. Neuringer & J. L. Michael (eds.), *Behavior modification in clinical psychology.* New York: Appleton-Century-Crofts, 1970.

Bandura, A. *Principles of behavior modification.* New York: Holt, Rinehart & Winston, 1969.

Bandura, A. *Social learning theory.* Englewood Cliffs, N.J.: Prentice-Hall, 1977.

Bandura, A., & Perloff, B. Relative efficacy of self-monitored and externally imposed reinforcement systems. *Journal of Personality and Social Psychology*, 1967, *7*, 111–116.

Banks, M., & Locke, B. J. *Self-injurious stereotypes and mild punishment with retarded subjects.* (Working paper No. 123.) Parsons, Kan.: Parsons Research Project, 1966.

Barkley, R. A., & Zupnick, S. Reduction of stereotypic body contortions using physical restraint and DRO. *Journal of Behavior Therapy and Experimental Psychiatry*, 1976, *7*, 167–170.

Barlow, J. A. Secondary motivation through classical conditioning: One trial nonmotor learning in the white rat. *American Psychologist*, 1952, *7*, 273.

Barlow, D. H., Leitenberg, H., & Agras, W. S. Experimental control of sexual deviation through manipulation of the noxious scene in covert sensitization. *Journal of Abnormal Psychology*, 1969, *74*, 596–601.

Barmann, B. C. Use of contingent vibration in the treatment of self-stimulatory hand-mouthing and ruminative vomiting behavior. *Journal of Behavior Therapy and Experimental Psychiatry*, 1980, *11*, 307–311.

Baroff, G. S. & Tate, B. G. The use of aversive stimulation in the treatment of chronic self-injurious behavior. *Journal of the American Academy of Child Psychiatry*, 1968, *7*, 454–470.

Baron, A. Functions of CS and UCS in fear conditioning. *Journal of Comparative and Physiological Psychology*, 1959, *52*, 591–593.

Baron, A., & Kaufman, A. Human, free-operant avoidance of "time-out" from monetary reinforcement. *Journal of the Experimental Analysis of Behavior*, 1966, *9*, 557–565.

Barrett, B. Behavior modification in the home: Parents adapt laboratory-developed tactics to bowel-train a 5½-year-hold. *Psychotherapy: Theory, Research and Practice*, 1969, *6*, 172–176.

Barrett, B. H. Reduction in rate of multiple tics by free operant conditioning methods. *Journal of Nervous and Mental Disease*, 1962, *135*, 187–195.

Barrett, R. P., & Shapiro, E. S. Treatment of stereotyped hair-pulling with overcorrection: A case study with long term follow-up. *Journal of Behavior Therapy and Experimental Psychiatry*, 1980, *11*, 317–320.

Barton, E. J., & Madsen, J. J. The use of awareness and omission training to control excessive drooling in a severely retarded youth. *Child Behavior Therapy*, 1980, *2*, 55–63.

Barton, E. J., & Osborne, J. G. The development of classroom sharing by a teacher using positive practice. *Behavior Modification*, 1978, *2*, 231–250.

Barton, E. S. Operant conditioning of appropriate and inappropriate social speech in the profoundly retarded. *Journal of Mental Deficiency Research*, 1973, *17*, 183–191.

Barton, E. S., Guess, D., Garcia, E., & Baer, D. M. Improvement of retardates' mealtime behaviors by timeout procedures using multiple baseline techniques. *Journal of Applied Behavior Analysis*, 1970, *3*, 77–84.

Bassett, J. E., Blanchard, E. B., & Koshland, E. On determining reinforcing stimuli: Armchair versus empirical procedures. *Behavior Therapy*, 1977, *8*, 205–212.

Baum, W. M. The correlation-based law of effect. *Journal of the Experimental Analysis of Behavior*, 1973, *20*, 137–153.

Baumeister, A. A., & Forehand, R. Effects of extinction of an instrumental response on stereo-typed body rocking in severe retardates. *The Psychological Record*, 1971, *21*, 235–240.

Baumeister, A. A., & Forehand, R. Effects of contingent shock and verbal command on body rocking of retardates. *Journal of Clinical Psychology*, 1972, *28*, 586–590.

Baumeister, A. A., & Rollings, J. P. Self-injurious behavior. In N. R. Ellis (ed.), *International review of research in mental retardation*. New York: Academic Press, 1976.

Becker, J. V., Turner, S. M., & Sajwaj, T. E. Multiple behavioral effects of the use of lemon juice with a ruminating toddler-age child. *Behavior Modification*, 1978, *2*, 267–278.

Becker, W. C. *Parents are teachers*. Champaign, Ill.: Research Press, 1971.

Begelman, D. A. Ethical and legal issues of behavior modification. In M. Hersen, R. M. Eisler, & P. M. Miller (eds.), *Progress in behavior modification* (Vol 1). New York: Academic Press, 1975.

Bellack, A. S., & Hersen, M. *Behavior modification: An introductory textbook*. New York: Oxford University Press, 1977.

Benjamin, A. *The helping interview*. Boston: Houghton Mifflin, 1974.

Bennett, D. Elimination of habitual vomiting using DRO procedures. *The Behavior Therapist*, 1980, *3*(1), 16–18.

Berecz, J. M. Aversion by fiat: The problem of "face validity" in behavior therapy. *Behavior Therapy*, 1973, *4*, 110–116.

Berecz, J. Treatment of smoking with cognitive conditioning therapy: A self-administered aversion technique. *Behavior Therapy*, 1976, *7*, 641–648.

Bigelow, G., Liebson, I., & Griffiths, R. Alcoholic drinking: Suppression by a brief time-out procedure. *Behaviour Research and Therapy*, 1974, *12*, 107–115.

Birnbrauer, J. S. Generalization of punishment effects—A case study. *Journal of Applied Behavior Analysis*, 1968, *1*, 201–211.

Birnbrauer, J. S., Wolf, M. M., Kidder, J. D., & Tague, C. E. Classroom behavior of retarded pupils with token reinforcement. *Journal of Experimental Child Psychology*, 1965, *2*, 19–39.

Bittle, R., & Hake, D. F. A multi-element design model for component analysis and cross-setting assessment of a treatment package. *Behavior Therapy*, 1977, *8*, 906–914.

Blakemore, C. B., Thorpe, J. G., Barker, J. C., Conway, C. G., & Lavin, N. I. The application of faradic aversion conditioning in a case of transvestism. *Behaviour Research and Therapy*, 1963, *1*, 29–34.

Blanchard, E. G., Libet, J. M., & Young, L. D. Apneic aversion and covert sensitization in the treatment of a hydrocarbon inhalation addiction: A case study. *Journal of Behavior Therapy and Experimental Psychiatry*, 1973, *4*, 383–387.

Boland, F. J., Mellor, C. S., & Revusky, S. Chemical aversion treatment of alcoholism: Lithium as the aversive agent. *Behaviour Research and Therapy*, 1978, *16*, 401–409.

Bootzin, R. R. *Behavior modification and therapy: An introduction.* Cambridge: Winthrop Publishers, 1975.

Bornstein, P. H., Hamilton, S. B. & Quevillon, P. R. Behavior modification by long-distance. Demonstration of functional control over disruptive behavior in a rural classroom setting. *Behavior Modification*, 1977, *1*, 369–394.

Bostow, D., & Bailey, J. B. Modification of severe disruptive and aggressive behavior using brief timeout and reinforcement procedures. *Journal of Applied Behavior Analysis*, 1969, *2*, 31–37.

Brady, J. V. Animal experimental evaluation of drug effects upon behavior. *Proceedings of the Association on Research in Nervous and Mental Disease*, 1969, *37*, 104–125.

Brandsma, J. M., & Stein, L. I. The use of punishment as a treatment modality: A case report. *Journal of Nervous and Mental Disease*, 1973, *156*, 30–37.

Braun, S. H. Ethical issues in behavior modification. *Behavior Therapy*, 1975, *6*, 51–62.

Brawley, E. R., Harris, F. R., Allen, K. E., Fleming, R. S., & Peterson, R. F. Behavior modification of an autistic child. *Behavioral Science*, 1969, *14*, 87–97.

Brethower, D. M., & Reynolds, G. S. A facilitative effect of punishment on unpunished behavior. *Journal of the Experimental Analysis of Behavior*, 1962, *5*, 191–199.

Bright, G. O., & Whaley, D. L. Suppression of regurgitation and rumination with aversive events. *Michigan Mental Health Research Bulletin*, 1968, *11*, 17–20.

Brodsky, G. The relation between verbal and non-verbal behavior change. *Behaviour Research and Therapy*, 1967, *5*, 183–191.

Bromberg, N. Is punishment dead? *American Journal of Psychiatry*, 1970, *127*, 245–248.

Brown, B. S., Wienckowski, L. A., & Stolz, S. B. *Behavior modification: Perspective on a current issue.* U.S. Department of Health, Education, and Welfare Publication No. (ADM) 75-202, Washington, D.C.: U.S. Government Printing Office, 1975.

Brownell, K. D., & Barlow, D. H. The behavioral treatment of sexual deviation. In A. Goldstein & E. B. Foa (eds.), *Handbook of behavioral interventions*. New York: John Wiley, 1980.

Browning, R. M. Treatment effects of a total behavior modification program with five autistic children. *Behaviour Research and Therapy*, 1971, *9*, 319–327.

Bucher, B., & King, L. W. Generalization of punishment effects in the deviant behavior of a psychotic child. *Behavior Therapy*, 1971, *2*, 68–77.

Bucher, B., & Lovaas, O. I. Use of aversive stimulation in behavior modification. In M. R. Jones (ed.), *Miami symposium on the prediction of behavior 1967: Aversive stimulation*. Coral Gables, Fla.: University of Miami Press, 1968.

Budd, K. S., & Baer, D. M. Behavior modification and the law: Implications of recent judicial decisions. *The Journal of Psychiatry and Law*, 1976, *4*, 171–244.

Burchard, J. D., & Barrera, F. An analysis of timeout and response cost in a programmed environment. *Journal of Applied Behavior Analysis*, 1972, *5*, 271–279.

Burchard, J. D., & Tyler, V., Jr. The modification of delinquent behavior through operant conditioning. *Behaviour Research and Therapy*, 1965, *2*, 245–250.

Bursten, B. Using mechanical restraints on acutely disturbed psychiatric patients. *Hospital and Community Psychiatry*, 1975, *26*, 757–759.

Butler, J. F. Toilet training a child with spina bifida. *Journal of Behavior Therapy and Experimental Psychiatry*, 1976, *7*, 63–65.

Butler, J. F. Treatment of encopresis by overcorrection. *Psychological Reports*, 1977, *40*, 639–646.

Butterfield, W. H. Electric shock—safety factors when used for the aversive conditioning of humans. *Behavior Therapy*, 1975, *6*, 98–110.

Byrd, L. D. Responding in the cat maintained under reponse-independent electric shock and response-produced electric shock. *Journal of the Experimental Analysis of Behavior*, 1969, *12*, 1–10.

Byrd, L. D. Responding in the squirrel monkey under second-order schedules of shock delivery. *Journal of the Experimental Analysis of Behavior*, 1972, *18*, 155–167.

Caddy, G. R., & Lovibond, S. H. Self-regulation and discriminated aversive conditioning in the modification of alcoholic's drinking behavior. *Behavior Therapy*, 1976, *7*, 223–230.

Cahoon, D. Symptom substitution and the behavior therapies: A reappraisal. *Psychological Bulletin*, 1968, *69*, 149–156.

Calhoun, K. S., & Lima, P. P. Effects of varying schedules of timeout on high and low rate of behaviors in a retarded girl. *Journal of Behavior Therapy and Experimental Psychiatry*, 1977, *8*, 189–194.

Calhoun, K. S., & Matherne, P. The effects of varying schedules of time-out on aggressive behavior of a retarded girl. *Journal of Behavior Therapy and Experimental Psychiatry*, 1975, *6*, 139–143.

Canter, S., & Canter, D. Building for therapy. In D. Canter & S. Canter (eds.), *Designing for therapeutic environments: A review of research*. New York: John Wiley, 1979.

Carlson, C. S., Arnold, C. R., Becker, W. C., & Madsen, C. H. The elimination of tantrum behavior of a child in an elementary classroom. *Behaviour Research and Therapy*, 1968, *6*, 117–119.

Carr, E. The motivation of self-injurious behavior. In R. L. Koegel, A. Rincover, & A. L. Egel (eds.), *Educating and understanding autistic children*. San Diego: College-Hill Press, 1982.

Carr, E. G., Newsom, C. D., & Binkoff, J. A. Stimulus control of self-destructive behavior in a psychotic child. *Journal of Abnormal Child Psychology*, 1976, *4*, 139–153.

Carr, E. G., Newsom, C. D., & Binkoff, J. A. Escape as a factor in the aggressive behavior of two retarded children. *Journal of Applied Behavior Analysis*, 1980, *13*, 101–117.

Cautela, J. R. Treatment of compulsive behavior by covert sensitization. *Psychological Record*, 1966, *16*, 33–41.

Cautela, J. R. Covert sensitization. *Psychological Reports*, 1967, *20*, 459–468.

Cautela, J. R. Covert reinforcement. *Behavior Therapy*, 1970, *1,* 33–50. (a)

Cautela, J. R. Treatment of smoking by covert sensitization. *Psychological Reports*, 1970, *26*, 415–420. (b)

Cautela, J. R. The use of covert sensitization in the treatment of alcoholism. *Psychotherapy: Theory, Research and Practice*, 1970, *7*, 86–90. (c)

Cautela, J. R. Covert conditioning. In A. Jacobs & L. B. Sachs (eds.), *The psychology of private events*. New York: Academic Press, *1971*.

Cautela, J. R. The treatment of over-eating by covert conditioning. *Psychotherapy: Theory, Research and Practice*, 1972, *9*, 211–216.

Cautela, J. R. The use of covert conditioning in modifying pain behavior. *Journal of Behavior Therapy and Experimental Psychiatry*, 1977, *8*, 45–52.

Cautela, J. R., & Rosenstiel, A. K. The use of covert conditioning in the treatment of drug abuse. *International Journal of the Addictions*, 1975, *10*, 277–303.

Cautela, J. R., & Wall, C. C. Covert conditioning in clinical practice. In A. Goldstein & E. B. Foa (eds.), *Handbook of behavioral interventions*. New York: John Wiley, 1980.

Cautela, J. R., & Wisocki, P. A. The use of imagery in the modification of attitudes toward the elderly: A preliminary report. *Journal of Psychology*, 1969, *73*, 193–199.

Cayner, J. J., & Kiland, J. R. Use of brief time out with three schizophrenic patients. *Journal of Behavior Therapy and Experimental Psychiatry*, 1974, *5*, 141–145.

Church, R. M. The varied effects of punishment on behavior. *Psychological Review*, 1963, *70*, 369–402.

Ciminero, A. R., Doleys, D. M., & Davidson, R. S. Free-operant avoidance of alcohol. *Journal of Behavior Therapy and Experimental Psychiatry*, 1975, *6*, 242–245.

Cinciripini, P. M., Epstein, L. H., & Kotanchik, N. L. Behavioral intervention for self-stimulatory, attending and seizure behavior in a cerebral palsied child. *Journal of Behavior Therapy and Exerpimental Psychiatry,* 1980, *11,* 313–316.

Clark, D. F. Behavior therapy of Gilles de la Tourette's syndrome. *British Journal of Psychiatry,* 1967, *113,* 375–381.

Clark, H. B., Greene, B. F., MacRae, J. W., McNees, M. P., Davis, J. L., & Risley, T. R. A parent advice package for family shopping trips: Development and evaluation. *Journal of Applied Behavior Analysis,* 1977, *10,* 605–624.

Clark, H. B., Rowbury, T., Baer, C. M., & Baer, D. M. Timeout as a punishing stimulus in continuous and intermittent schedules. *Journal of Applied Behavior Analysis,* 1973, *6,* 443–455.

Conway, J. B., & Bucher, B. D. Soap in the mouth as an aversive consequence. *Behavior Therapy,* 1974, *5,* 154–156.

Cook, J. W., Altman, K., & Haavik, S. Consent for aversive treatment: A model form. *Mental Retardation,* 1978, *16,* 47–51.

Cook, J. W., Altman, K., Shaw, J., & Blaylock, M. Use of contingent lemon juice to eliminate public masturbation by a severely retarded boy. *Behaviour Research and Therapy,* 1978, *16,* 131–134.

Corte, H. E., Wolf, M. M., & Locke, B. J. A comparison of procedures for eliminating self-injurious behavior of retarded adolescents. *Journal of Applied Behavior Analysis,* 1971, *4,* 201–213.

Cotler, S. B., Applegate, G., King, L. W., & Kristal, S. Establishing a token economy program in a state hospital classroom. A lesson in training student and teacher. *Behavior Therapy,* 1972, *3,* 209–222.

Craven, W. F. Protecting hospitalized patients from electrical hazards. *Hewlett-Packard Journal,* 1970, *21,* 11–17.

Crider, A., Schwartz, G. E., & Shapiro, D. Operant suppression of electrodermal response rate as a function of punishment schedule. *Journal of Experimental Psychology,* 1970, *83,* 333–334.

Cunningham, C. E., & Linscheid, T. R. Elimination of chronic infant ruminating by electric shock. *Behavior Therapy,* 1976, *7,* 231–234.

Curtis, R. H., & Presley, A. S. The extinction of homosexual behavior by covert sensitization: A case study. *Behaviour Research and Therapy,* 1972, *10,* 81–83.

Danaher, B. G., & Lichtenstein, E. Aversion therapy issues: A note of clarification. *Behavior Therapy,* 1974, *5,* 112–116.

Davis, J. R., Wallace, C. J., Liberman, R. P., & Finch, B. E. The use of brief isolation to suppress delusional and hallucinatory speech. *Journal of Behavior Therapy and Experimental Psychiatry,* 1976, *7,* 269–275.

Davison, G. C. A social learning theory programme with an autistic child. *Behaviour Research and Therapy,* 1964, *2,* 149–159.

Davison, G. C. The training of undergraduates as social reinforcers for autistic children. In L. P. Ullmann & L. Krasner (eds.), *Case studies in behavior modification.* New York: Holt, Rinehart & Winston, 1965.

Davison, G. C. Elimination of a sadistic fantasy by client-controlled counterconditioning technique: A case study. *Journal of Abnormal and Social Psychology*, 1968, *73*, 84–90.

DeCatanzaro, D. A., & Baldwin, G. Effective treatment of self-injurious behavior through a forced arm exercise. *American Journal of Mental Deficiency*, 1978, *82*, 433–439.

Deitz, S. M. An analysis of programming DRL schedules in educational settings. *Behaviour Research and Therapy*, 1977, *15*, 103–111.

Deitz, S. M., & Repp, A. C. Decreasing classroom misbehavior through the use of DRL schedules of reinforcement. *Journal of Applied Behavior Analysis*, 1973, *6*, 457–463.

Deitz, S. M., & Repp, A. C. Differentially reinforcing low rates of misbehavior with normal elementary school children. *Journal of Applied Behavior Analysis*, 1974, *4*, 622.

Deitz, S. M., Repp, A. C., & Deitz, D. E. D. Reducing inappropriate classroom behavior of retarded students through three procedures of differential reinforcement. *Journal of Mental Deficiency Research*, 1976, *20*, 155–170.

Deitz, S. M., Slack, D. J., Schwarzmueller, E. B., Wilander, A. P., Weatherly, T. J., & Hilliard, G. Reducing inappropriate behavior in special classrooms by reinforcing average interresponse times: Interval DRL. *Behavior Therapy*, 1978, *9*, 37–46.

Delgado, J. M. R. Cerebral heterostimulation in a monkey colony. *Science*, 1963, *141*, 161–163.

Detrich, R. Personal communication, February 1982.

Deur, J. L., & Parke, R. D. Resistance to extinction and continuous punishment in humans as a function of partial reward and partial punishment training. *Psychonomic Science*, 1968, *13*, 91–93.

Deutsch, M., & Parks, L. A. The use of contingent music to increase appropriate conversational speech. *Mental Retardation*, 1978, *16*, 33–36.

Devany, J., & Rincover, A. Self-stimulatory behavior and sensory reinforcement. In R. L. Koegel, A. Rincover, & A. L. Egel (eds.), *Educating and understanding autistic children*. San Diego: College-Hill Press, 1982.

Dinsmoor, J. A. A discrimination based on punishment. *Quarterly Journal of Experimental Psychology*, 1952, *4*, 27–45.

Dobes, R. W. Amelioration of psychosomatic dermatosis by reinforced inhibition of scratching. *Journal of Behavior Therapy and Experimental Psychiatry*, 1977, *8*, 185–188.

Doke, L. A., & Epstein, L. H. Oral overcorrection: Side effects and extended applications. *Journal of Experimental Child Psychology*, 1975, *20*, 460–511.

Doleys, D. M., Wells, K. C., Hobbs, S. A., Roberts, M. W., & Cartelli, L. M. The effects of social punishment on noncompliance: A comparison with time out and positive practice. *Journal of Applied Behavior Analysis*, 1976, *9*, 471–482.

Doljanac, R. F., Schrader, S. J., & Christian, J. G. *Development of verbal interaction skills in the mentally retarded.* Paper presented at the Association for the Advancement of Behavior Therapy, Atlanta, 1977.

Doty, D. W., McInnis, T., & Paul, G. L. Remediation of negative side effects of an ongoing response cost system with chronic mental patients. *Journal of Applied Behavior Analysis,* 1974, *7,* 191–198.

Dougherty, E. H., & Lane, J. R. Naturalistic alternatives to extinction: An application to self-injurious bedtime behavior. *Journal of Behavior Therapy and Experimental Psychiatry,* 1976, *7,* 373–376.

Drabman, R. Behavior modification in the classroom. In E. Craighead, M. Mahoney, & A. Kazdin (eds.), *Behavior modification: Principles, issues and applications.* Boston: Houghton Mifflin, 1976.

Drabman, R. S., Cruz, G. C., Ross, J., & Lynd, S. Suppression of chronic drooling in mentally retarded children and adolescents: Effectiveness of a behavioral treatment package. *Behavior Therapy,* 1979, *10,* 46–56.

Drabman, R. S., Ross, J. M., Lynd, R. S., & Cordua, E. D. Retarded children as observers, mediators, and generalization programmers using an icing procedure. *Behavior Modification,* 1978, *2,* 381–385.

Drabman, R., & Spitalnik, R. Social isolation as a punishment procedure: A controlled study. *Journal of Experimental Child Psychology,* 1973, *16,* 236–249.

Drabman, R. S., Spitalnik, R., & O'Leary, K. D. Teaching self-control to disruptive children. *Journal of Abnormal Psychology,* 1973, *82,* 10–16.

Duker, P. C. Behaviour control of self-biting in a Lesch-Nyham patient. *Journal of Mental Deficiency Research,* 1975, *19,* 11–19.

Duker, P. C. Remotely applied punishment versus avoidance conditioning in the treatment of self-injurious behaviours. *European Journal of Behavior Analysis and Modification,* 1976, *3,* 179–185.

Duker, P. C., & Seys, D. M. Elimination of vomiting in a retarded female using restitutional overcorrection. *Behavior Therapy,* 1977, *8,* 255–257.

Edwards, M., & Lilly, R. T. Operant conditioning: An application to behavioral problems in groups. *Mental Retardation,* 1966, *4,* 18–20.

Epstein, L. H., Doke, L. A., Sajwaj, T. E., Sorrell, S., & Rimmer, B. Generality and side effects of overcorrection. *Journal of Applied Behavior Analysis,* 1974, *7,* 385–390.

Erickson, J. R. Effects of punishment for errors on discrimination learning by humans. *Journal of Experimental Psychology,* 1970, *83,* 112–119.

Estes, W. K. An experimental study of punishment. *Psychological Monographs,* 1944, *57,* (3, Whole No. 263).

Evans, W. D. Producing either positive or negative tendencies to a stimulus associated with shock. *Journal of the Experimental Analysis of Behavior,* 1962, *5,* 335–337.

Favell, J. E., McGimsey, J. F., & Jones, M. L. The use of physical restraint in the treatment of self-injury and as positive reinforcement. *Journal of Applied Behavior Analysis,* 1978, *11,* 225–241.

Favell, J. E., McGimsey, J. F., & Schell, R. M. Treatment of self-injury by providing alternative sensory activities. *Analysis and Intervention in Developmental Disabilities*, 1982, *2*, 83–104.

Ferster, C. B., & Appel, J. B. Punishment of S^Δ responding in matching to sample by timeout from positive reinforcement. *Journal of the Experimental Analysis of Behavior*, 1961, *4*, 45–56.

Ferster, C. B., & Culbertson, S. A. *Behavior principles* (3rd ed.). Englewood Cliffs, N.J.: Prentice-Hall, 1982.

Ferster, C. B., & Skinner, B. F. *Schedules of reinforcement.* Englewood Cliffs, N.J.: Prentice-Hall, 1957.

Fineman, K. R. Shaping and increasing verbalizations in an autistic child in response to visual color stimulation. *Perceptual and Motor Skills*, 1968, *27*, 1071–1074. (a)

Fineman, K. R. Visual color reinforcement in establishment of speech by an autistic child. *Perceptual and Motor Skills*, 1968, *26*, 761–762. (b)

Fineman, K. R., & Ferjo, S. Establishing and increasing verbalizations in a deaf schizophrenic child through the use of contingent visual reinforcement. *Perceptual and Motor Skills*, 1969, *29*, 647–652.

Flanagan, B., Goldiamond, I., & Azrin, N. H. Operant stuttering: The control of stuttering behavior through response-contingent consequences. *Journal of the Experimental Analysis of Behavior*, 1958, *1*, 173–177.

Forehand, R., & Baumeister, A. A. Deceleration of aberrant behavior among retarded individuals. In M. Hersen, R. M. Eisler, & P. M. Miller (eds.), *Progress in behavior modification* (Vol. 2). New York: Academic Press, 1976.

Forehand, R., & MacDonough, S. Response contingent time out: An examination of outcome data. *European Journal of Behavioral Analysis and Modification*, 1975, *1*, 109–115.

Forehand, R., Roberts, M., Doleys, D., Hobbs, S., & Resnick, P. An examination of disciplinary procedures with children. *Journal of Experimental Child Psychology*, 1976, *21*, 109–120.

Foxx, R. M. Increasing a mildly retarded woman's attendance at self-help classes by overcorrection and instruction. *Behavior Therapy*, 1976, *7*, 390–396. (a)

Foxx, R. M. The use of overcorrection to eliminate the public disrobing (stripping) of retarded women. *Behaviour Research and Therapy*, 1976, *14*, 53–61. (b)

Foxx, R. M. Attention training: The use of overcorrection avoidance to increase the eye contact of autistic and retarded children. *Journal of Applied Behavior Analysis*, 1977, *10*, 489–499.

Foxx, R. M., & Azrin, N. H. Restitution: A method of eliminating aggressive–disruptive behavior of retarded and brain damaged patients. *Behaviour Research and Therapy*, 1972, *10*, 15–27.

Foxx, R. M., & Azrin, N. H. Dry pants: A rapid method of toilet training children. *Behaviour Research and Therapy*, 1973, *11*, 435–442. (a)

Foxx, R. M., & Azrin, N. H. The elimination of autistic self-stimulatory behavior by overcorrection. *Journal of Applied Behavior Analysis*, 1973, *6*, 1–14. (b)

Foxx, R. M., & Martin, E. D. Treatment of scavenging behavior (coprophagy and pica) by overcorrection. *Behaviour Research and Therapy*, 1975, *13*, 153–163.

Foxx, R. M., & Shapiro, S. T. The timeout ribbon: A nonexclusionary timeout procedure. *Journal of Applied Behavior Analysis*, 1978, *11*, 125–136.

Frank, J. *Persuasion and healing*. New York: Schocken, 1961.

Frankel, F., Moss, D., Schofield, S., & Simmons, J. Q. Case study: Use of differential reinforcement to suppress self-injurious and aggressive behavior. *Psychological Reports*, 1976, *39*, 843–849.

Franks, C. M. *Conditioning techniques in clinical practice and research*. New York: Springer, 1964.

Freeman, B. J., Graham, V., & Ritvo, E. R. Reduction of self-destructive behavior by overcorrection. *Psychological Reports*, 1975, *37*, 446.

Freeman, B. J., Moss, D., Somerset, T., & Ritvo, E. R. Thumbsucking in an autistic child overcome by overcorrection. *Journal of Behavior Therapy and Experimental Psychiatry*, 1977, *8*, 211–212.

Friedman, P. R. Legal regulation of applied behavior analysis in mental institutions and prisons. *Arizona Law Review*, 1975, *17*, 39–104.

Galbraith, D. A., Byrick, R. J., & Rutledge, J. T. An aversive conditioning approach to the inhibition of chronic vomiting. *Canadian Psychiatric Association Journal*, 1970, *15*, 311–313.

Garcia, E. E., & DeHaven, E. D. An experimental analysis of response acquisition and elimination with positive reinforcers. *Behavioral Neuropsychiatry*, 1976, *7*, 71–78.

Gardner, H., Forehand, R., & Roberts, M. W. Timeout with children: Effects of an explanation and brief parent training on child and parent behaviors. *Journal of Abnormal Child Psychology*, 1976, *4*, 277–288.

Gershman, L. Case conference: A transvestite fantasy treated by thought-stopping, covert sensitization, and aversive shock. *Journal of Behavior Therapy and Experimental Psychiatry*, 1970, *1*, 153–161.

Giles, D. K., & Wolf, M. M. Toilet training institutionalized, severe retardates: An application of operant behavior modification procedures. *American Journal of Mental Deficiency*, 1966, *70*, 766–780.

Glaven, J. P. *Behavioral strategies for classroom management*. Columbus, Ohio: Charles E. Merrill, 1974.

Golann, S., & Fremouw, W. J. (eds.). *The right to treatment for mental patients*. New York: Irvington, 1976.

Goldiamond, I. Stuttering and fluency as manipulable operant response classes. In L. Krasner & L. P. Ullmann (eds.), *Research in behavior modification*. New York: Holt, Rinehart & Winston, 1967.

Goldiamond, I., & Dyrud, J. E. Some applications and implications of behavior analysis for psychotherapy. In J. M. Shlien (ed.), *Research in psycho-*

therapy (Vol. 3). Washington, D.C.: American Psychological Association, 1968.

Gordon, K. S., & Zax, M. Once more unto the breach dear friends . . . A reconsideration of the literature on symptom substitution. *Clinical Psychology Review*, 1981, *1*, 33–47.

Greene, R. J., & Hoats, D. L. Reinforcing capabilities of television distortion. *Journal of Applied Behavior Analysis*, 1969, *2*, 139–141.

Greene, R. J., & Hoats, D. L. Aversive tickling: A simple conditioning technique. *Behavior Therapy*, 1971, *2*, 389–393.

Greene, R. J., Hoats, D. L., & Hornick, A. J. Music distortion: A new technique for behavior modification. *Psychological Record*, 1970, *20*, 107–109.

Greenblatt, M., York, R. H., & Brown, E. L. *From custodial to therapeutic patient care in mental hospitals*. New York: Russell Sage Foundation, 1955.

Griffin, J. C., & Locke, B. J. Self-injurious behavior: A bibliography and synopsis of procedural techniques. *JSAS Catalog of Selected Documents in Psychology*, 1974, *4*, 18.

Griffin, J. C., Locke, B. J., & Landers, W. F. Manipulation of potential punishment parameters in the treatment of self-injury. *Journal of Applied Behavior Analysis*, 1975, *8*, 458.

Griffiths, R. R., Bigelow, G., & Liebson, I. Comparison of social time-out and activity time-out procedures in suppressing ethanol self-administration in alcoholics. *Behaviour Research and Therapy*, 1977, *15*, 329–336.

Gump, P. V. Big schools–small schools. In R. H. Moos & P. M. Insel (eds.), *Issues in social ecology: Human milieus*. Palo Alto, Calif.: National Press Books, 1974.

Gutheil, T. G. Observations on the theoretical bases for seclusion of the psychiatric inpatient. *American Journal of Psychiatry*, 1978, *135*, 325–328.

Hake, D. F., & Azrin, N. H. Conditioned punishment. *Journal of the Experimental Analysis of Behavior*, 1965, *8*, 279–293.

Hall, R. V., Axelrod, S., Foundopoulos, M., Shellman, J., Campbell, R. A., & Cranston, S. S. The effective use of punishment to modify behavior in the classroom. *Educational Technology*, 1971, *11*, 24–26.

Hall, R. V., Fox, R., Willard, D., Goldsmith, L., Emerson, M., Owen, M., Davis, F., & Porcia, E. The teacher as observer and experimenter in the modification of disputing and talking-out behaviors. *Journal of Applied Behavior Analysis*, 1971, *4*, 141–149.

Hallam, R. S. Extinction of ruminations: A case study. *Behavior Therapy*, 1974, *5*, 565–568.

Hamilton, J., & Standahl, J. Suppression of stereotyped screaming behavior in a profoundly retarded institutionalized female. *Journal of Experimental Child Psychology*, 1969, *7*, 114–121.

Hamilton, J. W., & Stephens, L. Y. Reinstating speech in an emotionally disturbed, mentally retarded young woman. *Journal of Speech and Hearing Disorders*, 1967, *32*, 383–389.

Hamilton, J., Stephens, L., & Allen, P. Controlling aggressive and destructive behavior in severely retarded institutionalized residents. *American Journal of Mental Deficiency*, 1967, *71*, 852–856.

Hancock v. State, 402 S.W. 2d 906 (Tex. Crim. App. 1966).

Hannah, G. T., Christian, W. P., & Clark, H. B. (eds.). *Preservation of client rights*. New York: Free Press, 1981.

Hannah, G. T., & Surles, R. C. Client rights in clinical counseling services for adults. In G. T. Hannah, W. P. Christian, & H. B. Clark (eds.), *Preservation of client rights*. New York: Free Press, 1981.

Harmatz, M. G., & Lapuc, P. Behavior modification of overeating in a psychiatric population. *Journal of Consulting and Clinical Psychology*, 1968, *32*, 583–587.

Harris, S. L., & Ersner-Hershfield, R. Behavioral suppression of seriously disruptive behavior in psychotic and retarded patients: A review of punishment and its alternatives. *Psychological Bulletin*, 1978, *85*, 1352–1375.

Harris, S. L., Ernser-Hershfield, R., Kaffashan, L. C., & Romanczyk, R. G. The portable time-out room. *Behavior Therapy*, 1974, *5*, 687–688.

Harris, S. L., & Milch, R. E. Training parents as behavior therapists for their autistic children. *Clinical Psychology Review*, 1981, *1*, 49–63.

Harris, S. L., & Romanczyk, R. Treating self-injurious behavior of a retarded child by overcorrection. *Behavior Therapy*, 1976, *7*, 235–239.

Hart, B. M., Allen, K. E., Buell, J. S., Harris, F. R., & Wolf, M. M. Effects of social reinforcement on operant crying. *Journal of Experimental Child Psychology*, 1964, *1*, 145–153.

Hart, B. M., Reynolds, N. J., Baer, D. M., Brawley, E. R., & Harris, F. R. Effect of contingent and non-contingent social reinforcement on the cooperative play of a preschool child. *Journal of Applied Behavior Analysis*, 1968, *1*, 73–76.

Hart, B. M., & Risley, T. R. Environmental programming: Implications for the severely handicapped. In J. H. Prehm & S. J. Deitz (eds.), *Early intervention for the severely handicapped: Programming and accountability*. Portland, Ore.: University of Oregon, Severely Handicapped Learner Program Monogram No. 2, 1976.

Hasazi, J. E., Surles, R. C., & Hannah, G. T. Client rights in psychiatric facilities. In G. T. Hannah, W. P. Christian, & H. B. Clark (eds.), *Preservation of client rights*. New York: Free Press, 1981.

Hauck, L. P., & Martin, P. L. Music as a reinforcer in patient-controlled duration of time-out. *Journal of Music Therapy*, 1970, *7*, 43–53.

Hawkins, R. P., Peterson, R. F., Schweid, F., & Bijou, S. W. Behavior therapy in the home. Amelioration of problem parent–child relations with the parent in a therapeutic role. *Journal of Experimental Child Psychology*, 1966, *4*, 99–107.

Hayes, S., & Geddy, P. Suppression of psychotic hallucinations through time-out. *Behavior Therapy*, 1973, *4*, 123–127.

Hearst, E. Stress-induced breakdown of an appetitive discrimination. *Journal of the Experimental Analysis of Behavior*, 1965, *8*, 135–146.

Henricksen, K., & Doughty, R. Decelerating undesired mealtime behavior in a group of profoundly retarded boys. *American Journal of Mental Deficiency*, 1967, *72*, 40–44.

Herrnstein, R. J. Superstition: A corollary of the principles of operant conditioning. In W. K. Honig (ed.), *Operant behavior: Areas of research and application*. Englewood Cliffs, N.J.: Prentice-Hall, 1966.

Hersen, M., Eisler, R. M., Alford, G. S., & Agras, W. S. Effects of token economy on neurotic depression: An experimental analysis. *Behavior Therapy*, 1973, *4*, 392–397.

Hewitt, F. M. Teaching speech to autistic children through operant conditioning. *American Journal of Orthopsychiatry*, 1964, *17*, 613–618.

Hewitt, F. M. Teaching speech to an autistic child through operant conditioning. *American Journal of Orthopsychiatry*, 1965, *35*, 927–936.

Hewitt, F. M. *The emotionally disturbed child in the classroom*. Boston: Allyn & Bacon, 1968.

Hobbs, S. A. Modifying stereotyped behaviors by overcorrection: A critical review. *Rehabilitation Psychology*, 1976, *23*, 1–11.

Hobbs, S. A., & Forehand, R. Important parameters in the use of timeout with children: A re-examination. *Journal of Behavior Therapy and Experimental Psychiatry*, 1977, *8*, 365–370.

Hobbs, S. A., Forehand, R., & Murray, R. Effects of various durations of timeout on the noncompliant behavior of children. *Behavior Therapy*, 1978, *9*, 652–656.

Hobbs, S. A., & Goswick, R. A. Behavioral treatment of self-stimulation: An examination of alternatives to physical punishment. *Journal of Clinical Child Psychology*, 1977, *6*, 20–23.

Holland, J. G. Ethical considerations in behavior modification. In M. F. Shore & S. E. Golann (eds.), *Current ethical issues in mental health*. Rockville, Md.: National Institute of Mental Health, 1973.

Hollis, J. H. *Analysis of rocking behavior*. Parsons, Kan.: Parsons Research Center, Working Paper No. 193, 1963.

Hollis, J. H. Chlorpromazine: Direct measurement of differential behavioral effect. *Science*, 1968, *159*, 1487–1489.

Holz, W. C., & Azrin, N. H. Discriminative properties of punishment. *Journal of the Experimental Analysis of Behavior*, 1961, *4*, 225–232.

Holz, W. C., & Azrin, N. H. A comparison of several procedures for eliminating behavior. *Journal of the Experimental Analysis of Behavior*, 1963, *6*, 399–406.

Holz, W. C., Azrin, N. H., & Ayllon, T. Elimination of behavior of mental patients by response-produced extinction. *Journal of the Experimental Analysis of Behavior*, 1963, *6*, 407–412.

Homer, A. L., & Peterson, L. Differential reinforcement of other behavior:

A preferred response elimination procedure. *Behavior Therapy,* 1980, *11,* 449–471.

Homme, L. E. *How to use contingency contracting in the classroom.* Champaign, Ill.: Research Press, 1971.

Homme, L., Csanyi, A. P., Gonzales, M. A., & Rechs, J. R. *How to use contingency contracting in the classroom.* Champaign, Ill.: Research Press, 1970.

Honig, W. K., & Staddon, J. E. R. (eds.). *Handbook of operant behavior.* Englewood Cliffs, N.J.: Prentice-Hall, 1977.

Hops, H., & Greenwood, C. R. Social skills deficits. In E. J. Mash & L. G. Terdal (eds.), *Behavioral assessment of childhood disorders.* New York: Guilford Press, 1981.

Horner, D. R. The effects of an environmental "enrichment" program on the behavior of institutionalized profoundly retarded children. *Journal of Applied Behavior Analysis,* 1980, *13,* 473–491.

Hull, C. L. *Principles of behavior.* New York: Appleton, 1943.

Hull, C. L. *A behavior system.* New Haven, Conn.: Yale University Press, 1952.

Humphrey, L. L., Karoly, P., Kirschenbaum, D. S. Self-management in the classroom: Self-imposed response cost versus self-reward. *Behavior Therapy,* 1978, *9,* 592–601.

Hunt, H. F., & Brady, J. V. Some effects of punishment and intercurrent anxiety on a simple operant. *Journal of Comparative and Physiological Psychology,* 1955, *48,* 305–310.

Husted, J. R., Hall, P., & Agin, B. The effectiveness of time-out in reducing maladaptive behavior of autistic and retarded children. *Journal of Psychology,* 1971, *79,* 189–196.

Hutchinson, R. R., Azrin, N. H., & Hunt, G. M. Attack produced by intermittent reinforcement of a concurrent operant response. *Journal of the Experimental Analysis of Behavior,* 1968, *11,* 489–495.

Ingraham v. Wright. 525 F. 2d 909 (5th Cir. 1976), aff'd 97 S. Ct. 1401, 1977.

Irey, P. A. *Covert sensitization of cigarette smokers with high and low extraversion scores.* Unpublished master's thesis. Carbondale: Southern Illinois University at Carbondale, 1972.

Iwata, B. A., Dorsey, M. F., Slifer, K. J., Bauman, K. E., & Richman, G. S. Toward a functional analysis of self-injury. *Analysis and Intervention in Developmental Disabilities,* 1982, *2,* 3–20.

Iwata, B. A., & Lorentzson, A. M. Operant control of seizure-like behavior in an institutionalized retarded adult. *Behavior Therapy,* 1976, *1,* 247–251.

Janda, L. H., & Rimm, D. C. Covert sensitization in the treatment of obesity. *Journal of Abnormal Psychology,* 1972, *80,* 37–42.

Johnson, M., & Bailey, J. The modification of leisure behavior in a halfway house for retarded women. *Journal of Applied Behavior Analysis,* 1977, *10,* 273–282.

Johnson, W. L., Baumeister, A. A., Penland, M. J., & Inwald, C. Experimental analysis of self-injurious, stereotypic, and collateral behavior of retarded persons: Effects of overcorrection and reinforcement of alternative responding. *Analysis and Intervension in Developmental Disabilities,* 1982, *2,* 41–66.

Johnston, J. M. Punishment of human behavior. *American Psychologist,* 1972, *27,* 1033–1054.

Jones, M. L., Favell, J. E., & Risley, T. R. Socioecological programming in the mentally retarded. In J. L. Matson and F. Andrasik (eds.), *Treatment issues and innovations in mental retardation.* New York: Plenum, 1982.

Jones, R. T., & Kazdin, A. E. Childhood behavior problems in the school. In S. M. Turner, K. S. Calhoun, & H. E. Adams (eds.), *Handbook of clinical behavior therapy.* New York: John Wiley, 1981.

Kagen, J., & Kagan, N. Individual variation in cognitive processes. In P. Mussen (ed.), *Carmichael's manual of child psychology* (3rd ed.). New York: John Wiley, 1970.

Kaimowitz v. Michigan Department of Mental Health. 42 U.S.L. Week 2063, Michigan Circuit Court, Wayne County, July 10, 1973.

Kanfer, F., & Phillips, J. *Learning foundations of behavior therapy.* New York: John Wiley, 1970.

Katz, J. *Experimentation with human beings.* New York: Russell Sage Foundation, 1972.

Kaufman, K. F., & O'Leary, K. D. Reward, cost and self-evaluation procedures for disruptive adolescents in a psychiatric hospital school. *Journal of Applied Behavior Analysis,* 1972, *5,* 293–309.

Kazdin, A. E. The effect of response cost in suppressing behavior in a prepsychotic retardate. *Journal of Behavior Therapy and Experimental Psychiatry,* 1971, *2,* 137–140.

Kazdin, A. E. The effect of response cost and aversive stimulation in suppressing punished and nonpunished speech dysfluencies. *Behavior Therapy,* 1973, *4,* 73–82.

Kazdin, A. E. *Behavior modification in applied settings.* Homewood, Ill.: Dorsey Press, 1975.

Kazdin, A. E. *The token economy: A review and evaluation.* New York: Plenum, 1977.

Kazdin, A. E. Acceptability of alternative treatments for deviant child behavior. *Journal of Applied Behavior Analysis,* 1980, *13,* 259–273. (a)

Kazdin, A. E. *Behavior modification in applied settings.* Second Edition. Homewood, Ill.: Dorsey Press, 1980. (b)

Kazdin, A. E. Acceptability of child treatment techniques: The influence of treatment efficacy and adverse side effects. *Behavior Therapy,* 1981, *4,* 493–506.

Kazdin, A. E., & Moyer, W. Teaching teachers to use behavior modification. In S. Yen & R. McIntire (eds.), *Teaching behavior modification.* Kalamazoo, Mich.: Behaviordelia, 1976.

Kazdin, A. E., & Wilson, G. T. *Evaluation of behavior therapy: Issues, evidence, and research strategies.* Cambridge, Mass.: Ballinger, 1978.

Kelleher, R. T. Chaining and conditioned reinforcement. In W. K. Honig (ed.), *Operant behavior: Areas of research and application.* New York: Appleton, 1966.

Kelleher, R. T., & Morse, W. H. Schedules using noxious stimuli, III: Responding maintained with response-produced electric shocks. *Journal of the Experimental Analysis of Behavior,* 1968, *11,* 819–838.

Kelleher, R. T., Riddle, W. C. & Cook, L. Persistent behavior maintained by unavoidable shocks. *Journal of the Experimental Analysis of Behavior,* 1963, *6,* 507–517.

Kelly, J. A., & Drabman, R. S. Generalizing response suppression of self-injurious behavior through an overcorrection punishment procedure: A case study. *Behavior Therapy,* 1977, *8,* 468–472.

Kemper, R. W., & Hall, R. V. Reduction of industrial absenteeism: Results of a behavioral approach. *Journal of Organizational Behavior Management,* 1977, *1,* 1–21.

Kendall, P. C., Nay, W. R., & Jeffers, J. Timeout duration and contrast effects: A systematic evaluation of a successive treatments design. *Behavior Therapy,* 1975, *6,* 609–615.

Kimble, G. A. *Hilgard and Marquis' conditioning and learning.* New York: Appleton-Century-Crofts, 1961.

Kircher, A. S., Pear, J. J., & Martin, G. L. Shock as punishment in a picture-naming task with retarded children. *Journal of Applied Behavior Analysis,* 1971, *4,* 227–233.

Klinge, V., Thrasher, P., & Myers, S. Use of bed-rest overcorrection in a chronic schizophrenic. *Journal of Behavior Therapy and Experimental Psychiatry,* 1975, *6,* 69–73.

Knight, M. F., & McKenzie, H. S. Elimination of bedtime thumbsucking in home settings through contingent reading. *Journal of Applied Behavior Analysis,* 1974, *7,* 33–38.

Koegel, R. L., & Covert, A. The relationship of self-stimulation to learning in autistic children. *Journal of Applied Behavior Analysis,* 1972, *5,* 381–387.

Koegel, R. L., Firestone, P. B., Kramme, K. W., & Dunlap, G. Increasing spontaneous play by suppressing self-stimulation in autistic children. *Journal of Applied Behavior Analysis,* 1974, *7,* 521–528.

Koegel, R. L., Rincover, A., & Russo, D. C. Classroom management: Progression from special to normal classrooms. In R. L. Koegel, A. Rincover, & A. L. Egel (eds.), *Educating and understanding autistic children.* San Diego: College-Hill Press, 1982.

Koegel, R. L., Russo, D. C., Rincover, A., & Schreibman, L. Assessing and training teachers. In R. L. Koegel, A. Rincover, & A. L. Egel (eds.), *Educating and understanding autistic children.* San Diego: College-Hill Press, 1982.

Kohlenberg, R. J. The punishment of persistent vomiting: A case study. *Journal of Applied Behavior Analysis*, 1970, *3*, 241–245.

Kohlenberg, R. J., Levin, M., & Belcher, S. Skin conductance changes and the punishment of self-destructive behavior: A case study. *Mental Retardation*, 1973, *11*, 11–13.

Kolvin, I. "Aversive imagery" treatment in adolescents. *Behaviour Research and Therapy*, 1967, *5*, 245–248.

Krantz, P. J., & Risley, T. R. Behavioral ecology in the classroom. In K. D. O'Leary (eds.), *Classroom management: The successful use of behavior modification* (2nd ed.). New York: Pergamon Press, 1977.

Krapfl, J., & Vargas, E. (eds.). *Behaviorism and ethics*. Kalamazoo, Mich.: Behaviordelia, 1977.

Kushner, M. The operant control of intractable sneezing. In C. D. Spielberger, R. Fox, & B. Masterson (eds.), *Contributions to general psychology*. New York: Ronald Press, 1968.

Lahey, B. B., McNees, M. P., & McNees, M. C. Control of an obscene "verbal tic" through time-out in an elementary school classroom. *Journal of Applied Behavior Analysis*, 1973, *6*, 101–104.

Lamon, S. G., Wilson, T., & Leaf, R. C. Human classical aversion conditioning: Nausea versus electric shock in the reduction of target beverage consumption. *Behaviour Research and Therapy*, 1977, *15*, 313–320.

Landesman-Dwyer, S., & Sackett, G. P. Behavior changes in non-ambulatory, mentally retarded individuals. In C. E. Meyers (ed.), *Quality of life in severely and profoundly mentally retarded people: Research foundations for improvement*. Washington, D.C.: American Association on Mental Deficiency, 1978.

Lang, P. J., & Melamed, B. G. Case report: Avoidance conditioning of an infant with chronic ruminative vomiting. *Journal of Abnormal Psychology*, 1969, *74*, 1–8.

Lattal, K. A., & Poling, A. D. Describing response-event relations: Babel revisited. *The Behavior Analyst*, 1981, *4*, 143–152.

Laws, D. R., Brown, R. A., Epstein, J., & Hocking, N. Reduction of inappropriate social behavior in disturbed children by an untrained paraprofessional therapist. *Behavior Therapy*, 1971, *2*, 519–533.

Lawson, D. M., & May, R. B. Three procedures for the extinction of smoking behavior. *Psychological Record*, 1970, *20*, 151–157.

Lawson, R. *Frustration*. New York: Macmillan, 1965.

LeBlanc, J. M., Busby, K. H., & Thomson, C. L. The functions of timeout for changing the aggressive behaviors of a preschool child: A multiple-baseline analysis. In R. Ulrich, T. Stachnik, & J. Mabry (eds.), *Control of human behavior* (Vol. 3). New York: Scott Foresman, 1974.

LeBoeuf, A., & Boeverts, M. Automatic detection and modification of aberrant behaviors: Two case studies. *Journal of Behavior Therapy and Experimental Psychiatry*, 1981, *12*, 153–157.

Leitenberg, H. Is time-out from positive reinforcement an aversive event? A review of the experimental evidence. *Psychological Bulletin*, 1965, *64*, 428–441.

Leitenberg, H., Burchard, D., Burchard, N., Fuller, E. J., & Lysaght, T. V. Using positive reinforcement to suppress behavior: Some experimental comparisons with sibling conflict. *Behavior Therapy*, 1977, *8*, 168–182.

Liberman, R. P., & Davis, J. Drugs and behavior analysis. In M. Hersen, R. M. Eisler, & P. M. Miller (eds.), *Progress in behavior modification* (Vol. 1). New York: Academic Press, 1975.

Liberman, R. P., Teigen, J., Patterson, R., & Baker, V. Reducing delusional speech in chronic, paranoid schizophrenics. *Journal of Applied Behavior Analysis*, 1973, *6*, 57–64.

Lichstein, K. L., & Schreibman, L. Employing electric shock with autistic children. *Journal of Autism and Childhood Schizophrenia*, 1976, *6*, 163–173.

Lichtenstein, E., & Brown, R. A. Smoking cessation methods: Review and recommendations. In W. R. Miller (ed.), *The addictive behaviors: Treatment of alcoholism, drug abuse, smoking, and obesity*. New York: Pergamon Press, 1980.

Linkenhoker, D. D. Increasing the effectiveness of timeout from reinforcement. *Psychotherapy: Theory, Research, and Practice*, 1974, *11*, 326–328.

Linn, L. Other psychiatric emergencies. In A. M. Freedman, H. I. Kaplan, & B. J. Sadock (eds.), *Comprehensive textbook of psychiatry* (Vol. 2). Baltimore: Williams and Wilkins, 1975.

Lipman, R. S. The use of psychopharmacological agents in residential facilities for the retarded. In F. Menolascino (ed.), *Psychiatric approaches to mental retardation*. New York: Basic Books, 1970.

Lott, D. F., & Sommer, R. Seating arrangement and status. *Journal of Personality and Psychology*, 1967, *7*, 90–95.

Lovaas, O. I. A program for the establishment of speech in psychotic children. In J. K. Wing (ed.), *Early childhood autism*. Oxford, England: Pergamon Press, 1966.

Lovaas, O. I. Some studies in the treatment of childhood schizophrenia. In J. M. Schlien (ed.), *Research in psychotherapy*. Washington, D.C.: American Psychological Association, 1968.

Lovaas, O. I., Berberich, J. P., Perloff, B. F., & Schaeffer, B. Acquisition of imitative speech by schizophrenic children. *Science*, 1966, *151*, 705–707.

Lovaas, O. I., Freitag, G., Gold, U. J., & Kassorla, I. C. Experimental studies in childhood schizophrenia: Analysis of self-destructive behavior. *Journal of Experimental Child Psychology*, 1965, *2*, 76–84.

Lovaas, O. I. Freitag, G., Kinder, M. I., Rubenstein, B. D., Schaeffer, B., & Simmons, J. Q. Establishment of social reinforcers in two schizophrenic children on the basis of food. *Journal of Experimental Child Psychology*, 1966, *4*, 109–125.

Lovaas, O. I., Litrownik, A., & Mann, R. Response latencies to auditory stimuli in autistic children engaged in self-stimulatory behavior. *Behaviour Research and Therapy*, 1971, *9*, 39–49.

Lovaas, O. I., Schaeffer, B., & Simmons, J. Q. Building social behavior in autistic children by use of electric shock. *Journal of Experimental Research in Personality,* 1965, *1,* 99–109.

Lovaas, O. I., & Simmons, J. Q. Manipulation of self-destruction in three retarded children. *Journal of Applied Behavior Analysis,* 1969, *2,* 143–157.

Lovibond, S. H., & Caddy, G. R. Discriminated aversive control in the moderation of alcoholics' drinking behavior. *Behavior Therapy,* 1970, *1,* 437–444.

Lowitz, G. H., & Suib, M. R. Generalized control of persistent thumbsucking by differential reinforcement of other behaviors. *Journal of Behavior Therapy and Experimental Psychiatry,* 1978, *9,* 343–346.

Luce, S. C., & Hall, R. V. Contingent exercise: A procedure used with differential reinforcement to reduce bizarre verbal behavior. *Education and Treatment of Children,* 1981, *4,* 309–327.

Luckey, R. E., Watson, C. M., & Musick, J. K. Aversive conditioning as a means of inhibiting vomiting and rumination. *American Journal of Mental Deficiency,* 1968, *73,* 139–142.

Ludwig, A. M., Marx, A. J., Hill, P. A., & Browning, R. M. The control of violent behavior through faradic shock. *Journal of Nervous and Mental Disease,* 1969, *148,* 624–637.

Luiselli, J. K. Behavioral treatment of self-stimulation: Review and recommendations. *Education and Treatment of Children,* 1981, *4,* 375–392.

Luiselli, J. K., Colozzi, G., Donellon, S., Helfen, C. S., & Pemberton, B. W. Training and generalization of a greeting exchange with a mentally retarded language-deficient child. *Education and Treatment of Children,* 1978, *1,* 23–30.

Luiselli, J. K., Colozzi, G. A., Helfen, C. S., & Pollow, R. S. Differential reinforcement of incompatible behavior (DRI) in treating classroom management problems of developmentally disabled children. *The Psychological Record,* 1980, *30,* 261–270.

Luiselli, J. K., Helfen, C. S., Pemberton, B. W., & Reisman, J. The elimination of a child's in-class masturbation by overcorrection and reinforcement. *Journal of Behavior Therapy and Experimental Psychiatry,* 1977, *8,* 201–204.

Luiselli, J. K., & Krause, S. Reducing sterotypic behavior through a combination of DRO, cueing, and reinforcer isolation procedures. *The Behavior Therapist,* 1981, *4,* 2–3.

Luiselli, J. K., Pemberton, B. W., & Helfen, C. S. Effects and side effects of a brief overcorrection procedure in reducing multiple self-stimulatory behavior: A single-case analysis. *Journal of Mental Deficiency Research,* 1978, *22,* 287–294.

Luiselli, J. K., & Reisman, J. Some variations in the use of differential reinforcement procedures with mentally retarded children in specialized treatment settings. *Applied Research in Mental Retardation,* 1980, *1,* 277–288.

Luiselli, J. K., Reisman, J., Helfen, C. S., & Pemberton, B. W. Toilet training in the classroom: An adaptation of Azrin and Foxx's rapid toilet training procedures. *Behavioral Engineering,* 1979, *5,* 89–93.

Luiselli, J. K., & Townsend, N. M. *Effects of punishment in behavior modification programs with children: A review.* Unpublished manuscript, 1980.

Lutzker, J. R. Reducing self-injurious behavior by facial screening. *American Journal of Mental Deficiency,* 1978, *82,* 510–513.

Lutzker, J. R., Frame, R. E., & Rice, J. M. Project 12-ways: An ecobehavioral approach to the treatment and prevention of child abuse and neglect. *Education and Treatment of Children,* 1982, *5,* 141–155.

MacCulloch, M. J., Williams, C., & Birtles, C. J. The successful application of aversion therapy to an adolescent exhibitionist. *Journal of Behavior Therapy and Experimental Psychiatry,* 1971, *2,* 61–65.

MacDonough, T. S., & Forehand, R. Response-contingent timeout: Important parameters in behavior modification with children. *Journal of Behavior Therapy and Experimental Psychiatry,* 1973, *4,* 231–236.

Mackey v. Procunier, 477 F. 2d 877 (9th Cir.), 1973.

Madsen, C. H., Jr., Becker, W. C., & Thomas, D. R. Rules, praise and ignoring: Elements of elementary classroom control. *Journal of Applied Behavior Analysis,* 1968, *1,* 139–150.

Madsen, C. H., Jr., Becker, W. C., Thomas, D. R., Koser, L., & Plager, E. An analysis of the reinforcing function of "sit down" commands. In R. K. Parker (ed.), *Readings in educational psychology.* Boston: Allyn & Bacon, 1968.

Maley, R. F., Feldman, G. L., & Ruskin, R. S. Evaluation of patient improvement in a token economy treatment program. *Journal of Abnormal Psychology,* 1973, *82,* 141–144.

Manno, B., & Marston, A. R. Weight reduction as a function of negative covert reinforcement (sensitization) versus covert positive reinforcement. *Behaviour Research and Therapy,* 1972, *10,* 201–207.

Mansdorf, I. J. Reinforcer isolation: An alternative to subject isolation in time-out from positive reinforcement. *Journal of Behavior Therapy and Experimental Psychiatry,* 1977, *8,* 391–393.

Marholin, D., & Gray, D. Effects of group response-cost procedures on cash shortages in a small business. *Journal of Applied Behavior Analysis,* 1976, *9,* 25–30.

Marholin, D., Luiselli, J. K., Robinson, M., & Lott, I. Response-contingent taste aversion in treating chronic ruminative vomiting of institutionalized profoundly retarded children. *Journal of Mental Deficiency Research,* 1980, *24,* 47–56.

Marholin, D., Luiselli, J. K., & Townsend, N. M. Overcorrection: An examination of its rationale and treatment effectiveness. In M. Hersen, R. M. Eisler, & P. M. Miller (eds.), *Progress in behavior modification* (Vol. 9). New York: Academic Press, 1980.

Marholin, D., & Touchette, P. E. Transfer and maintenance. In A. P. Goldstein & F. H. Kanfer (eds.), *Maximizing treatment gains.* New York: Academic Press, 1979.

Marholin, D., & Townsend, N. M. An experimental analysis of side effects and response maintenance of a modified overcorrection procedure: The case of the persistent twiddler. *Behavior Therapy,* 1978, *9,* 383–390.

Marks, J., Sonoda, B., & Schalock, R. Reinforcement vs. relationship therapy for schizophrenics. *Journal of Abnormal Psychology,* 1968, *73,* 397–402.

Marshall, G. R. Toilet training of an autistic eight-year-old through conditioning therapy: A case report. *Behaviour Research and Therapy,* 1966, *4,* 242–245.

Marshall, W. L., Boutilier, J., & Minnes, P. The modification of phobic behavior by covert reinforcement. *Behavior Therapy,* 1974, *5,* 469–480.

Martin, G. Brief time-outs as consequences for errors during training programs with autistic and retarded children: A questionable procedure. *Psychological Record,* 1975, *25,* 71–87.

Martin, G., & Pallotta-Cornick, A. Behavior modification in sheltered workshops and community group homes: Status and future. In L. A. Hamerlynck (ed.), *Behavioral systems for the developmentally disabled: Institutional, clinic, and community environments.* New York: Brunner/Mazel, 1979.

Martin, G., Pallotta-Cornick, A., Johnstone, G., & Goyos, A. C. A supervisory strategy to improve work performance for lower-functioning clients in a sheltered workshop. *Journal of Applied Behavior Analysis,* 1980, *13,* 183–190.

Martin, G. L., MacDonald, S., & Omichinski, M. An operant analysis of response interactions during meals with severely retarded girls. *American Journal of Mental Deficiency,* 1971, *76,* 68–75.

Martin, J., & Matson, J. L. Eliminating the inappropriate vocalizations of a retarded adult by overcorrection. *Scandinavian Journal of Behavior Therapy,* 1978, *7,* 203–209.

Martin, J., Weller, S., & Matson, J. L. Eliminating object-transferring by a profoundly retarded female by overcorrection. *Psychological Reports,* 1977, *40,* 779–782.

Martin, P. L. & Foxx, R. M. Victim control of the aggression of an institutionalized retardate. *Journal of Behavior Therapy and Experimental Psychiatry,* 1973, *4,* 161–165.

Martin, R. *Legal challenges to behavior modification: Trends in schools, corrections, and mental health.* Champaign, Ill: Research Press, 1975.

Martin, R. The right to receive or refuse treatment. *The Behavior Therapist,* 1980, *3,* (1), 8.

Martin, R. Legal issues in preserving client rights. In G. T. Hannah, W. P. Christian, & H. B. Clark (eds.), *Preservation of client rights.* New York: Free Press, 1981.

Masters, J. C., Furman, W., & Barden, R. C. Effects of achievement standards, tangible rewards, and self-dispensed achievement evaluations on children's task mastery. *Child Development*, 1977, *48*, 217–224.

Masters, J. C., & Santrock, J. Studies in the self-regulation of behavior: Effects of contingent cognitive and affective events. *Developmental Psychology*, 1976, *12*, 334–348.

Matson, J. L. Some practical considerations for using the Foxx and Azrin rapid method of toilet training. *Psychological Reports*, 1975, *37*, 350.

Matson, J. L. Training socially appropriate behaviors to moderately retarded adults with contingent praise, instructions, feedback, and a modified self-recording procedure. *Scandinavian Journal of Behavior Therapy*, 1978, *7*, 167–175.

Matson, J. L., & Adkins, J. Teaching institutionalized mentally retarded adults socially appropriate leisure skills. *Mental Retardation*, 1980, *18*, 249–252.

Matson, J. L. & Cahill, T. Overcorrection: A technique for eliminating resistant behaviors. *JSAS Catalog of Selected Documents in Psychology*, 1976, *6*, 20.

Matson, J. L., Esvelt-Dawson, K., & O'Donnell, D. Overcorrection, modeling and reinforcement procedures for reinstating speech in a mute boy. *Child Behavior Therapy*, 1979, *1*, 363–371.

Matson, J. L., Horne, A. M., Ollendick, D., & Ollendick, T. H. A further evaluation of the components of overcorrection. *Journal of Behavior Therapy and Experimental Psychiatry*, 1979, *10*, 295–298.

Matson, J. L., & Kazdin, A. E. Punishment in behavior modification: Pragmatic, ethical and legal issues. *Clinical Psychology Review*, 1981, *1*, 197–210.

Matson, J. L., & Marchetti, A. A comparison of leisure skills training procedures for the mentally retarded. *Applied Research in Mental Retardation*, 1980, *1*, 113–122.

Matson, J. L., & Martin, J. E. A social learning approach to vocational training of the severely retarded. *Journal of Mental Deficiency Research*, 1979, *23*, 9–16.

Matson, J. L., & Ollendick, T. H. Elimination of low frequency biting. *Behavior Therapy*, 1976, *1*, 410–412.

Matson, J. L., & Ollendick, T. H. Issues in toilet training. *Behavior Therapy*, 1977, *8*, 549–553.

Matson, J. L., Ollendick, T. H., & DiLorenzo, T. M. Time-out and the characteristics of mentally retarded institutionalized adults who do or do not receive it. *Mental Retardation*, 1980, *18*, 181–184.

Matson, J. L., & Stephens, R. M. Overcorrection of aggressive behavior in a chronic psychiatric patient. *Behavior Modification*, 1977, *1*, 559–564.

Matson, J. L., & Stephens, R. M. Increasing appropriate behavior of explosive chronic psychiatric patients with social skills training package. *Behavior Modification*, 1978, *2*, 61–75.

Matson, J. L., & Stephens, R. M. Overcorrection treatment of stereotyped behaviors. *Behavior Modification*, 1981, *5*, 491–502.

Matson, J. L., Stephens, R. M., & Horne, A. M. Overcorrection and extinction-reinforcement as rapid methods of eliminating the disruptive behaviors of relatively normal children. *Behavioral Engineering*, 1978, *4*, 89–94.

Matson, J. L., Stephens, R. M., & Smith, C. Treatment of self-injurious behavior with overcorrection. *Journal of Mental Deficiency Research*, 1978, *22*, 175–178.

Matson, J. L., & Zeiss, R. A. Group training of social skills in chronically explosive, severely disturbed psychiatric patients. *Behavioral Engineering*, 1978, *5*, 41–50.

Matson, J. L., & Zeiss, R. A. The buddy system: A method for generalized reduction of inappropriate interpersonal behavior of retarded psychiatric patients. *British Journal of Social and Clinical Psychology*, 1979, *18*, 401–405.

Matson, J. L., Zeiss, A. M., Zeiss, R. A., & Bowman, W. A comparison of social skills training and contingent attention to improve behavioral deficits of chronic psychiatric patients. *British Journal of Social and Clinical Psychology*, 1980, *19*, 57–64.

May, J. G., Risley, T. R., Twardosz, S., Friedman, P., Bijou, S., & Wexler, D. *Guidelines for the use of behavioral procedures in state programs for retarded persons*. Arlington, Tex: Association for Retarded Citizens, 1976.

McConaghy, N., Armstrong, M. S., & Blaszczynski, A. Controlled comparison of aversive therapy and covert sensitization in compulsive homosexuality. *Behaviour Research and Therapy*, 1981, *19*, 425–434.

McFarlain, R. A., Andy, O. J. , Scott, R. W., & Wheatley, M. L. Suppression of head banging on the ward. *Psychological Reports*, 1975, *36*, 315–321.

McKearney, J. W. Maintenance of responding under a fixed-interval schedule of electric shock presentation. *Science*, 1968, *160*, 1249–1251.

McKearney, J. W. Fixed-interval schedules of electric shock presentation: Extinction and recovery of performance under different shock intensities and fixed-interval durations. *Journal of the Experimental Analysis of Behavior*, 1969, *12*, 301–313.

McLaughlin, J.G., & Nay, W.R. Treatment of trichotillomania using positive coverants and response cost: A case report. *Behavior Therapy*, 1975, *6*, 87–91.

McLaughlin, T., & Malaby, J. Reducing and measuring inappropriate verbalizations in a token classroom. *Journal of Applied Behavior Analysis*, 1972, *5*, 329–333.

McReynolds, L.V. Application of timeout from positive reinforcement for increasing the efficiency of speech training. *Journal of Applied Behavior Analysis*, 1969, *2*, 199–205.

Measel, L. J., & Alfieri, P. A. Treatment of self-injurious behavior by a combination of reinforcement for incompatible behavior and overcorrection. *American Journal of Mental Deficiency*, 1976, *2*, 147–153.

Melin, K., & Gotestam, K. G. The effects of rearranging ward routines on communication and eating behavior of psychogeriatric patients. *Journal of Applied Behavior Analysis,* 1981, *14,* 47–51.

Merbaum, M. The modification of self-destructive behavior by a mother therapist using aversive stimulation. *Behavior Therapy,* 1973, *4,* 442–447.

Meyer, W. J. , & Offenbach, S. I. Effectiveness of reward and punishment as a function of task complexity. *Journal of Comparative and Physiological Psychology,* 1962, *55,* 532–534.

Miller, A. J., & Kratochwill, T. R. Resolution of frequent stomachache complaints by time-out. *Behavior Therapy,* 1979, *10,* 211–218.

Miller, L. M. *Behavior management: The new science of managing people to work.* New York: John Wiley, 1978.

Miller, W. R., & Hester, R. K. Treating the problem drinker: Modern approaches. In W. R. Miller (ed.), *The addictive behaviors: Treatment of alcoholism, drug abuse, smoking, and obesity.* New York: Pergamon Press, 1980.

Montes, F., & Risley, T. R. Evaluating traditional day care practices: An empirical approach. *Child Care Quarterly,* 1975, *4,* 208–215.

Morris, G. H. (ed.), *The mentally ill and the right to treatment.* Springfield Ill.: Charles C Thomas, 1970.

Morris, R. J. & Brown, D. K. Legal and ethical issues in behavior modification with mentally retarded persons. In J. L. Maston & F. Andrasik (ed.), *Treatment issues and innovations in mental retardation.* New York: Plenum Press, 1983.

Morrison, D. Issues in the application of reinforcement theory in the treatment of a child's self-injurious behavior. *Psychotherapy: Therapy, Research and Practice,* 1972, *9,* 40–45.

Morse, W. H. Intermittent reinforcement. In W. K. Honig (ed.), *Operant behavior: Areas of research and application.* Englewood Cliffs, N.J.: Prentice-Hall, 1966.

Morse, W. H., & Kelleher, R. T. Determinants of reinforcement and punishment. In W.K. Honig & J. E. R. Staddon (eds.), *Handbook of operant behavior.* Englewood Cliffs, N.J.: Prentice-Hall, 1977.

Mowrer, O. H., & Aiken, E. G. Contiguity vs. drive-reduction in conditioned fear: Temporal variations in conditioned and unconditioned stimulus. *American Journal of Psychology,* 1954, *67,* 26–38.

Mowrer, O. H., & Solomon, L. N. Contiguity vs. drive-reduction in conditioned fear: The proximity and abruptness of drive-reduction. *American Journal of Psychology,* 1954, *67,* 15–25.

Mulhern, T., & Baumeister, A. A. An experimental attempt to reduce stereotype by reinforcement procedures. *American Journal of Mental Deficiency,* 1969, *74,* 69–74.

Mullen, F. G. *The effect of covert sensitization on smoking behavior.* Unpublished study, Queens College, 1968.

Murray. R. G., & Hobbs, S. A. The use of a self-imposed timeout procedure in the modification of excessive alcohol consumption. *Journal of Behavior Therapy and Experimental Psychiatry,* 1977, *8,* 377–380.

Myers, J. J., & Deibert, A. N. Reduction of self-abusive behavior is a blind child by using a feeding response. *Journal of Behavior Therapy and Experimental Psychiatry*, 1971, *2*, 141–144.

Neisworth, J. T., Madle, R. A., & Goeke, K. K. "Errorless" elimination of separation anxiety; A case study. *Journal of Behavior Therapy and Experimental Psychiatry*, 1975, *6*, 79–82.

Neisworth, J. T., & Moore, F. Operant treatment of asthmatic responding with the parent as therapist. *Behavior Therapy*, 1972, *3*, 95–99.

Neuringer, A. J. Superstitious key pecking after three peck-produced reinforcements. *Journal of the Experimental Analysis of Behavior*, 1970, *13*, 127–134.

New York Association for Retarded Citizens v. Carey. 393 F. Supp. 715 (E.D. N.Y.) 1975.

New York Association for Retarded Citizens v. Rockefeller. 357 F. Supp. 752 (E.D. N.Y.) 1973.

Nordquist, V. M., & Wahler, R. G. Naturalistic treatment of an autistic child. *Journal of Applied Behavior Anaylsis*, 1973, *6*, 79–87.

Nunes, D. L., Murphy, R. J. & Ruprecht, M. L. Reducing self-injurious behavior of severely retarded individuals through withdrawal of reinforcement procedures. *Behavior Modification*, 1977, *1*, 499–516.

Nunn, R. G., & Azrin, N. H. Eliminating nail-biting by the habit reversal procedure. *Behaviour Research and Therapy*, 1976, *14*, 65–67.

O'Brien, F., & Arzin, N. H. Developing proper mealtime behaviors of the institutionalized retarded. *Journal of Applied Behavior Analysis*, 1972, *5*, 389–399.(a)

O'Brien, F., & Azrin, N. H. Symptom reduction by functional displacement in a token economy: A case study. *Journal of Behavior Therapy and Experimental Psychiatry*, 1972, *3*, 205–207.(b)

O'Brien, F., Azrin, N. H., & Bugle, C. Training profoundly retarded children to stop crawling. *Journal of Applied Behavior Analysis*, 1972, *5*, 131–137.

O'Brien, F., Bugle, C., & Azrin, N. H. Training and maintaining a retarded child's proper eating. *Journal of Applied Behavior Analysis*, 1972, *5*, 67–72.

O'Leary, K. D., Kaufman, K. F., Kass, R., & Drabman, R. The effects of loud and soft reprimands on the behavior of disruptive students. *Exceptional Children*, 1970, *37*, 145–155.

O'Leary, K. D., O'Leary, S., & Becker, W. C. Modification of a deviant sibling interaction pattern in the home. *Behaviour Research and Therapy*, 1967, *5*, 113–120.

Ollendick, T. H. Self-monitoring and self-administered overcorrection: The modification of nervous tics in children. *Behavior Modification*, 1981, *5*, 75–84.

Ollendick, T. H., & Matson, J. L. An initial investigation into the parameters of overcorrection. *Psychological Reports*, 1976, *39*, 1139–1142.

Ollendick, T. H., & Matson, J. L. Overcorrection: An overview. *Behavior Therapy*, 1978, *9*, 830–842.

Ollendick, T. H., Matson, J. L., & Martin, J. E. Effectiveness of hand overcorrection for topographically similar and dissimilar self-stimulatory behaviors. *Journal of Experimental Child Psychology*, 1978, *25*, 396–403.

O'Neil, P. M., White, J. L., King, C. R., & Carek, D. J. Controlling childhood rumination through differential reinforcement of other behavior. *Behavior Modification*, 1979, *3*, 355–372.

Osborne, J. G. Overcorrection and behavior therapy: A reply to Hobbs. *Rehabilitation Psychology*, 1976, *23*, 13–31.

Paloutzian, R. F., Hasazi, J., Streifel, J., & Edgar, C. L. Promotion of positive social interaction in severely retarded young children. *American Journal of Mental Deficiency*, 1971, *75*, 519–524.

Patterson, G. R., & White, G. D. It's a samll world: The application of "timeout from reinforcement." In F. H. Kanfer & J. S. Phillips (eds.), *Learning foundations of behavior therapy*. New York: John Wiley, 1970.

Pendergrass, V. E. Effects of length of timeout from positive reinforcements and schedule of applications in suppression of aggressive behavior. *Psychological Record*, 1971, *21*, 75–80.

Pendergrass, V. E. Time-out from positive reinforcement following persistent, high-rate behavior in retardates. *Journal of Applied Behavior Analysis*, 1972, *5*, 85–91.

Peterson, R. F., & Peterson, L. R. The use of positive reinforcement in the control of self-destructive behavior in a retarded boy. *Journal of Experimental Child Psychology*, 1968, *6*, 351–360.

Pfeiffer, E. A., & Johnson, J. B. A new electrode for the application of electrical shock in aversive conditioning therapy. *Behaviour Research and Therapy*, 1968, *6*, 393–394.

Phillips, E. L. Achievement Place: Token reinforcement procedures in a home-style rehabilitation setting for "pre-delinquent" boys. *Journal of Applied Behavior Analysis*, 1968, *1*, 213–223.

Phillips, E. L., Phillips, E. A., Fixsen, D. L., & Wolf, M. M. Achievement place: Modification of the behaviors of pre-delinquent boys within a token economy. *Journal of Applied Behavior Analysis*, 1971, *4*, 45–59.

Pinkston, E. M., Reese, N. M., LeBlanc, J. M., & Baer, D. M. Independent control of a pre-school child's aggression and peer interaction by contingent teacher attention. *Journal of Applied Behavior Analysis*, 1973, *6*, 115–124.

Plummer, S., Baer, D. M., & LeBlanc, J. M. Functional considerations in the use of procedural time-out and an effective alternative. *Journal of Applied Behavior Analysis*, 1977, *10*, 689–705.

Plutchik, R., Karasu, T. B., Conte, H. R., Siegel, B., & Jerrett, M. A. Toward a rationale for the seclusion process. *The Journal of Nervous and Mental Disease*, 1978, *166*, 571–579.

Pohl, R. W., Revusky, S., & Mellor, C. S. Drugs employed in the treatment of alcoholism: Rat data suggest they are unnessarily severe. *Behaviour Research and Therapy*, 1980, *18*, 71–78.

Pollow, R. S., McPhee, D. F., Luiselli, J. K., & Marholin, D., II. Assessment and treatment of high rate vocal disruption in a developmentally disabled child: Contingent application of mouth wash as a response-inhibitory technique. Unpublished manuscript, 1980.

Porterfield, J., Blunden, R., & Blewitt, E. Improving environments for profoundly handicapped adults: Using prompts and social attention to maintain high group engagement. *Behavior Modification*, 1980, *4*, 225–241.

Porterfield, J. K., Herbert-Jackson, E., & Risley, T. R. Contingent observation: An effective and acceptable procedure for reducing disruptive behavior of young children in a group. *Journal of Applied Behavior Analysis*, 1976, *9*, 55–64.

Prochaska, J., Smith, N. Marzilli, R. Colby, J., & Donovan, W. Remote-control aversive stimulation in the treatment of head banging in a retarded child. *Journal of Behavior Therapy and Experimental Psychiatry*, 1974, *5*, 285–289.

Rachman, S., & Teasdale, J. *Aversion therapy and behaviors disorders: An analysis.* Coral Gables, Fla.: University of Miami Press, 1969.

Ramp. E., Ulrich, R., & Dulaney, S. Delayed time-out as a procedure for reducing disruptive classroom behavior: A case study. *Journal of Applied Behavior Analysis*, 1971, *4.* 235–239.

Rapoff, M. A., Altman, K., & Christophersen, E. R. Elimination of a retarded blind child's self-hitting by response-contingent brief restraint. *Education and Treatment of Children*, 1980, *3*, 231–236.

Redd, W. H. Effects of mixed reinforcement contingencies on adults' control of children's behavior. *Journal of Applied Behavior Analysis*, 1969, *2*, 249–254.

Reichle, J., Brubakken, D., & Tetreault, G. Eliminating perseverative speech by positive reinforcement and time-out in a psychotic child. *Journal of Behavior Therapy and Experimental Psychiatry*, 1976, *1*, 179–183.

Reisinger, J. J. The treatment of anxiety–depression via positive reinforcement and response cost. *Journal of Applied Behavior Analysis*, 1972, *5*, 125–130.

Rekers, G. A., & Lovaas, O. I. Behavioral treatment of deviant sex-role behaviors in a male child. *Journal of Applied Behavior Analysis*, 1974, *7.* 173–190.

Rennie v. Klein. 462 F. Supp. 1131 (D.N.J.), 1978, CA 77-2624, Sept. 14, 1979.

Repp, A. C., & Barton, L. E. Naturalistic observations of institutionalized retarded persons: A comparison of licensure decisions and behavioral observations. *Journal of Applied Behavior Analysis*, 1980, *13*, 333–341.

Repp, A. C., & Brulle, A. R. Reducing aggressive behavior of mentally retarded persons. In J. L. Matson & J. R. McCartney (eds.), *Handbook of behavior modification with the mentally retarded.* New York: Plenum Press, 1980.

Repp, A. C., & Deitz, D. E. D. On the selective use of punishment—Suggested guidelines for adminstrators. *Mental Retardation,* 1978, *16,* 250–254.

Repp, A. C. , & Deitz, S. M. Reducing aggressive and self-injurious behavior of institutionalized retarded children through reinforcement of other behavior. *Journal of Applied Behavior Analysis,* 1974, *7,* 313–325.

Repp, A. C., Deitz, S. M., & Deitz, D. E. D. Reducing inappropriate behaviors in classrooms and in individual sessions through DRO schedules of reinforcement. *Mental Retardation,* 1976,*14,* 11–15.

Repp, A. C., Deitz, S. M., & Speir, N. C. Reducing stereotypic responding of retarded persons by the differential reinforcement of other behaviors. *American Journal of Mental Deficiency,* 1974, *79,* 279–284.

Resnick, P. A., Forehand, R., & McWhorter, A. Q. The effect of parental treatment of one child on an untreated sibling. *Behavior Therapy,* 1976, *7,* 544–548.

Reynolds, G. S. *A primer of operant conditioning.* Glenview, Ill.: Scott, Foresman, 1968.

Rilling, M. Stimulus control and inhibitory processes. In W. K. Honig & J. E. R. Straddon (eds.), *Handbook of operant behavior.* Englewood Cliffs, N.J.: Prentice-Hall, 1977.

Rimm, D. C., & Masters, J. C. *Behavior therapy: Techinques and empirical findings,* New York: Academic Press, 1974.

Rimm, D. C., & Masters, J. C. *Behavior therapy: Techniques and empirical findings* (2nd ed.), New York: Academic Press, 1979.

Rincover, A. Sensory extinction: A procedure for eliminating self-stimulatory behavior in psychotic children. *Journal of Abnormal Child Psychology,* 1978, *6,* 299–310.

Rincover, A., Cook, R., Peoples, A., & Packard, D. Using sensory extinction and sensory reinforcement principles for programming multiple adaptive behavior change. *Journal of Applied Behavior Analysis,* 1979, *12,* 221–233.

Rincover, A., Newsom, C. D., Lovaas, O. I., & Koegel, R. L. Some motivational properties of sensory stimulation in psychotic children. *Journal of Experimental Child Psychology,* 1977, *24,* 312–323.

Risley, T. R. The effects and side effects of punishing the autistic behaviors of a deviant child. *Journal of Applied Behavior Analysis,* 1968, *1,* 21–34.

Risley, T. R., & Cataldo, M. F. Evaluation of planned activities: The PLA-check measure of classroom participation. Unpublished paper. Lawrence, Kan.: Center for Applied Behavior Analysis, 1974.

Risley, T. R., & Wolf, M. M. Establishing functional speech in echolalic children, *Behaviour Research and Therapy,* 1967, *5,* 73–88.

Ritschl, C., Mongrella, J., & Presbie, R. J. Group time-out from rock and roll music and out-of-seat behavior of handicapped children while riding a school bus. *Psychological Reports,* 1972, *31,* 967–973.

Roberts, M. W., McMahon, R. J., Forehand, R., & Humphreys, L. The effect of parental instruction giving on child compliance. *Behavior Therapy*, 1978, *9*, 793–798.

Robinson, E., Hughes, H., Wilson, D., Lahey, B. B., & Haynes, S. N. *Modification of self-stimulatory behaviors of autistic children through contingent water squirts*. Paper presented at the meeting of the Association for the Advancement of Behavior Therapy, Chicago, November, 1974.

Rollings, J. P., Baumeister, A. A., & Baumeister, A. A. The use of overcorrection procedures to eliminate the stereotyped behaviors of retarded individuals: An analysis of collateral behaviors and generalization of suppressive effects. *Behavior Modification*, 1977, *1*, 29–46.

Romanczyk, R. G. Intermittent punishment of key-press responding: Effectiveness during application and extinction. *Psychological Record*, 1976, *26*, 203–214.

Romanczyk, R. G. Intermittent punishment of self-stimulation: Effectiveness during application and extinction. *Journal of Consulting and Clinical Psychology*, 1977, *45*, 53–60.

Romanczyk, R. G., Colletti, G. & Lockshin, S. *Developing a policy concerning the use of aversive procedures: Ethical, legal, and empirical issues*. Paper presented at the Association for Behavior Analysis, Milwaukee, May, 1981.

Romanczyk, R. G., Colletti, G., & Plotkin, R. Punishment of self-injurious behavior: Issues of behavior analysis, generalization, and the right to treatment. *Child Behavior Therapy*, 1980, *2*, 37–54.

Romanczyk, R. G., & Goren, E. R. Severe self-injurious behavior: The problem of clinical control. *Journal of Consulting and Clinical Psychology*, 1975, *43*, 730–739.

Romanczyk, R. G., Kistner, J. A., & Crimmins, D. B. Institutional treatment of severely disturbed children: Fact, possibility, or nonsequitur? In B. B. Lahey & A. E. Kazdin (eds.), *Advances in clinical child psychology* (Vol. 3). New York: Plenum Press, 1980.

Romanczyk, R. G. & Lockshin, S. *The Individualized Goal Selection Curriculum*. Vestal, New York: Clinical Behavior Therapy Associates, 1982.

Roos, P. Human rights and behavior modification. *Mental Retardation*, 1974, *12*, 3–6.

Rose, T. L. The corporal punishment cycle: A behavioral analysis of the maintenance of corporal punishment in the tools. *Education and Treatment of Children*, 1981, *4*, 157–169.

Rosen, H., & DiGiacomo, J. N. The role of physical restraint in the treatment of psychiatric illness. *The Journal of Clinical Psychiatry*, 1978, *135*, 325–328.

Ross, J. A. Parents modify thumbsucking: A case study. *Journal of Behavior Therapy and Experimental Psychiatry*, 1975, *6*, 248–249.

Roth, L. H., Meisel, A. & Lidz, C. W. Tests of competency to consent to treatment. *American Journal of Psychiatry*. 1977, *134*, 279–284.

Royer, F. L., Rynearson, R., Rice, W., & Upper, D. An inexpensive quickly built shockgrid for use with humans. *Behavior Therapy*, 1971, *2*, 251–252.

Sachs, D. A. The efficacy of time-out procedures in a variety of behavior problems. *Journal of Behavior Therapy and Experimental Psychiatry*, 1973, *4*, 237–242.

Sachs, D. A., & Mayhall, B. Behavioral control of spasms using aversive conditioning with a cerebral palsied adult. *Journal of Nervous and Mental Disorders*. 1971, *152*, 362–363.

Sachs, L. B., Bean, H., & Morrow, J. E. Comparison of smoking treatments. *Behavior Therapy*, 1970, *1*, 465–472.

Sailor, W., Guess, D., Rutherford, G., & Baer, D. M. Control of tantrum behavior by operant techniques during experimental verbal training. *Journal of Applied Behavior Analysis*, 1968, *1*, 237–243,

Sajwaj, T. Issues and implications of establishing guidelines for the use of behavioral techniques. *Journal of Applied Behavior Analysis*, 1977, *10*, 531–540.

Sajwaj, T., Libet, J., & Agras, S. Lemon juice therapy: The control of life-threatening rumination in a six-month-old infant. *Journal of Applied Behavior Analysis*, 1974, *7*, 557–563.

Sajwaj, T., Twardosz, S., & Burke, M. Side effects of extinction procedures in a remedial preschool. *Journal of Applied Behavior Analysis*, 1972, *5*, 163–175.

Sanok, R. L., & Striefel, S. Elective mutism: Generalization of verbal responding across people and settings. *Behavior Therapy*, 1979, *10*, 357–371.

Saposnek, D. T., & Watson, L. S. The elimination of the self-destructive behavior of a psychotic child: A case study. *Behavior Therapy*, 1974, *5*, 79–89.

Scarboro, M. E., & Forehand, R. Effects of two types of response-contingent timeout on compliance and oppositional behavior of children. *Journal of Experimental Child Psychology*, 1975, *19*, 252–264.

Schaefer, H. Vibration as a reinforcer with infant children. *Journal of the Experimental Analysis of Behavior*, 1960, *3*, 160.

Schiefelbusch, R. L. A philosophy of intervention. *Analysis and Intervention in Developmental Disabilities*, 1981, *1*, 373–388.

Schleien, S., Kiernan, J., & Wehman, P. Evaluation of an age-appropriate leisure skills program for moderately retarded adults. *Education and Training of the Mentally Retarded*, 1981, *16*, 13–19.

Schleien, S. J., Wehman, P., & Kiernan, J. Teaching leisure skills to severely handicapped adults: An age-appropriate darts game. *Journal of Applied Behavior Analysis*, 1981, *14*, 513–519.

Schmauk, F.J. Punishment, arousal, and avoidance learning in sociopaths. *Journal of Abnormal Psychology*, 1970, *76*, 325–335.

Schneider, H. C. , Ross, J. S. G., & Drubin, W. J. Practical alternative for the treatment of tantrum and self-injurious behavior. *Journal of Behavior Therapy and Experimental Psychiatry*, 1979, *10*, 73–75.

Schreibman, L., & Koegel, R. L. A guideline for planning behavior modification programs for autistic children. In S. M. Turner, K. S. Calhoun, & H. E. Adams (eds.), *Handbook of Clinical Behavior Therapy.* New York: John Wiley, 1981.

Schwitzgebel, R. L., & Schwitzgebel, R. K. *Law and psychological practice.* New York: John Wiley, 1980.

Scovern, A. W., & Kilmann, P. R. Status of electroconvulsive therapy: Review of the outcome literature. *Psychological Bullentin,* 1980, *87,* 260–303.

Sears, B. R., Maccoby, E. E., & Levin, H. *Patterns of child rearing.* Evanston, Ill.: Row-Peterson, 1957.

Segal, B., & Sims, J. Covert sensitization with a homosexual: A controlled replication. *Journal of Consulting and Clinical Psychology,* 1972, *39,* 259–263.

Sewell, E., McCoy, J. F., & Sewell, W. R. Modification of an antagonistic social behavior using positive reinforcement for other behavior. *Psychological Record,* 1973, *23,* 499–504.

Shafto, F., & Sulzbacher, S. Comparing treatment tactics with a hyperactive preschool child: Stimulant medication and programmed teacher intervention. *Journal of Applied Behavior Analysis,* 1977, *10,* 13–20.

Shelton v. Tucker. 364 U.S. 479, 1960.

Sibley, S., Abbott, M., & Cooper, B. Modification of the classroom behavior of a "disadvantaged" kindergarden boy by social reinforcement and isolation. *Journal of Experimental Child Psychology,* 1969, 7, 203–219.

Silverman, P. J. The role of social reinforcement in maintaining an obsessive-compulsive neurosis. *Journal of Behavior Therapy and Experimental Psychiatry,* 1977, *8,* 325–326.

Simmons, J. Q., & Lovaas, O. I. Use of pain and punishment as treatment techniques with childhood schizophrenics, *American Journal of Psychotherapy,* 1969, *23,* 23–36.

Singh, R. Experiments in two cases of hysterical fits. *Journal of Behavior Therapy and Experimental Psychiatry,* 1975, 6, 351–353.

Skinner, B. F. *The behavior of organisms,* New York: Appleton-Century-Crofts, 1938.

Skinner B. F. *Science and human behavior.* New York: Free Press, 1953.

Skinner, B. F. *Contingencies of reinforcement: A theoretical analysis,* New York, Appleton-Century-Crofts, 1969.

Skinner, B. F. Reward or punishment: Which works better? *U.S. News & World Report,* November 3, 1980, pp. 79–80.

Sloane, H. N., Johnston, M. K., & Bijou, S. W. Successive modification of aggressive fantasy play by management of contingencies. *Journal of Child Psychology and Psychiatry,* 1967, *8,* 217–226.

Sloane, R. B., Staples, F. R., Cristol, A. H., Yorkston, N. J., & Whipple, K. *Psychotherapy versus behavior therapy.* Cambridge, Mass: Harvard University Press, 1975.

Smeets, P. M., Elson, L. E., & Clement, A. Eliminating nasal discharge in a multi-handicapped deaf child. *Journal of Behavior Therapy and Experimental Psychiatry,* 1975, *6,* 264–266.

Solnick, J. V., Rincover, A., & Peterson, C. R. Some determinants of the reinforcing and punishing effects of timeout. *Journal of Applied Behavior Analysis,* 1977, *10,* 415–424.

Solomon, R. L. Punishment. *American Psychologist,* 1964, *19,* 239–253.

Song, A. Y., Song, R. H., & Grant, P. A. Toilet training in the school and its transfer in the living unit. *Journal of Behavior Therapy and Experimental Psychiatry,* 1976, *7,* 281–284.

Spence, J. T., & Segner, L. L. Verbal versus nonverbal reinforcement combinations in the discrimination learning of middle and lower-class children. *Child Development,* 1967, *38,* 29–38.

Spencer, T., & Lutzker, J. R. *Punishment of self-injurious behavior in retardates by application of a harmless face cover.* Paper presented at the meeting of the American Psychological Association, New Orleans, 1974.

Spitalnik, R., & Drabman, R. A classroom timeout procedure for retarded children. *Journal of Behavior Therapy and Experimental Psychiatry,* 1976, *7,* 17–21.

Sprague, R. L., & Baxley, G. B. Drugs for behavior management with comment on some legal aspects. In J. Wortis (ed.), *Mental retardation and developmental disabilities* (Vol. 10). New York: Brunner/Mazel, 1978.

Staddon, J. E. R. Schedule-induced behavior. In W. K. Honig & J. E. R. Staddon (eds.), *Handbook of operant behavior.* Englewood Cliffs, N.J.: Prentice-Hall, 1977.

Stark, J., Meisel, J., & Wright, T. S. Modifying maladaptive behavior in a non-verbal child. *British Journal of Disorders of Communication,* 1969, *4,* 67–72.

Steeves, J. M., Martin, G. L., & Pear, J. J. Self-imposed time-out by autistic children during an operant training program. *Behavior Therapy,* 1970, *1,* 371–381.

Stevenson, H. W., Weir, M. W., & Zigler, E. F. Discrimination learning in children as function of motive–incentive conditions. *Psychological Reports,* 1959, *5,* 95–98.

Stokes, T. F., & Baer, D. M. An implicit technology of generalization. *Journal of Applied Behavior Analysis,* 1977, *10,* 349–367.

Stolz, S. B. Why no guidelines for behavior modification? *Journal of Applied Behavior Analysis,* 1977, *10,* 541–547.

Stolz, S. B., & Associates. *Ethical issues in behavior modification.* San Francisco, Calif.: Jossey-Bass, 1978.

Stuart, R. B. Behavioral control over eating. *Behaviour Research and Therapy,* 1967, *5,* 357–365.

Stuart, R. B. Ethical guidelines for behavior therapy. In S. M. Turner, K. S. Calhoun, & H. E. Adams (eds.), *Handbook of clinical behavior therapy.* New York: John Wiley, 1981.

Sulzer-Azaroff, B., & Mayer, G. R. *Applying behavior-analysis procedures with children and youth.* New York: Holt, Rinehart and Winston, 1977.

Sumner, J. G., Meuser, S. T., Hsu, L., & Morales, R. G. Overcorrection treatment for radical reduction of aggressive–disruptive behavior in institutionalized mental patients. *Psychological Reports,* 1974, *35,* 655–662.

Tanner, B. A. A comparison of automated aversive conditioning and a waiting list control in the modification of homosexual behavior in males. *Behavior Therapy,* 1974, *5,* 29–32.

Tanner, B. A., & Zeiler, M. Punishment of self-injurious behavior using aromatic ammonia as the aversive stimulus. *Journal of Applied Behavior Analysis,* 1975, *8,* 53–57.

Tate, B. G., & Baroff, G. S. Aversive control of self-injurious behavior in a psychotic boy. *Behaviour Research and Therapy,* 1966, *4,* 281–287.

Taylor, C. B., Zlutnick, S. I., & Hoehle, W. The effects of behavioral procedures on tardive dyskinesias. *Behavior Therapy,* 1979, *10,* 37–45.

Terrell, G., & Ware, R. Role of delay of reward in speed of size and form discrimination learning in children. *Child Development,* 1961, *32,* 409–415.

Thomas, D. R., & Murphy, R. J. Practitioner competencies needed for implementing behavior management guidelines. *The Behavior Therapist,* 1981, *4*(1), 7–10.

Thompson, T., Kodluboy, S., & Heston, L. Behavioral treatment of obesity in Prader-Willi Syndrome. *Behavior Therapy,* 1980, *11,* 588–593.

Toister, R. P., Colin, J., Worley, L. M., & Arthur, D. Faradic therapy of chronic vomiting in infancy: A case study. *Journal of Behavior Therapy and Experimental Psychiatry,* 1975, *6,* 55–59.

Tooley, J. T., & Pratt, S. An experimental procedure for the extinction of smoking behavior. *Psychological Record,* 1967, *17,* 209–218.

Townsend, N. M., & Marholin, D. Practice makes perfect: The elimination of stereotyped body-rocking through positive practice. *Scandinavian Journal of Behaviour Therapy,* 1978, *7,* 195–201.

Traugott, M. A., & Campbell, C. O. *Reduction of self-injurious behaviors through the use of contingent electric shock.* Paper presented at the Association for Behavior Analysis, Milwaukee, May 1981.

Turner, S. M., Sajwaj, T. E., & Becker, J. V. Treatment of institutionalized ruminators with lemon juice used as a punishing stimulus. In C. R. King (chair), *Rumination: A life-threatening disorder of childhood.* Symposium presented at the meeting of the American Association of Psychiatric Services for Children, Washington, D.C., 1977.

Twardosz, S., & Sajwaj, T. Multiple effects of a procedure to increase sitting in a hyperactive, retarded boy. *Journal of Applied Behavior Analysis,* 1972, *5,* 73–78.

Tyler, V. O., & Brown, G. D. The use of swift, brief isolation as a group control device for institutionalized delinquents. *Behaviour Research and Therapy,* 1967, *5,* 1–9.

Ullmann, L., & Krasner, L. (eds.). *Case studies in behavior modification.* New York: Holt, Rinehart & Winston, 1965.

Ulrich, R. E., & Azrin, N. H. Reflexive fighting in response to aversive stimulation. *Journal of the Experimental Analysis of Behavior,* 1962, *5,* 511–520.

United States Department of Health, Education and Welfare. Regulations for intermediate care facility services for the mentally retarded. *Federal Register,* 1974, *39,* 2220–2235.

Upper, D. A. A "ticket" system for reducing ward rule violations on a token economy program. *Journal of Behavior Therapy and Experimental Psychiatry,* 1973, *4,* 137–140.

VanBiervliet, A., Spangler, P. F., & Marshall, A. M. An ecobehavioural examination of a simple strategy for increasing mealtime language in residential facilities. *Journal of Applied Behavior Analysis,* 1981, *14,* 295–305.

VanHorn, R. W., Mein, K., Rich, B., Tison, C., Trout, C., Watterson, M., & Wilfong, S. Environmental psychology in the classroom: Four studies. *Education and Treatment of Children,* 1981, *4,* 171–178.

Vargas, J. M., & Adesso, V. J. A comparison of aversion therapies for nail-biting behavior. *Behavior Therapy,* 1976, *7,* 322–329.

Varni, J. W., Boyd, E. F., & Cataldo, M. F. Self-monitoring, external reinforcement, and timeout procedures in the control of high rate tic behaviors in a hyperactive child. *Journal of Behavior Therapy and Experimental Psychiatry,* 1978, *9,* 353–358.

Vogler, R. E., Lunde, S. E., Johnson, G. R., & Martin, P. L. Electrical aversion conditioning with chronic alcoholics. *Journal of Consulting and Clinical Psychology,* 1970, *34,* 302–307.

Vogler, R. E., Lunde, S. E., & Martin, P. L. Electrical aversion conditioning with chronic alcoholics: Follow-up and suggestions for research. *Journal of Consulting and Clinical Psychology,* 1971, *36,* 450.

Vukelich, R., & Hake, D. R. Reeducation of dangerously aggressive behavior in a severely retarded resident through a combination of positive reinforcement procedures. *Journal of Applied Behavior Analysis,* 1971, *4,* 215–225.

Wagner, M. K., & Bragg, R. A. Comparing behavior modification approaches to habit decrement—smoking. *Journal of Consulting and Clinical Psychology,* 1970, *34,* 258–263.

Wahler, R. G. Oppositional children: A quest for parental reinforcement control. *Journal of Applied Behavior Analysis,* 1969, *2,* 159–170.

Wahler, R. G. Some structural aspects of deviant child behavior. *Journal of Applied Behavior Analysis,* 1975, *8,* 27–42.

Wahler, R. G., & Fox, J. J. Solitary toy play and time out: A family treatment package for children with aggressive and oppositional behavior. *Journal of Applied Behavior Analysis,* 1980, *13,* 23–39.

Wahler, R., Winkel, G., Peterson, R., & Morrison, D. Mothers as behavior therapists for their own children. *Behaviour Research and Therapy*, 1965, *3*, 113–124.

Walker, H., Mattson, R., & Buckley, N. Special class placement as a treatment alternative for deviant behavior in children. In F. Benson (ed.), *Modifying deviant social behavior in various classroom settings*. Eugene: University of Oregon, 1968.

Waller, M. B., & Waller, P. F. The effects of unavoidable shocks on a multiple schedule having an avoidance componeent. *Journal of the Experimental Analysis of Behavior*, 1963, *6*, 29–37.

Walton, D. The application of learning theory to the treatment of a case of neurodermatitis. In H. J. Eysenck (ed.), *Behaviour therapy and the neuroses*. Oxford, England: Pergamon Press, 1960.

Walton, D. Experimental psychology and the treatment of a tiquer. *Journal of Child Psychology and Psychiatry*, 1961, *2*, 148–155.

Walton, D. Massed practice and simultaneous reduction in drive level: Further evidence of the efficacy of this approach to the treatment of tics. In H. J. Eysenck (ed.), *Experiments in behavior therpay*. Oxford, England: Pergamon Press, 1964.

Ward, E. M. Overcorrection: A component analysis of its effects and side effects on the appropriate and inappropriate behavior of retarded children and adults. Unpublished manuscript. Notre Dame, Ind.: University of Notre Dame, 1976.

Warren, S. A. Behavior modification—Boon, bane or both? *Mental Retardation*, 1971, *9*, 2.

Wasik, B., Senn, K., Welch, R., & Cooper, B. Behavior modification with culturally deprived school children: Two case studies. *Journal of Applied Behavior Analysis*, 1969, *2*, 181–194.

Watkins, J. T. Treatment of chronic vomiting and extreme emaciation by an aversive stimulus: Case study. *Psychological Reports*, 1972, *31*, 803–805.

Watson, J. B., & Rayner, R. Conditioned emotional reactions. *Journal of Experimental Psychology*, 1920, *3*, 1–14.

Watson, L. S., Jr., & Uzzell, R. A program for teaching behavior modification skills to institutional staff. *Applied Research in Mental Retardation*, 1980, *112*, 41–54.

Webster, D. R., & Azrin, N. H. Required relaxation: A method of inhibiting agitative–disruptive behavior of retardates. *Behaviour Research and Therapy*, 1973, *11*, 67–78.

Wehman, P. Leisure skill programming for the severely and profoundly handicapped: State of the art. *British Journal of Social and Clinical Psychology*, 1978, *17*, 217–231.

Wehman, P. (ed.). *Recreation programming for developmentally disabled persons*. Baltimore, Md.: University Park Press, 1979.

Wehman, P., Karan, O., & Rettie, C. Developing independent play in three severely retarded women. *Psychological Reports*, 1976, *39*, 995–998.

Wehman, P., Renzaglia, A., Berry, A., Schutz, R., & Karan, O. D. Development of a leisure skill repertoire in severely and profoundly retarded adolescents and adults. *AAESPH Review*, 1978, *3*, 162–172.

Weiher, R. G., & Harman, R. E. The use of omission training to reduce self-injurious behavior in a retarded child. *Behavior Therapy*, 1975, *6*, 261–268.

Weiner, H. Some effects of response cost upon human operant behavior. *Journal of the Experimental Analysis of Behavior*, 1962, *5*, 201–208.

Weiner, H. Response cost and the aversive control of human operant behavior. *Journal of the Experimental Analysis of Behavior*, 1963, *6*, 415–421.

Weisberg, P., Passman, R. H., & Russell, J. E. Modification of bizarre gestures of retardates through imitative reinforcement procedures. *Journal of Applied Behavior Analysis*, 1973, *6*, 487–495.

Weitzel, W. B., Horan, J. J., & Addis, J. W. A new olfactory aversion apparatus. *Behavior Therapy*, 1977, *8*, 83–88.

Wells, D. A. The use of seclusion on a university hospital psychiatric floor. *Archives of General Psychiatry*, 1972, *26*, 410–413.

Wells, K. C., & Forehand, R. Childhood behavior problems in the home. In S. M. Turner, K. S. Calhoun, & H. E. Adams (eds.), *Handbook of clinical behavior therapy*. New York: John Wiley, 1981.

Wells, K. C., Forehand, R., & Hickey, K. Effects of a verbal warning and overcorrection on stereotyped and appropriate behaviors. *Journal of Abnormal Child Psychology*, 1977, *5*, 387–403.

Wells, K. C., Forehand, R., Hickey, K., & Green, R. Effects of a procedure derived from the overcorrection principle on manipulated and nonmanipulated behaviors. *Journal of Applied Behavior Analysis*, 1977, *10*, 679–687.

Wetzel, R. J., Baker, J., Roney, M., & Martin, M. Outpatient treatment of autistic behavior. *Behaviour Research and Therapy*, 1966, *4*, 169–177.

Wexler, D. B. Reflections on the legal regulation of behavior modification in institutional settings. *Arizona Law Review*, 1975, *17*, 132–143.

Whalen, C. K., & Henker, B. The pitfalls of politicization: A response to Conrad's "The discovery of hyperkinesis: Notes on the medicalization of deviant behavior." *Social Problems*, 1977, *24*, 590–595.

Whalen, C. K., Henker, B., Collins, B. E., Finck, D., & Dotemoto, S. A social ecology of hyperactive boys: Medication effects in structured classroom environments. *Journal of Applied Behavior Analysis*, 1979, *12*, 65–81.

Whaley, D. L., & Tough, J. Treatment of a self-injuring mongoloid with shock induced suppression and avoidance. In R. Ulrich, T. Stachnik, & J. Mabry (eds.), *Control of human behavior* (Vol. 2). Glenview, Ill.: Scott, Foresman, 1970.

White, G. D., Nielsen, G., & Johnson, S. M. Timeout duration and the suppression of deviant behavior in children. *Journal of Applied Behavior Analysis*, 1972, *5*, 111–120.

White, J. C., Jr., & Taylor, D. J. Noxious conditioning as a treatment for rumination. *Mental Retardation*, 1967, *5*, 30–33.

Wiesen, A. E., & Watson, E. Elimination of attention seeking behavior in a retarded child. *American Journal of Mental Deficiency,* 1967, *72,* 50–52.

Wilbur, R. L., Chandler, P. J., & Carpenter, B. L. Modification of self-mutilative behavior by aversive conditioning. *Behavioral Engineering,* 1974, *1,* 14–25.

Willems, E. P. Behavioral technology and behavioral ecology. *Journal of Applied Behavior Analysis,* 1974, *7,* 151–165.

Willems, E. P. Ecological psychology. In D. Stokols (ed.), *Perspectives on environment and behavior: Theory, research and applications.* New York: Plenum Press, 1977.

Williams, C. D. The elimination of tantrum behaviors by extinction procedures. *Journal of Abnormal and Social Psychology,* 1959, *59,* 269.

Wilson, G. T., & Davison, G. C. Aversion techniques in behavior therapy: Some theoretical and metatheoretical considerations. *Journal of Consulting and Clinical Psychology,* 1969, *33,* 327–329.

Winkler, R. C. Management of chronic psychiatric patients by a token reinforcement system. *Journal of Applied Behavior Analysis,* 1970, *3,* 47–55.

Winkler, R. C. Reinforcement schedules for individual patients in a token economy. *Behavior Therapy,* 1971, *2,* 534–537.

Winston, F. Restraints in delirium tremens. *American Journal of Psychiatry,* 1977, *134,* 98.

Wisocki, P. A. The successful treatment of a heroin addict by covert conditioning techniques. *Journal of Behavior Therapy and Experimental Psychiatry,* 1973, *4,* 55–61.

Wolf, M. M., Birnbrauer, J. S., Williams, T., & Lawler, J. A note on apparent extinction of the vomiting behavior of a retarded child. In L. P. Ullmann & L. Krasner (eds.), *Case studies in behavior modification.* New York: Holt, Rinehart and Winston, 1965.

Wolf, M. M., Hanley, E. L., King, L. A., Lachowicz, J., & Giles, D. K. The timer-game: A variable interval contingency for the management of out-of-seat behavior. *Exceptional Children,* 1970, *37,* 113–117.

Wolf, M. M., Risley, T., Johnston, M., Harris, F., & Allen, E. Application of operant conditioning procedures to the behavior problems of an autistic child: A follow-up and extension. *Behaviour Research and Therapy,* 1967, *5,* 103–111.

Wolf, M., Risley, T., & Mees, H. Application of operant conditioning procedures to the behaviour problems of an autistic child. *Behaviour Research and Therapy,* 1964, *1,* 305–312.

Wolpe, J. *Psychotherapy by reciprocal inhibition.* Stanford, Calif.: Stanford University Press, 1958.

Wright, L. Aversive conditioning of self-induced seizures. *Behavior Therapy,* 1973, *4,* 712–713.

Wulbert, M., & Dries, R. The relative efficacy of methylphenidate (Ritalin) and behavior modification techniques in the treatment of a hyperactive child. *Journal of Applied Behavior Analysis,* 1977, *10,* 21–31.

Wulbert, M., Nyman, B. H., Snow, D., & Owen, Y. The efficacy of stimulus fading and contingency management in the treatment of elective mutism. A case study. *Journal of Applied Behavior Analysis,* 1973, *6,* 435–441.

Wyatt v. Stickney. 344 F. Supp. at 379–384, 1972.

Yates, A. *Behavior therapy.* New York: John Wiley, 1970.

Yeakel, M. H., Salisbury, L. L., Greer, S. L., & Marcus, L. F. An appliance for autoinduced adverse control of self-injurious behavior. *Journal of Experimental Child Psychology,* 1970, *10,* 159–169.

Yen, S., & McIntire, R. (eds.). *Teaching behavior modification.* Kalamazoo, Mich.: Behaviordelia, 1976.

Young, J. A., & Wincze, J. P. The effects of the reinforcement of compatible and incompatible alternative behaviors on the self-injurious and related behaviors of a profoundly retarded female adult. *Behavior Therapy,* 1974, *5,* 614–623.

Zegiob, L., Alford, G. S., & House, A. Response suppressive and generalization effects of facial screening on multiple self-injurious behaviors in a retarded boy. *Behavior Therapy,* 1978, *9,* 688.

Zegiob, L., Becker, J. V., Jenkins, J. O., & Bristow, A. Facial screening: Effects on appropriate and inappropriate behaviors. *Journal of Behavior Therapy and Experimental Psychiatry,* 1976, *7,* 355–357.

Zehr, M. D., & Theobald, D. E. Manual guidance used in a punishment procedure: The active ingredient in overcorrection. *Journal of Mental Deficiency Research,* 1977, *22,* 263–272.

Zeilberger, J., Sampen, S., & Sloane, H., Jr. Modification of a child's problem behaviors in the home with the mother as the therapist. *Journal of Applied Behavior Analysis,* 1968, *1,* 47–53.

Zeiler, M. Other Behavior: Consequence of reinforcing not responding. *Journal of Psychology,* 1970, *74,* 149–155.

Zeiler, M. Schedules of reinforcement: The controlling variables. In W. K. Honig & J. E. R. Staddon (eds.), *Handbook of operant behavior.* Englewood Cliffs, N.J.: Prentice-Hall, 1977.

Zimmerman, E. H., & Zimmerman, J. The alteration of behavior in a special classroom situation. *Journal of the Experimental Analysis of Behavior,* 1962, *5,* 59–60.

Zimmerman, J., & Bayden, N. T. Punishment of S^{Δ} responding of humans in conditional matching to sample by time-out. *Journal of the Experimental Analysis of Behavior,* 1963, *6,* 589–597.

Zimmerman, J., & Ferster, C. B. Intermittent punishment of S^{Δ} responding in matching to sample. *Journal of the Experimental Analysis of Behavior,* 1963, *6,* 349–356.

Index

Index